Hard · Disk · Manager

Also by the Authors

Hard Disk Management for the IBM PC XT, AT and Compatible Systems

Hard · Disk · Manager

25 UTILITIES
TO CUSTOMIZE,
ORGANIZE,
AND MANAGE
YOUR HARD DISK SYSTEM

Nancy Woodard Cain
Thomas Cain

A Brady Utility
Published by Prentice Hall Press
New York, NY 10023

Copyright © 1987 by Nancy Woodard Cain and Thomas Cain
All rights reserved
including the right of reproduction
in whole or in part in any form

A Brady Utility
Published by Prentice Hall Press
A Division of Simon & Schuster, Inc.
Gulf + Western Building
One Gulf + Western Plaza
New York, New York 10023

PRENTICE HALL PRESS is a trademark of Simon & Schuster, Inc.

Manufactured in the United States of America

1 2 3 4 5 6 7 8 9 10

Library of Congress Cataloging-in-Publication Data

Cain, Nancy Woodard.
  Hard Disk Manager [computer file].

  1 computer disk; 5¼ in.+reference manual.
  System requirements: IBM PC, XT, AT or other compatibles; PC-DOS or MS-DOS 2.0 or higher; hard disk; monochrome monitor.
  Title from reference manual.
  "A Brady utility."
  Not copy protected.
  Intended audience: Business computer users.
  Summary: Provides twenty-five DOS-based utilities that can be customized for common hard disk management and organization tasks.
  1. Utilities (Computer programs)—Software.
I. Cain, Thomas. II. Title.
QA76.76.U84C35 1987   005.4′46   87-17994

ISBN 0-13-383779-3

Trademarks

COMPAQ is a trademark of COMPAQ Computer Corp.
dBASE II and *dBASE III* are trademarks of Ashton-Tate Inc.
IBM, AT, PC/XT, PC-DOS, and *DisplayWrite3* are trademarks of International Business Machines Corp.
Lotus 1-2-3 is a trademark of Lotus Development Corp.
Microsoft and *MS-DOS* are trademarks of Microsoft Corp.
MultiMate is a trademark of Ashton-Tate Inc.

Acknowledgments

A number of persons helped make this effort worthwhile. The authors would like to thank our editor Terry Anderson for seeing us through yet another project. Joe and Lulu Hamilton deserve thanks for their moral support; they patiently listened to us continually talk about this project, even though they had no personal interest in computers. We also would like to thank Bruce Bernstein and Tony Schmitz, who contributed support and ideas for this effort. Finally, the authors would like to acknowledge the contributions of James Cain and Steve Dashefsky for their invaluable critiques and suggestions on the software.

Contents

Preface	*xiii*
Quick Start	*xv*

chapter 1 AN INTRODUCTION TO THE *HARD DISK MANAGER* 1

chapter 2 BEHIND THE UTILITIES 5
2.1 Programming with DOS 8
2.2 Programming with DOS's Advanced Features 10
2.3 A Summary of DOS Features Behind the Utilities 14

chapter 3 INSTALLING *HARD DISK MANAGER* 16
3.1 Requirements 16
3.2 Installing the Entire Program 17
3.3 Installing Part of *Hard Disk Manager* 19
3.4 Troubleshooting 21
3.5 Removing All Utilities from the Hard Disk 24

chapter

4	**DISK ORGANIZATION UTILITIES**	*28*
	4.1 The Disk/Directory Utilities	*32*
	The Menu/Directory Setup Utility	*32*
	The Disk & Directory View/Print Utilities	*49*
	The Format Utilities	*54*
	4.2 Modifying the Disk/Directory Utilities	*57*
	4.3 Some Background Information on Data Storage and Directories	*61*

chapter

5	**CUSTOMIZED DISPLAY UTILITIES**	*70*
	5.1 The Customized Display Utilities	*73*
	The Change Foreground Color Utility	*73*
	The Change Background Color Utility	*78*
	The Change Screen Attributes Utility	*79*
	The Change Screen Attributes Program Files	*81*
	5.2 Modifying the Customized Display Utilities	*82*
	5.3 Some Background Information on Display and Keyboard Control	*87*

chapter

6	**SCREEN DESIGN UTILITY**	*95*
	6.1 The Screen Design Utility	*98*
	6.2 Planning a Screen for Use with the Design Utility	*101*
	Some Information on the EDLIN REPLACE TEXT Command	*107*
	Using the REPLACE TEXT Command in Screen Design	*107*
	6.3 Modifying the Screen Design Utility	*116*

chapter

7	**BACKUP/RESTORE UTILITIES**	*121*
	7.1 The Backup/Restore Utilities	*125*
	The Full Backup Utility	*125*

Contents ix

	The Partial Backup Utility	*129*
	The Backup Files by Date Utility	*132*
	The New File/Modified File Backup Utility	*134*
	The Full Restore Utility	*137*
	The Partial Restore Utility	*139*
7.2	Modifying the Backup/Restore Utilities	*142*
7.3	Some Background Information on Data Security	*145*

chapter 8 FILE MANAGEMENT UTILITIES — *148*

8.1	The File Management Utilities	*151*
	The File Archive Utility	*151*
	The Move File Utility	*153*
	The File Combine Utility	*156*
	The Text Search Utility	*158*
	The File Locate Utility	*162*
	The Diskcopy Utility	*166*
	The File Protect/Unprotect Utilities	*167*
8.2	Modifying the File Management Utilities	*171*
8.3	Some Background Information on File Management and Hard Disk Maintenance	*178*

chapter 9 HELP SCREEN UTILITIES — *185*

9.1	The HELP Screen Utilities	*188*
9.2	Modifying the HELP Screen Utilities	*195*
9.3	Some Background Information on HELP Screens	*199*

chapter 10 MODIFYING THE HARD DISK UTILITIES — *201*

10.1	Analyzing Utility File Changes	*201*
	Some Basic Utility Information	*202*
10.2	Some Basic Tools for Editing Files	*204*

10.3	Adding, Modifying, and Deleting Screen Files	207
10.4	Adding, Modifying, and Deleting Batch Files	215

chapter

11 CREATING YOUR OWN UTILITIES: TIPS AND TECHNIQUES FOR PROGRAMMING WITH DOS — 219

11.1	Screen and Batch File Techniques	222
	Using the Hard Disk Manager *Techniques*	223
11.2	Ten Techniques for Creative Screen Design	223
	Using the ASCII Extended Character Set	223
	Control Codes: Changing Full-Screen Attributes	224
	Control Codes: Used in Screen Design	225
	Controlling the Cursor and System Prompt	226
	Using "What If" in Screen Design	226
	Forced Line Spacing in Information Screens	227
	Displaying Information Screens	227
	Multiple Information Screens	228
	Executing Menu Selections	229
	Screen and Menu Layout: Organization and Brevity	229
11.3	Ten Techniques for Creative Batch File Design	230
	User-Interactive Batch Files	230
	Redirecting Input from a File	230
	Redirecting Output to Files and Devices	231
	Key Reassignment	231
	Validation of User Input	232
	Using Batch File Subroutines	233
	Confirmation Prompts	233
	Different Uses of Replaceable Parameters	234
	Chaining Together Batch Files	234
	Self-Modifying Batch Files	235

appendix

A AN OVERVIEW OF SELECTED DOS COMMANDS — 237

Contents   xi

appendix

B   A BATCH FILE REFERENCE GUIDE   *266*

    Creating Batch Files   *266*
    Batch File Subroutines   *269*
    Batch File Commands   *270*
    Using Replaceable Parameters with Batch Files   *275*
    A Special Batch File: AUTOEXEC.BAT   *276*

appendix

C   AN EDLIN REFERENCE GUIDE   *277*

appendix

D   CONTROL CHARACTER SEQUENCES   *282*

appendix

E   ASCII EXTENDED CHARACTER SET: SELECTED VALUES   *284*

appendix

F   EXTENDED ASCII CODES FOR KEY REASSIGNMENT   *285*

    Index   *289*

Preface

This is not an ordinary book, nor is it an ordinary utility software package. It is a book about using and creating utilities, in which the disk is an integral part of the story. It is a software package that encourages the use as well as the modification of its utility programs. Use of the programs does not depend on additional hardware or software, nor does one have to be a programmer to modify existing programs. All of the programs are uncompiled and written using functions and features available within the operating system.

Why is this book written from this perspective? Because utilities, by definition, are supposed to be useful. Less technical users need utilities that simplify the day-to-day use of a microcomputer. A number of "desk top" applications have surfaced to meet these needs. However, unknown to many users are free utilities—commands and features of the operating system that can be customized to any user's needs. With this package, you can not only modify programs to create your own utilities, but you can also customize a hard disk management system that will grow as your needs change.

All of the utility programs in the *Hard Disk Manager* are "DOS-Based Utilities." They utilize a number of Disk Operating System (DOS) tools and commands that allow you to set up, organize, and maintain disks full of information. These utilities take full advantage of DOS's advanced features—those features that are hidden away in the back of the reference manual or, in the case of DOS 3.X, included in the DOS Technical Reference Manual. Since they are written in DOS, even nonprogrammers can use these utilities to create a well-organized and controlled systems environment.

Features of This Book/Disk

    1. An overview of the operating system and some basic information on its contents.

2. A well-documented guide to installing the utilities without any surprises and with minimal confusion.
3. Complete and understandable summaries of batch file, DOS, and EDLIN commands.
4. Explanations of *how* and *why* to use the utilities.
5. User-oriented descriptions of each utility and the contents of its program files.
6. Ideas for modifying existing program files and creating new ones.
7. Step-by-step, hands-on explanations for modifying screen and program files.

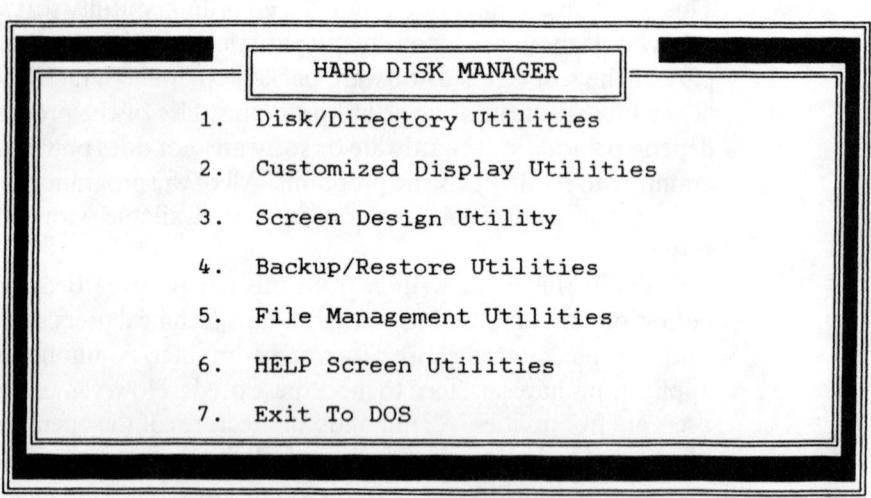

Hard Disk Manager Main Menu

Quick Start

Here are the procedures for quickly getting the *Hard Disk Manager* programs on your system. These steps install the entire program. For more detailed explanations, see Chapter 3.

Before you begin, make sure you know the directory location of DOS on your hard disk. During installation, you will be required to enter the drive and path for DOS files (for example, **C:\DOS**).

1. Turn on the computer. After the DOS system prompt is displayed, insert the *Hard Disk Manager* disk in drive A.
2. Enter the following command:

    a:install
3. When prompted, enter the DOS directory name, including the drive and path. Include any other directories that should be in the command search path; separate each with a semicolon. Press **<F6>**, then Enter.
4. The installation program takes 5 to 10 minutes, depending on the speed of your system. When the completion message is displayed, remove the *Hard Disk Manager* program disk and reboot your computer.
5. Make sure that you are in the root directory. If not, enter the command:

    cd\
6. At the system prompt, enter the command:

    hdu

Once installed, the command **hdu** should always display the *Hard Disk Manager* menu. Menu items are activated by typing the menu number and pressing Enter.

Consult Chapter 3 for partial installation of *Hard Disk Manager* and other installation-related information.

c·h·a·p·t·e·r 1

An Introduction to the *Hard Disk Manager*

The individuals who need hard disk utilities most probably don't realize it. These less technical users need utilities that simplify the day-to-day use of a microcomputer.

Any number of good utilities can be found for improving the performance of a hard disk system, for dealing with disasters, and so on. After all, it only takes one accidental formatting of a 10-MB disk to be convinced that everyone ought to have at least one trustworthy utilities package. However, utilities as powerful as these are not always for the fainthearted; the user may have to be prepared to decipher a screen full of hexidecimal values or to interpret all kinds of system and error messages.

The *Hard Disk Manager* utilities are based on the premise that you do not have to settle for a "rocket scientist's" concept of what is useful, nor must you purchase the most recent best-selling generic program. Instead, this is a hard disk management system that addresses your current needs and can grow in functionality as your requirements change.

What Is the Hard Disk Manager?

The *Hard Disk Manager* is a book/disk package for both new and serious computer users. It provides a comprehensive library of utility programs and illustrates techniques on which to build additional utilities. The *Hard Disk Manager* contains the following features:

- easily installed utility programs that provide users with an integrated hard disk management system
- DISK/DIRECTORY UTILITIES: Menu creation tools and utilities for directory and disk setups
- DISPLAY UTILITIES: Utilities to change the color of the display foreground and background, and to enhance certain aspects of the display screen through use of highlighting, reverse video images, etc.
- DESIGN UTILITY: An EDLIN-based screen design tool
- BACKUP/RESTORE UTILITIES: Various options for backing up and restoring data files according to date, files last modified, etc.
- FILE MANAGEMENT UTILITIES: Utilities to write-protect data files, archive unused files, conduct text searches, find files, move files from one directory to another, etc.
- HELP SCREEN UTILITIES: Ten HELP facilities that provide basic information on using many features of the operating system
- explanations for the use and modification of the utility programs and ideas for creating new utilities
- information on little-known capabilities of DOS
- reference guides for DOS, EDLIN, and batch file commands

What Does the Hard Disk Manager Do for You?

The *Hard Disk Manager* is a utility software package that can be installed as is. It is used to *organize* and *customize* your hard disk to meet your individual needs:

- It is used to establish your own hierarchical directory and file structure.
- It provides greater security around your hard disk system.
- Its menu-driven environment is used to perform routine housekeeping tasks but does not require a working knowledge of DOS.

As your knowledge and requirements grow, your disk management system can be modified to meet your changing needs. Since the program is written entirely with DOS, it is easy to modify. It is not written in a higher-level language nor is it compiled code. This means that it can be modified by you or any other user. Or, since it is built within DOS, programs in the *Hard Disk Manager* can also be incorporated into other, larger micro-based systems.

An Introduction to the Hard Disk Manager

Who Can Use This Book?

The *Hard Disk Manager* utilities are written for two types of users:

- NEW BUSINESS USERS who need and will use a menu management system but have no desire to program.
- EXPERIENCED USERS who know computers and create systems for end users—those who will incorporate the *Hard Disk Manager* and its ideas into bundled systems.

How You Can Use This Book

For less experienced users who wish to read about the program before beginning, Chapter 2, "Behind the Utilities," is a good place to start. This chapter provides an overview of those DOS features that make up the guts of the utilities. It includes information on: DOS command files, DOS's file management capabilities, DOS's built-in utility commands, programming with DOS, and programming with DOS's advanced features.

Each type of utility (e.g., Disk/Directory, File Management, etc.) is described in a separate chapter. In these chapters, you will find documentation on the batch files or program files that make up each utility. You also will find some background information on how to make optimal use of the utilities and how various DOS features were used in the construction of specific utilities. Finally, you will find ideas on how to add to and modify the utilities.

If you are the adventurous type and wish to try your own hand at creating utilities, separate chapters are devoted to this topic. Refer to Chapter 10, "Modifying the Hard Disk Utilities," and Chapter 11, "Creating Your Own Utilities," for tips on creating your own utilities.

QUICK START

> If you wish to jump right in and begin playing with the utilities, turn to the "Quick Start" section preceding this chapter. You will find that installing this program is straightforward and requires only a few steps. Thereafter, you can follow the instructional screens included with each utility. You need not refer to the documentation for each utility, although there you will find many helpful tips for using and modifying the utility programs.

HARD DISK MANAGER

About the Utility Programs

This package contains 25 different DOS-based utilities for organizing and customizing your hard disk system. Some are just short batch files. Others are more complex routines that employ programming techniques such as conditional logic, subroutines, validation of user input, and concatenation. All are understandable and modifiable by nonprogrammers.

Some of these routines are available through generic "desk top" applications. These "desk top" applications, however, leave you with little individual choices and lock you into certain limitations. In contrast, the *Hard Disk Manager* utilities can be tailored to individual requirements. For the novice user, the programs can be installed as is. For the more experienced user, you can have the satisfaction of knowing that you designed and installed your own hard disk management system. And, any time the need arises, you can change them again . . . and again.

chapter 2

Behind the Utilities

For hard disk users, interacting with the operating system is a fact of life. It is the operating system that coordinates and integrates all aspects of one's hardware and software. The Disk Operating System (DOS) is a highly powerful tool that controls a computer's input and output, that loads and executes programs, and that is responsible for managing files in a floppy or hard disk environment.

DOS also can be viewed as a programming language for setting up and managing a hard disk system. Behind DOS's basic commands lies the ability to combine various commands and advanced features of DOS into powerful utility programs. The point of these utilities is that you, the user, can install them as is, customize them to your own system, or use them as a basis for creating new ones.

This chapter is an overview of those features of DOS that make up the guts of the utilities. A quick scan of the chapter before you install the utilities will give you some insight into their design and construction. This chapter is relevant particularly for the individual who wants to know *what* is behind the utilities. On the other hand, when you're convinced that you want to write some on your own, this summary is perhaps the best place to begin.

A Functional Overview of the Operating System

A number of versions of PC-DOS have been released. The earliest versions of DOS (1.0 and 1.1) were written exclusively for the PC. Many features were added to versions 2.0 and greater so that later versions of DOS could accommodate the needs of hard disk users.

The DOS Command Files

At the heart of DOS are three command files: IBMBIO.COM, IBM-DOS.COM, and COMMAND.COM. At the time a system is first set up, DOS is installed on the hard disk. During this process, some files are copied onto the hard disk automatically, and others must be copied manually by the user. The three files mentioned above are automatically copied. In addition, every time DOS is loaded or the system is initialized, these three files are placed in memory.

IBMBIO.COM establishes the system's Basic Input/Output System (BIOS) that is located in the computer's ROM (Read-Only Memory) chips. In doing so, it determines how the system is configured and initializes the system's peripherals (e.g., the printer, display, and so on). IBMBIO.COM in turn loads COMMAND.COM into memory.

IBMDOS.COM is DOS's file management system. It initializes the internal working tables of DOS. These internal working tables are established each time a disk is formatted and serve as an index of disk files and file status.

COMMAND.COM is the DOS file most users are familiar with. Also known as the command processor, it is the largest of the three essential operating system files and is the guts of DOS's programming capabilities. The COMMAND.COM file contains the DOS internal commands. These are fundamental DOS commands that are placed in resident memory since they are frequently accessed by the user.

DOS's File Management Capabilities

Certain aspects of DOS not only determine where data are physically held on a hard disk, but also where they are logically located. DOS organizes the disk storage space into physical locations and provides a mechanism for indexing data stored in those locations. At the same time, multiple indices, hierarchically arranged, can be established to group data into logical locations.

Physical Data Storage

During the formatting process, DOS marks the hard disk, dividing it into a number of concentric circles called tracks. These tracks are further divided into sectors, each containing up to 512 bytes, or characters of information. The formatting process also establishes a directory and a File Allocation

Table (FAT). The directory contains an index of what is stored on the disk and the FAT contains pointers to the sectors in which information is stored.

Each time a file is saved, DOS searches for free sectors and places the file contents in them. It is interesting to note that this file organization process is quite a bit different from a manual filing system. Instead of placing like information in a single area, DOS places information in any available sector; one large file could be spread all over the disk. It is up to the FAT to keep track of the pointers to each sector.

Logical Data Storage

Perhaps the most useful feature added to the hard disk versions of DOS was the inclusion of hierarchical directories. As mentioned above, a directory is an index. It contains a list of files stored on a disk along with reference information that tells DOS where each file is physically stored. This index can contain references to sub-indices; that is, directories may be arranged in a hierarchy in which directory entries contain names of lower-level directories. The feature allows the user to logically group data into a number of levels of subdirectories. In the jargon of the operating system, this is termed setting up a "tree-structured directory." The starting point for all hierarchical directories is the DOS master directory (the Root Directory) that is established during the initial setup of the hard disk.

Although the operating system can keep track of where any file is stored, it is not nearly so easy for the user to search through a single index of hundreds of files. Logically grouping files with like contents into a number of subdirectories is essential for the efficient management of a hard disk system.

DOS's Built-in Utilities and Commands

A number of useful utilities are provided with the operating system. These utilities can be used as stand-alone routines. Or, by using DOS as a programming language, a number of DOS utility commands can be combined to create multifaceted utility programs. Included in the DOS programs are some 50 commands. Included in these are utilities for disk management; utilities for manipulating files and directories; utilities for searching, sorting, and combining the contents of files; and a text editor called EDLIN.

Each utility is activated by using a DOS command. Activation of a DOS command can take one of two forms: Commands can be entered by the user, one by one, or commands can be programmed into sequences and entered in a batch mode through use of a DOS batch file. Batch files, which are user-designed executable programs that contain one or more DOS commands, are described in more detail in the next section.

2.1 PROGRAMMING WITH DOS

There are any number of reasons why one might want to program with DOS using batch file sequences. For example, it may not be necessary or practical for users to enter DOS commands individually. One might be building an integrated application in which a number of DOS commands must be chained together with other applications software. Or one might be dealing with a user who has little or no understanding of DOS.

For example, a File Archive program could be written that allows the user to: Copy an infrequently used file from the current directory to a floppy disk; erase the file in the current directory; and in an Archive Log File, add an entry that includes the name of the file and the date it was archived. All the user would have to type is the command **ARCHIVE** and the filename, as in:

```
ARCHIVE [filename.ext]
```

Behind that simple English command would be DOS commands that copy the file from the current directory to a floppy disk, delete the file from the current directory, capture the archival information, and append the archival information to the end of a log file.

Batch files are extraordinarily versatile. Ranging from several lines of code to more elaborate programs with decision-making logic, they can be written and modified by nonprogrammers.

Batch File Characteristics

Batch files are programs written in ASCII text format, and they can be written with any text editor. One does not have to go out and buy a special text editor; EDLIN, included with the DOS program files, will suffice. Tips on using DOS functions to write batch files are included in Appendix B.

As is the case with any other DOS file, batch file names must be eight characters or less. In addition, a unique requirement of batch files is that they must have the extension **.BAT**. This is because all files with the exten-

Behind the Utilities

sion .BAT are automatically executed by DOS when the filename is typed. For example, if the user creates a batch file named ARCHIVE.BAT, a batch routine will be activated any time the user types the word **ARCHIVE** at the DOS prompt.

As batch files are executed, each line of the program is displayed on the screen unless the display is suppressed by using a special batch file command.

Depending on the technical sophistication of the user and the need for complex command routines, batch files can be created to perform most any disk or file management task. In general, batch files can be categorized into two types, based upon their complexity:

1. Batch files that contain only the usual DOS commands.
2. Batch files that also use a special set of DOS batch file commands; some of these have decision-making capabilities and permit the use of higher-level programming techniques, including conditional statements and subroutines.

Batch File Contents

Any DOS command that can be typed interactively by the user may be placed in a batch file. This includes both DOS internal commands (commands loaded into memory when DOS is initialized) and DOS external commands (those that must be loaded into memory at the time of use). Batch files also may contain non-DOS program names such as BASICA, LOTUS, etc. These are programs that use DOS to communicate with the computer. In addition, batch files can also contain names of other batch files, allowing the user to chain together one batch file after another.

A useful feature of batch files is the ability to use variables. These variables, known as replaceable parameters or dummy parameters, allow the user to construct a generic batch file that can accept different input each time it is executed. This process is discussed in detail in Appendix B.

Batch File Uses

Perhaps the most common use of batch files is to insulate the user from the operating system. Any command or operation that someone might want to perform on his or her hard disk can be programmed as a batch file. With minimal knowledge of the operating system, the user can make maximal use of DOS's file and disk management utilities. For example, the likelihood of a user backing up files on a routine basis can be greatly enhanced by providing menu-driven batch file backup routines.

Batch files also can be used to standardize certain routines that must be performed. By programming all command sequences into a batch file, one can ensure that the same routine is followed regardless of the user or the situation. Such a use of batch files might be required in order to maintain an organized hard disk when several users are sharing a hard disk system.

Efficiency is another major advantage of using batch files. Preprogrammed command sequences eliminate the need to perform the same commands over and over again.

Lastly, batch files greatly simplify the use of a hard disk system. Once command sequences are programmed into a batch file, it is no longer necessary to remember elaborate command sequences or arcane syntax.

DOS Programming Commands for Batch Files

A number of DOS's commands are used exclusively in batch files. These commands include:

```
REM
ECHO
PAUSE
IF
GOTO
FOR
SHIFT
```

The user may recognize several of these commands such as IF, GOTO, and FOR as commands frequently found in other more sophisticated programming languages. It is these commands in particular that permit DOS to be a powerful tool to both programmers and nonprogrammers.

Descriptions of each of these commands can be found in Appendix B.

2.2

PROGRAMMING WITH DOS'S ADVANCED FEATURES

In addition to a number of utility-oriented commands, DOS contains a number of features that allow the user to alter the computer's basic input/output system to suit individual needs. These features include the setup of a configuration file (CONFIG.SYS), redirection of the traditional modes of input and output, and the ability to alter characteristics of the display.

Configuration Files (CONFIG.SYS)

A configuration file, just like a batch file, is an ASCII file (text file) created by the user. DOS requires that such a file be called CONFIG.SYS, and that this file be located in the root directory. This allows the file to be checked by DOS when the system is booted; thus, the file tells DOS how the user has configured his or her system.

Configuration File Format

The format of a CONFIG.SYS file is always the same. Each configurational feature is listed on a line of the file, followed by an equal (=) sign, and a value or filename. For example, a CONFIG.SYS file might have the following entry:

```
BUFFERS=10
```

This entry means that the number of buffers or memory blocks has been set to 10.

Configuration File Contents

Five to eight different configurational features can be used with the CONFIG.SYS file, depending on the version of DOS. These include features that are beneficial to the average user as well as features typically needed only by programmers. The three features utilized by the average user are:

> BUFFERS= The ability to set the size of memory blocks from 1 to 99.
>
> Whenever a file is written to or read, DOS brings portions of the file into the memory buffer. Increasing the buffer size increases the amount of that file that can be held in the buffer. Up to a point, increasing the buffer size will speed up processing. By having this information at the point of initialization, DOS will always use a buffer size of 10 unless the number of buffers is reconfigured by modifying the CONFIG.SYS file.

DEVICE = The ability to specify files containing device drivers. Device drivers are hardware-specific programs to which DOS transfers control when accessing that particular hardware device or peripheral.

The device driver of most interest to users is ANSI.SYS, which is included in DOS's program contents. ANSI.SYS contains the American National Standards Institute (ANSI) set of terminal codes. These are standard codes for controlling a system's display or video screen. It is only through use of this device driver that the user can access DOS's extended screen and keyboard functions. For example, to change the display's background color or to highlight a character by making it blink, this device driver must be set. Other enhanced keyboard features accessible by setting ANSI.SYS are: character (or foreground) color, reverse video capabilities, intensified characters, invisible characters, and underscored characters.

It should be noted that when the *Hard Disk Manager* utilities are installed, a CONFIG.SYS file is automatically installed if one does not exist on the hard disk. This file contains the command:

```
device=ansi.sys
```

FILES = The ability to set the maximum number of files that may be open at any one time.

Although the default value of FILES= is 8, this value might have to be increased if the user is working with an application that requires more than 8 files to be opened at a time (such as dBASE III).

Redirection of Input and Output

DOS allows the user to alter a system's standard input and output devices. Typically, input is via the keyboard, whereas output is directed toward the display screen. By using DOS's redirection capabilities, for example, input can come from a file and the output can be redirected to a file, a printer, or to a device called "nul" in which the output is suppressed. Redirection of output is signified in DOS by a greater-than sign (>) followed by the output device name. For example, to obtain a printout of the contents of a directory, redirection might be used as follows

```
C:\ DIR>PRN
```

in which PRN is the DOS device name for the printer. Redirection of input is signified by a lesser-than sign (<).

DOS's redirection capabilities give the DOS programmer a good deal of flexibility. For example, whenever log files or audit trails are required for a particular operation, the output can be sent automatically to another file or to the printer. The ability to save information in a file and then use that file as input to another operation also is quite useful. For example, a batch file could prompt the user for input, save that information in a temporary file, and then refer to the contents of that file later on in the program.

Key Reassignment

A lesser-known form of redirected input is the ability to reassign the meaning of various keys. In this case, it is the ANSI.SYS device driver that gives the user the ability to assign new values or functions to the keys on the computer's keyboard. Unfortunately, most users assume that it is necessary to purchase special software packages to do this.

Entire operations can be assigned to a single function key in which the function key activates a batch file. For example, in the *Hard Disk Manager* utilities, this process is used to make the <F1> key redisplay the *Hard Disk Manager* utilities menu (or the Main Menu if one has been installed). The process is simple. When <F1> is pressed, it activates a batch file that in turn redisplays the menu.

The procedures for key reassignment are described in detail in Chapter 5.

Using DOS's Extended Screen and Keyboard Functions

DOS uses special character sequences, known as control codes or character control sequences, to manipulate various aspects of the video screen and terminal. For example, these control codes can be used to accentuate various attributes of a screen's design, to change the cursor position, or to alter the color of the display.

Control Character Sequences

All of DOS's extended screen and keyboard control functions must be activated by using a special control code known as an escape character (ASCII 27). This escape character either can be typed at the keyboard or placed within a text file. Control codes that are preceded by an escape character are intercepted by the file ANSI.SYS. As mentioned earlier, the ANSI.SYS file, which must be resident in memory, contains the American National Standard Institute set of terminal codes for altering display attributes.

Chapter 5 describes the procedures for placing control character sequences in a text file.

Changing Display Attributes

Control character sequences can be used to alter or enhance many attributes of the display. They can be used in screen design to make characters typed on the screen invisible; to make portions of the display screen blink, to increase the intensity of display characters, to reverse the video screen image, to underscore display characters, to set the cursor position, and to change the color of the screen foreground and/or background.

Using the ASCII Extended Character Set

In addition to regular text characters (letters, numerals, etc.) and control character sequences, DOS text files may contain the ASCII (American Standard Code for Information Interchange) extended character set as well. These are ASCII symbols with numeric values from ASCII 128 through ASCII 255. These characters can be used to design professional-looking informational and menu screens. A number of the ASCII extended character set values are intended specifically for border designs. A table of these values is presented in Appendix E.

Characters forming the ASCII extended character set are entered into a text file by depressing the Alt key and typing the ASCII value *on the numeric keypad.* The most frequently used of these characters can be found in the ASCII Help screen on the accompanying disk.

2.3
A SUMMARY OF DOS FEATURES BEHIND THE UTILITIES

1. DOS has three essential system files that are sent to memory every time DOS is loaded. These files control the system's basic input and output, initialize the system, and serve as a file management system.
2. Formatting a disk divides it into tracks and sectors and establishes a directory and File Allocation Table (FAT). The directory contains

an inventory of the disk. The FAT contains pointers to sectors where each file is stored.
3. DOS's subdirectory capabilities allow the user to hierarchically organize the directories and files on his or her disk.
4. DOS's commands can be entered interactively from the keyboard. Or DOS commands can be entered automatically in a batch mode through the creation of batch files.
5. DOS programs can be written that include special batch file commands with decision-making capabilities.
6. DOS programs are written as batch files. They must be written in ASCII format (using any text editor or EDLIN). They also must have the extension **.BAT**.
7. DOS programs can be written with variables called "replaceable parameters." These variables permit the construction of generic batch file utilities.
8. Batch files are used to insulate the user from the operating system, to standardize certain routines, and to make a hard disk system more efficient and easier to use.
9. A configuration file (CONFIG.SYS) is created to tailor a computer's basic input and output system to the user's needs. It is used to activate the DOS device driver ANSI.SYS.
10. DEVICE=ANSI.SYS can be set in the configuration file. When the device driver ANSI.SYS is called, the user can gain far greater control over attributes of the video display. These attributes include the ability to alter the color of both the display foreground and background.
11. The ANSI.SYS device driver gives the user the ability to perform key reassignment functions. This is particularly useful for assigning specific routines to the function keys.
12. Control character sequences are used to manipulate various aspects of the display. An escape character precedes all character sequences for DOS's extended screen and keyboard control functions.
13. The ASCII extended character set (ASCII values 128 to 255) can be used for generating graphic designs. These characters are generated by holding down the <Alt> key and typing the ASCII value on the numeric keypad.

c·h·a·p·t·e·r 3

Installing *Hard Disk Manager*

This chapter describes the installation of the *Hard Disk Manager*. All or part of the utility programs may be installed.

This chapter is not just a description of the installation steps. It is important to understand exactly what operations are being performed during installation. This does not mean that anything radical is being done to your hard disk. On the contrary, the routines are fairly uncomplicated.

This chapter is for those users want to know what is happening when anything, no matter how minor, is being done to their systems. Many experienced users will say that they never run the installation routine of an unknown program without first checking to see what it does. This chapter explains the process.

3.1 REQUIREMENTS

The system requirements for the use of these programs are minimal. There are no system memory requirements because none of these routines is memory resident. The only requirements are as follows:

1. The user's hard disk must contain all of the DOS programs (the DOS disk and the Supplemental Programs disk). The user must know the directory location of DOS on the hard disk. The DOS version may be 2.0 or later.
2. It is assumed that all individuals using *Hard Disk Manager* are using a hard disk system with a C drive.

Hard Disk Manager

REPLACEMENT ORDER FORM

Please use this form when ordering a replacement for a defective diskette.

A. If Ordering within Thirty Days of Purchase
If a diskette is reported defective within thirty days of purchase, a replacement diskette will be provided free of charge. *This card must be totally filled out and accompanied by the defective diskette and a copy of the dated sales receipt.* In addition, please complete and return the Limited Warranty Registration Card.

B. If Ordering after Thirty Days of Purchase but within One Year
If a diskette is reported defective after thirty days but within one year of purchase and the Warranty Registration Card has been properly filed, a replacement diskette will be provided to you for a nominal fee of $5.00 (send check or money order only). *This card must be totally filled out and accompanied by the defective diskette, a copy of the dated sales receipt, and a $5.00 check or money order made payable to Simon & Schuster, Inc.*

NAME _____ PHONE NUMBER (___) _____
ADDRESS _____
CITY _____ STATE _____ ZIP _____
PURCHASE DATE _____
PURCHASE PRICE _____
COMPUTER BRAND & MODEL _____

Please send all requests to MicroService Customer Service, Simon & Schuster/Prentice Hall Press, 200 Old Tappan Road, Old Tappan, NJ 07675; ATTN: Replacements

NOTE: Simon & Schuster reserves the right, at its option, to refund your purchase price in lieu of providing a replacement diskette.

0-13-383779-3

Hard Disk Manager

LIMITED WARRANTY REGISTRATION CARD

In order to preserve your rights as provided for in the limited warranty, this card must be on file with Simon & Schuster within thirty days of purchase.

Please fill in the information requested:

NAME _____ PHONE NUMBER (___) _____
ADDRESS _____
CITY _____ STATE _____ ZIP _____
COMPUTER BRAND & MODEL _____ DOS VERSION _____ MEMORY ____K

Where did you purchase this product?
DEALER NAME _____
ADDRESS _____
CITY _____ STATE _____ ZIP _____
PURCHASE DATE _____ PURCHASE PRICE _____

How did you learn about this product? (Check as many as applicable.)
STORE DISPLAY _____ SALESPERSON _____ MAGAZINE ARTICLE _____ ADVERTISEMENT _____
OTHER (Please explain) _____

How long have you owned or used this computer?
LESS THAN 30 DAYS _____ LESS THAN 6 MONTHS _____ 6 MONTHS TO A YEAR _____ OVER 1 YEAR _____

What is your primary use for the computer?
BUSINESS _____ PERSONAL _____ EDUCATION _____ OTHER (Please explain) _____

Where is your computer located?
HOME _____ OFFICE _____ SCHOOL _____ OTHER (Please explain) _____

0-13-383779-3

PUT
FIRST-
CLASS
STAMP
HERE

Simon & Schuster, Inc.
Brady Books
One Gulf+Western Plaza
New York, New York 10023

ATTN: **PRODUCT REGISTRATION**

Installing Hard Disk Manager

If the user can answer "yes" to the above requirements, the installation of all of *Hard Disk Manager* is a straightforward process. If the hard disk does not contain the DOS programs, the DOS manual should be consulted for instructions on how to install all of the DOS programs on the hard disk.

It should also be noted that the program disk does not contain any operating system files; the computer cannot be started using this program disk as a "boot" disk.

3.2
INSTALLING THE ENTIRE PROGRAM

The amount of disk space occupied by the *Hard Disk Manager* varies with the size of the hard disk. For example, on a 20-MB hard disk, the program uses approximately 700 KB of disk space. A directory structure is created and the files are copied into these directories. There should be no overlap with any existing directories since there is only one directory created at the second level under the root directory: \HDU. All of the other directories created are subdirectories of \HDU.

Steps

The only information required of the user is the directory containing the DOS files. During the installation process, the user is prompted for this information. Otherwise, the process is as follows:

1. Turn on the computer. After the DOS system prompt (the C> symbols) is displayed, insert the *Hard Disk Manager* disk in drive A.
2. Enter the following command:

    ```
    a:install
    ```
3. An information screen that describes the installation process will be displayed. A "Strike any key when ready" message appears at the bottom of the screen; press a key for the installation process to proceed.
4. After a few moments, a prompt for the name of the directory containing the DOS program files appears. You must:
    - Enter the directory name (including the drive and path). The path should include all path parameters currently on your disk. Consult the DOS manual or Appendix A if you need further assistance with the syntax for the path designation.

18   HARD DISK MANAGER

- Press the <F6> function key.
- Press <Enter>.

Pressing the <F6> key causes the symbols ^Z to be displayed; this is normal. The installation process then continues.

5. A check is made to determine if the DOS directory input is valid (i.e., if the specified directory does indeed contain the DOS program files). If the input is not valid, an error message is displayed and the installation is aborted. (Refer to the "Troubleshooting" section of this chapter.)
6. If the DOS directory specification is valid, the installation proceeds to create the necessary directories and to copy program files into them. This section takes about 5 to 10 minutes, depending on the speed of one's system.
7. A message is displayed when the installation is complete. Figure 3.1 shows the final installation message.
8. YOU MUST THEN REBOOT THE COMPUTER (press <Ctrl> <Alt> <Del>).
9. To start the program, change the current directory to the root directory (by entering the command CD\). Then, enter the command

    hdu

to display the *Hard Disk Manager* main menu.

That is all there is to the installation of *Hard Disk Manager*. Be sure you make a backup copy of the program disk. The program is always started by executing the command **hdu** from the root directory. The following section describes the action that is taken during the installation process.

What the INSTALL.BAT File Does to the Hard Disk

The installation of all of *Hard Disk Manager* begins with INSTALL.BAT and is completed with CONTINUE.BAT. Basically, the installation can be divided into the operations listed on the next page.

```
Installation is now complete.  To start the program . . .
    1. Remove disk from drive A
    2. Reboot the system ( by pressing [Ctrl] [Alt] [Del] )
    3. Enter the command CD \
    4. Then, enter the command HDU
These steps are found in Figure 3-1 of Chapter 3.
```

Figure 3.1. *Hard Disk Manager* Final Installation Message

1. The directory containing the DOS program files is specified by the user.
2. The user's DOS directory input is added to a file that becomes CONTINUE.BAT.
3. The validity of the DOS directory information is checked.
4. The ANSI.SYS file is copied to the root directory.
5. The necessary directories are created.
6. The *Hard Disk Manager* programs are copied into the new directories.
7. A check is made to determine if a CONFIG.SYS file exists. (CONFIG.SYS is a configuration file required to run some of the *Hard Disk Manager* utilities.) If CONFIG.SYS does not exist, this file is copied to the root directory; if it does exist, then the command DEVICE=ANSI.SYS is appended to the existing file.
8. The DOS directory information is appended to a PATH command that is stored in a separate file for future use. This PATH command also is added to the beginning of the HDU.BAT file. This is the batch file that calls up the *Hard Disk Manager* main menu.

The INSTALL.BAT and CONTINUE.BAT files are shown at the end of this chapter for readers interested in examining the process in detail (Figures 3.3 and 3.4).

3.3
INSTALLING PART OF *HARD DISK MANAGER*

For users interested in installing only certain components of *Hard Disk Manager*, the installation process is somewhat different. A directory structure is created, but only the directories necessary for the desired utility are created. Like the complete installation, there should be no overlap with any existing directories since there is only one directory created at the first level under the root directory: \HDU. The other directories created are subdirectories of the \HDU directory.

The partial installation process can be divided into two parts. The first part is automated, whereas the second part is menu driven. The automated process performs the initial configuration routines that are necessary for all the programs on *Hard Disk Manager*. It is executed only once.

Steps

The first part of the installation performs the following operations: The user is asked to specify the location of the DOS program files; the validity of the user's entry is checked; a CONFIG.SYS file is created or the command DEVICE=ANSI.SYS is appended to an existing one; the \HDU directory is created; and some key files are copied to the new directory. Here are the specific steps.

1. Turn on the computer. After the DOS system prompt (the C> symbols) is displayed, insert the *Hard Disk Manager* disk in drive A.
2. Enter the following command:

    a: partial

3. You are prompted for the name of the directory containing the DOS program files. You must:
   - Enter the directory name (including the drive and path).
   - Press the <F6> function key.
   - Press <Enter>.

   Pressing the <F6> key causes the symbols ^Z to be displayed; this is normal. The preparation routine then continues.
4. A check is made to determine if the user's DOS directory input is valid (i.e., if the specified directory does indeed contain the DOS program files). If it is not valid, an error message is displayed and the preparation process is aborted. (The user should refer to the "Troubleshooting" section of this chapter.)
5. If the DOS directory specification is valid, the necessary directories are created and certain files are copied into them. This section takes a few minutes. A message informs the user when the preparation routine is complete. Pressing any key will display a menu of installation options (shown in Figure 3.2).
6. The Installation Menu contains the following options:

   Install Disk/Directory Utilities

   Install Customized Display Utilities

   Install Screen Design Utility

   Install Backup/Restore Utilities

   Install File Management Utilities

   Install HELP Utilities

   Install All Utilities

   Exit To DOS

   You may select one or more of these components of *Hard Disk Manager* for installation. All utilities may be installed even if individual components have previously been installed.
7. When the desired portions of *Hard Disk Manager* have been installed, select the Exit To DOS option.

Installing Hard Disk Manager   21

```
┌─────────────────────────────────────────────────┐
│              ┌─────────────────┐                │
│              │ INSTALLATION MENU│               │
│              └─────────────────┘                │
│                                                 │
│         1. Install Disk/Directory Utilities     │
│         2. Install Customized Display Utilities │
│         3. Install Screen Design Utility        │
│         4. Install Backup/Restore Utility       │
│         5. Install File Management Utilities    │
│         6. Install HELP Screen Utilities        │
│         7. Install ALL Hard Disk Utilites       │
│         8. Exit to DOS                          │
│                                                 │
└─────────────────────────────────────────────────┘
```

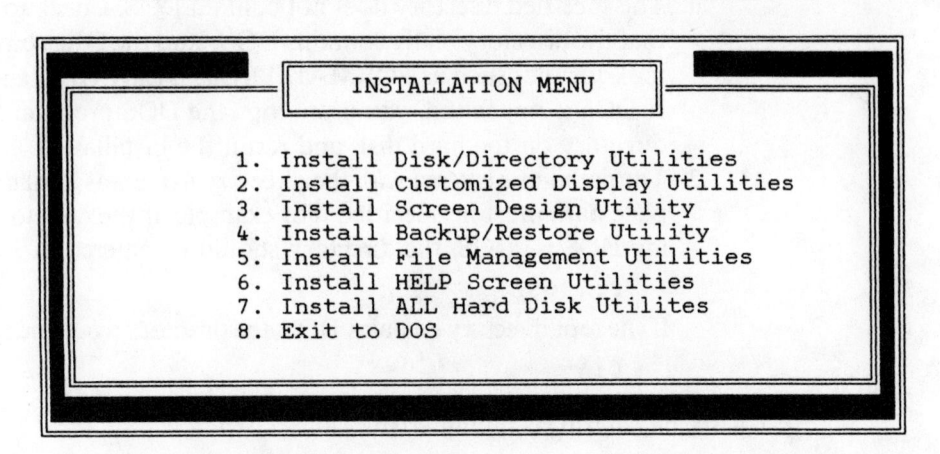

Figure 3.2. Menu of Installation Options (Partial Installation)

8. Each selected utility is now installed. The following commands call up the menu associated with the specific utility from the \HDU directory:

Disk/Directory:	DISK
Display:	DISPLAY
Screen Design:	DESIGN
Backup/Restore:	BACK
File Management:	FILE
Help Utilities:	HELP

9. *You must then reboot the computer* (press <Ctrl> <Alt> <Del>).
10. Then, change the current directory to C:\HDU and execute the appropriate command.

3.4 TROUBLESHOOTING

This section briefly covers some problems that may be encountered during installation and use of *Hard Disk Manager*.

Invalid Directory Specification

This is the problem when the user encounters the error message "Your DOS directory specification was not specified correctly." Here are some possible errors:

1. The specified directory does not contain DOS. Check to make sure that the directory really contains DOS. Run the DIR command and look for files such as FORMAT, TREE, DISKCOPY, and EDLIN. If DOS is not found, you must copy the DOS program files into a directory on the hard disk and rerun the installation.
2. The pathname entered with the directory name was invalid. The complete path must be specified. For example, if the directory containing DOS is \DOS, the directory should be entered as

    ```
    c:\DOS
    ```

    If the root directory contains DOS, the directory would be specified as

    ```
    c:\
    ```

Also, be careful of typing errors.

Strange Characters After the Prompt

Odd characters may appear at the bottom of the menu as a prompt, below the ENTER SELECTION line, such as

```
[0,59;"return",13p; [22;18H
```

This is a result of an absent CONFIG.SYS file. If this file does not exist on your system when *Hard Disk Manager* is installed (either partially or totally), the installation routines should create it. If you have just installed *Hard Disk Manager* utilities, you must restart (reboot) your system before using any of the utilities. The CONFIG.SYS file is only read by DOS at start-up time. If you have already done this, here are some possible solutions:

1. Enter the following command:

    ```
    type c:\config.sys
    ```

    The contents should contain the following line:

    ```
    device=ansi.sys
    ```

2. If DOS responds with a "File not found" message, then place the *Hard Disk Manager* disk in drive A and enter this command:

    ```
    copy a:\hdu\disk\auto\config.tmp c:\config.sys
    ```

3. If the CONFIG.SYS file exists, but does not contain the line shown above, then place the *Hard Disk Manager* disk in drive A and enter this command:

    ```
    copy c:\config.sys + a:\hdu\disk\auto\config.tmp
    ```

Installing Hard Disk Manager

4. If the CONFIG.SYS file exists and contains the required line shown above, then try entering this command:

    ```
    dir c:\ansi.sys
    ```

    If a "File not found" message is the response, then you must copy the ANSI.SYS file from your DOS directory to the root directory, as in:

    ```
    copy c:\dos\ansi.sys c:\
    ```

One of the above steps should solve the problem. *Be sure to reboot the system after performing any of the above steps.*

Conflicts with Additional PATH Commands

In order for *Hard Disk Manager* to work, it is necessary for the user to specify the directory containing the DOS programs. This information is placed in a PATH command at the beginning of a file called HDU.BAT. (This is the command file that calls the *Hard Disk Manager* program.)

If the user's system contains an AUTOEXEC.BAT file, and that file also contains a PATH command, there may be problems if the specified paths are not the same in both files. The problems will only be evident when the other programs are executed *after Hard Disk Manager* has been run. Here are the steps for investigating this possibility.

1. Enter the following command:

    ```
    type c:\hdu\hdu.bat
    ```

    The first line of this file should contain the PATH command.

2. Now enter this command:

    ```
    type c:\autoexec.bat
    ```

    If your system responds with the message "File not found," or no PATH command is found in the displayed file, then the PATH command is not causing a problem.

3. However, if there is a PATH command in the AUTOEXEC.BAT file, compare its contents to the same command in the HDU.BAT file. Disregard differences in upper- and lowercase letters or the presence or absence of the "equals" (=) sign.

4. If any directories are shown in the AUTOEXEC.BAT file's PATH command, these should be added to the HDU.BAT file. For example, suppose the HDU.BAT file contains the command

    ```
    path c:\;c:\dos
    ```

and the AUTOEXEC.BAT file contains this PATH command:
```
path c:\;c:\dos;c:\utility
```
5. The additional directory (c:\utility) must be added to HDU.BAT. Here is the procedure for editing HDU.BAT:

   a. Change your current directory to the directory containing your DOS program files.
   b. Enter the following command:
   ```
   edlin c:\hdu.bat
   ```
   EDLIN will respond with the message "End of file."
   c. To edit the first line, enter the number 1. EDLIN will display the contents of the existing line 1.
   d. Type the existing line exactly as it appears, and add the additional directory at the end of the line; then press <Enter>.
   e. End the EDLIN session by entering the command
   ```
   E
   ```

Pressing <Ctrl><Break>: No Menu, No Prompt

The user may encounter problems when the <Ctrl> <Break> is activated during the running of some of the utilities. Under normal execution, all the utilities will return to a menu screen. However, if <Ctrl> <Break> is pressed during the execution of a utility and a menu does not reappear, the user can press the <F1> key to redisplay the menu.

3.5 REMOVING ALL UTILITIES FROM THE HARD DISK

If the user, alas, wishes to remove all of the *Hard Disk Manager* from his or her hard disk, a batch file has been included on the program disk that will do the entire process. This routine will erase *all* files in the directory system of the *Hard Disk Manager*. If any nonprogram files are stored in those directories, they too will be erased. After the directories are emptied, they will be removed. There will be no trace of *Hard Disk Manager* on the user's system.

Installing Hard Disk Manager

Hard Disk Manager is removed by placing the *Hard Disk Manager* program disk in drive A, and entering the following command:

    a:remove

Of course, if the user later decides that this was folly, the *Hard Disk Manager* can simply be reinstalled.

```
        INSTALL.BAT
 1:     echo off
 2:     cls
 3:     type a:title.scr
 4:     pause
 5:     cls
 6:     a:
 7:     echo  This routine installs all of Hard Disk Manager on your
 8:     echo        hard disk.  The program is installed on drive C.

 9:     echo  DOS must already be installed on the hard disk.  You will
10:     echo       be prompted to enter its path and directory name.
11:     echo  Those unfamiliar with DOS should read Chapter 3 prior to
12:     echo       proceeding. The installation process is explained in this
              chapter.
13:     echo  To abort the installation, press [Ctrl] [Break], and
14:     echo       then a "Y" in response to "Terminate batch job (Y/N)?"

15:     pause
16:     cls
17:     type dospath.scr
18:     copy con:dospath.tmp
19:     if not exist dospath.tmp goto ABORT
20:     copy dospath1.txt+dospath.tmp+continue.txt continue.bat
21:     continue
22:     :ABORT
23:     echo DOS directory information was not specified correctly;
24:     echo      installation aborted.
25:     echo      Please refer to Chapter 3 for installation procedures.
26:     c:
```

Figure 3.3. INSTALL.BAT Batch File

```
    CONTINUE.BAT
 1: cd [DOS directory name added here in INSTALL.BAT]
 2: if not exist format.com goto ERROR
 3: if not exist edlin.com goto ERROR
 4: echo Making directories and copying files . . .
 5: echo      This will take about 5-10 minutes.
 6: copy ansi.sys \ansi.sys
 7: md c:\hdu
 8: md c:\hdu\protect
 9: md c:\hdu\disk
10: md c:\hdu\file
11: md c:\hdu\display
12: md c:\hdu\backgrnd
13: md c:\hdu\foregrnd
14: md c:\hdu\design
15: md c:\hdu\view
16: md c:\hdu\backup
17: md c:\hdu\help
18: md c:\hdu\help\dos
19: md c:\hdu\help\batch
20: md c:\hdu\help\edlin
21: md c:\hdu\backup\partial
22: md c:\hdu\backup\dateback
23: md c:\hdu\backup\modify
24: md c:\hdu\backup\fullrest
25: md c:\hdu\backup\partrest
26: md c:\hdu\disk\auto
27: md c:\hdu\disk\mp
28: md c:\hdu\display\screen
29: copy a:\hdu\*.* c:\hdu\*.*
30: copy a:\hdu\protect\*.* c:\hdu\protect\*.*
31: copy a:\hdu\disk\*.* c:\hdu\disk\*.*
32: copy a:\hdu\file\*.* c:\hdu\file\*.*
33: copy a:\hdu\display\*.* c:\hdu\display\*.*
34: copy a:\hdu\backgrnd\*.* c:\hdu\backgrnd\*.*
35: copy a:\hdu\foregrnd\*.* c:\hdu\foregrnd\*.*
36: copy a:\hdu\design\*.* c:\hdu\design\*.*
37: copy a:\hdu\view\*.* c:\hdu\view\*.*
38: copy a:\hdu\backup\*.* c:\hdu\backup\*.*
39: copy a:\hdu\help\*.* c:\hdu\help\*.*
40: copy a:\hdu\help\dos\*.* c:\hdu\help\dos\*.*
41: copy a:\hdu\help\batch\*.* c:\hdu\help\batch\*.*
42: copy a:\hdu\help\edlin\*.* c:\hdu\help\edlin\*.*
43: copy a:\hdu\backup\partial\*.* c:\hdu\backup\partial\*.*
44: copy a:\hdu\backup\dateback\*.* c:\hdu\backup\dateback\*.*
45: copy a:\hdu\backup\modify\*.* c:\hdu\backup\modify\*.*
46: copy a:\hdu\backup\fullrest\*.* c:\hdu\backup\fullrest\*.*
47: copy a:\hdu\backup\partrest\*.* c:\hdu\backup\partrest\*.*
48: copy a:\hdu\disk\auto\*.* c:\hdu\disk\auto\*.*
49: copy a:\hdu\disk\mp\*.* c:\hdu\disk\mp\*.*
50: copy a:\hdu\display\screen\*.* c:\hdu\display\screen\*.*
51: copy a:\return.bat c:\
52: copy a:\setscrn.bat c:\
```

(continued)

```
53: cd \
54: if not exist config.sys goto NOCONFIG
55: :CONFIG
56: copy config.sys + \hdu\disk\auto\config.tmp
57: goto FINAL
58: :NOCONFIG
59: copy \hdu\disk\auto\config.tmp \config.sys
60: :FINAL
61: cd \hdu\disk\auto
62: copy dospath2.txt + a:dospath.tmp \hdu\dospath.txt
63: copy \hdu\dospath.txt + hdu.tmp \hdu.bat
64: del a:dospath.tmp
65: cls
66: echo Installation is now complete.  To start the program . . .
67: echo     1. Remove disk from drive A
68: echo     2. Reboot the system (by pressing [Ctrl] [Alt] [Del])
69: echo     3. Enter the command CD \
70: echo     4. Then, enter the command HDU
71: echo These steps are found in Figure 3-1 of Chapter 3.
72: goto DONE
73: :ERROR
74: del a:dospath.tmp
75: cd\
76: echo Your DOS directory was not specified correctly.
77: echo     See the "Trouble Shooting" section in Chapter 3.
78: echo     Installation aborted.
79: :DONE
80: c:
```

Figure 3.4. CONTINUE.BAT Batch File

chapter 4

Disk Organization Utilities

How much data can be stored on a disk and how those data are stored are issues of primary concern to users. When a vast amount of data are stored electronically, the user wants some assurance that the data can be retrieved reliably and with a minimal amount of effort. Although the operating system manages how the data are physically stored, it is up to the user to determine the media (hard disk, floppy disk, tape, etc.) and the logical groupings of the data into directories, subdirectories, and files. The Disk/Directory utilities guide users through the development of a logical directory structure and assist in the management and organization of their storage media.

What Are the Disk/Directory Utilities?

There are five Disk/Directory utilities. They include routines for:

- setting up a logical directory structure and linking it to a master menu for easy access to any subdirectory
- viewing and/or printing the contents of directories and subdirectories
- formatting floppy disks under a number of different conditions

Why Are They Used?

The key to a well-managed hard disk system is having an easily accessible and well-organized directory and file structure. Particularly when a number of different users will be retrieving and storing data, the administrative tasks associated with maintaining many data files can be overwhelming.

The Disk/Directory utilities address this problem. They provide menu-driven access to all of the necessary directories, subdirectories, and software programs. Such menu-based programs can navigate even the most inexperienced user through a hierarchical directory structure. In addition, these utilities eliminate the need to memorize complicated DOS commands and minimize potential errors associated with using certain disk-related commands.

How to Use the Utilities

The Disk/Directory utilites are accessed when selection 1 is chosen from the *Hard Disk Manager* main menu. This selection changes the directory to \HDU\DISK and displays the Disk Directory Menu. Any of the five selections on the screen can be chosen simply by entering the number of the desired utility. After the selection is made, the user is prompted for any required input; informational screens, when necessary, guide the user through the utility. If at any time the user chooses not to proceed with a utility, the <F1> key can be pressed to return to the previous menu.

For the those who would like additional information on electronic storage media and DOS's directory capabilities, overviews of these topics can be found at the end of this chapter.

Organization of the Disk/Directory Utilities

The disk organization utilities contained on the *Hard Disk Manager* program disk are made up of numerous files in several different directories. The principal directory is the \HDU\DISK directory. It contains the routines for all the Disk/Directory utilities except the second menu choice on the Disk/Directory menu.

Although there are over 70 files in the \HDU\DISK directory, most of these are used by the Menu/Directory Setup utility. This is a fairly extensive program, and there are two subdirectories also used by this utility: \HDU\DISK\MP and \HDU\DISK\AUTO. The first of these contains the programs for installing the Miscellaneous Programs option on the main menu. The \HDU\DISK\AUTO directory contains the files used for installation of the main menu onto the system.

```
C:\HDU\DISK      <DIR>

        1.BAT       1DBINPUT.TXT      3DBINPUT.TXT      5DBINPUT.TXT
        2.BAT       1EXINPUT.TXT      3EXINPUT.TXT      5EXINPUT.TXT
        3.BAT       1HDINPUT.TXT      3HDINPUT.TXT      5HDINPUT.TXT
        4.BAT       1MPINPUT.TXT      3MPINPUT.TXT      5MPINPUT.TXT
        5.BAT       1SSINPUT.TXT      3SSINPUT.TXT      5SSINPUT.TXT
                    1WPINPUT.TXT      3WPINPUT.TXT      5WPINPUT.TXT
        A.BAT       2DBINPUT.TXT      4DBINPUT.TXT      6DBINPUT.TXT
        B.BAT       2EXINPUT.TXT      4EXINPUT.TXT      6EXINPUT.TXT
        C.BAT       2HDINPUT.TXT      4HDINPUT.TXT      6HDINPUT.TXT
        D.BAT       2MPINPUT.TXT      4MPINPUT.TXT      6MPINPUT.TXT
        E.BAT       2SSINPUT.TXT      4SSINPUT.TXT      6SSINPUT.TXT
        F.BAT       2WPINPUT.TXT      4WPINPUT.TXT      6WPINPUT.TXT
        G.BAT
                    DBBEGIN.TXT       EXIT2DOS.BAT      SSBEGIN.TXT
                    DISKMENU.SCR      MAINMENU.TMP      WPBEGIN.TXT
                    END.TXT           MENU.BAT          SETUP.SCR
                    CR.TXT

                    DOCOPYC1.BAT      DOFORM3.BAT       DOFORM5.BAT
                    DOCOPYC2.BAT      DOFORM4.BAT

                    SSSTART.TXT       WPSTART.TXT       DBSTART.TXT
                    SSSTART.BAT       WPSTART.BAT       DBSTART.BAT


C:\HDU\DISK\VIEW    <DIR>

        1.BAT       INSTRUCT.SCR      VIEW.BAT          DOTREE2.BAT
        2.BAT       VIEW.SCR          DOVIEW.BAT        DOTREE3.BAT
        3.BAT       PRINT.BAT         DOPRINT.BAT


C:\HDU\DISK\AUTO    <DIR>

        Y.BAT       MANUAL.BAT        INSTRUCT.SCR      AUTOEXEC.TMP
        N.BAT       AUTO.BAT          MAKEAUTO.SCR      RETURN.TMP
                                      CONFIG.TMP        DOSPATH2.TXT
                                      HDU.TMP           NURETURN.TMP


C:\HDU\DISK\MP      <DIR>

        Y.BAT       MP2BEGIN.TXT      MP2.SCR           MISCPROG.SCR
        N.BAT       MP3BEGIN.TXT      MP3.SCR           DOCOPYC3.BAT
        1.BAT       MP4BEGIN.TXT      MP4.SCR
    MISCPROG.BAT    MP5BEGIN.TXT      MP5.SCR
                    MP6BEGIN.TXT      MP6.SCR
                    MPBEGIN.TXT       MPLINE.SCR
                    MPEND.TXT         MPINSTRU.SCR
```

Figure 4.1. Directory and File Structure for Disk/Directory Utilities

Disk Organization Utilities

The \HDU\VIEW directory contains the files that run the second menu choice, Disk and Directory View/Print Utilities.

Figure 4.1 shows the structure of the files and directories for the Disk/Directory utilities. As is shown in Figure 4.1, there are basically three file types used by the Disk/Directory utilities: the batch files (.BAT extensions), information/instruction screens (.SCR extensions), and EDLIN input files (.TXT extensions). The .TXT files serve as input to batch files where the EDLIN program is executed inside the batch file.

Activation of the Utilities

Selection of choice **1** on the main utility menu accesses the Disk/Directory utilities by activating the 1.BAT file in the \HDU directory. It contains the following commands:

```
   1.BAT
1: echo off
2: cls
3: cd disk
4: type diskmenu.scr
5: echo ENTER SELECTION:
6: prompt $e[22;18H
7: setscrn
```

```
================= DISK/DIRECTORY MENU =================

    1.  Main Menu and Directory Setup Utility

    2.  Disk and Directory View/Print Utilities

    3.  Format a Floppy (Data Disk)

    4.  Format a Floppy (System Disk)

    5.  Format a 360 KB Floppy in High-Capacity Drive


            <<<<< Press F1 to Return >>>>>
```

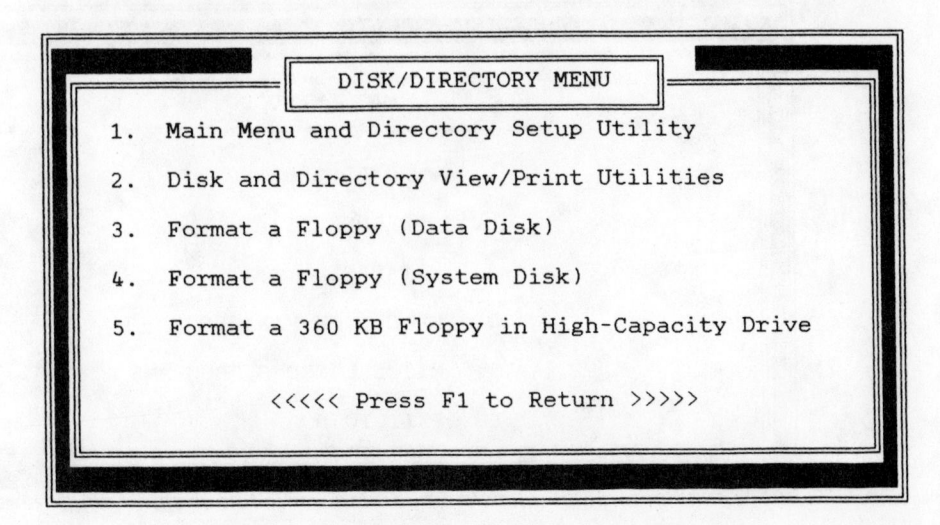

Figure 4.2. Disk/Directory Utility Menu Screen

HARD DISK MANAGER

The functions of this file are to change the current directory to \HDU\DISK, display the Disk/Directory menu (DISKMENU.SCR), position the cursor at the end of the ENTER SELECTION: prompt, and to reset the screen display attributes (setscrn). Figure 4.2 shows the Disk/Directory screen.

4.1
THE DISK/DIRECTORY UTILITIES

The Menu/Directory Setup Utility

This is one of the key utilities in the *Hard Disk Manager*. This utility allows the user to create a directory structure for common microcomputer applications (such as spreadsheet and word processing programs), and a menu system that accesses these applications. The user decides what the contents of the main menu should be.

The Menu Choices

The choices that can appear on the main menu include: Word Processing, Spreadsheet, Database, Exit To DOS, Hard Disk Manager, and Miscel-

```
                    MAIN MENU

            1.   WORD PROCESSING

            2.   SPREADSHEET

            3.   DATABASE

            4.   HARD DISK MANAGER

            5.   MISCELLANEOUS PROGRAMS

            6.   EXIT TO DOS
```

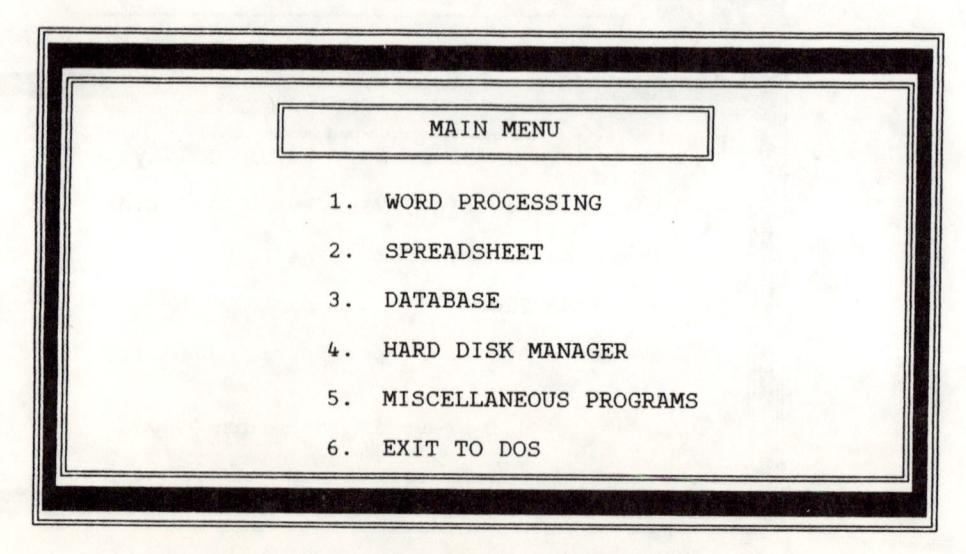

Figure 4.3. Main Menu Screen with Six Options

Disk Organization Utilities

laneous Programs. The menu choice Miscellaneous Programs is a submenu to which the user can add any program or application not found on the main menu. The user selects one or more of these six items (in any order) for inclusion in the main menu. The main menu can be installed in the system so that it is displayed automatically every time the system is turned on or restarted, or it may be installed so that it is displayed whenever the user manually enters the command **MENU** at a DOS prompt. Figure 4.3 shows the appearance of this main menu when all six menu choices have been placed on the menu.

It should be noted at the onset that this simple menu system is just that—it is a simple menu structure that is created entirely with DOS commands and utilities. Because it involves no compiled code, it can be modified to meet the needs of individual users. Without the cost of purchasing a menu-creation program, one can create a menu system that gives the average hard disk user the ability to organize and easily access hard disk applications.

Choosing Menu Selections

The Main Menu Setup Utility screen (shown in Figure 4.4) is displayed when selection 1 is chosen on the Disk/Directory menu. From here, the menu and directory structure is created in a two-step process, as shown on page 34.

```
                       MAIN MENU SETUP UTILITY

This utility creates and installs a main menu. Selections A-C will
   prompt you for the following information:
      -The name of the directory where the program resides (the directory
       will be created if it does not exist);
      -The commmand that runs the program (e.g.,"lotus" for Lotus 1-2-3).

Add Selections A-F one at a time, in any order, as needed. You MUST
   execute Selection G when the last menu choice has been added.

    ┌─────────────────────────────────────────────────────────────────┐
    │  A. Add WORD PROCESSING Menu Choice                             │
    │  B. Add SPREADSHEET Menu Choice                                 │
    │  C. Add DATABASE Menu Choice                                    │
    │  D. Add EXIT TO DOS Menu Choice                                 │
    │  E. Add HARD DISK MANAGER Menu Choice                           │
    │  F. Add MISCELLANEOUS PROGRAMS Submenu (Directory: \MISC)       │
    │  G. Install Completed Main Menu                                 │
    └─────────────────────────────────────────────────────────────────┘

                  <<<<< Press F1 to Return >>>>>
```

Figure 4.4. Main Menu/Directory Setup Utility

1. A menu item can be added to the main menu by entering the letter of the desired item (letters A through F). This step is repeated for each item that is to be placed on the main menu.
2. The last menu choice (letter G, Install Completed Main Menu) is entered after all the desired menu items have been added to the main menu.

These two steps are described in more detail below.

Constructing the Menu

In step 1, when selections A, B, C, or F are entered, directories are created for the respective applications. With selections A–C, the user is prompted to supply the name of the directory; in selection F, the directory is automatically called \MISC.

Also, in selections A, B, and C, since these menu selections will activate specific applications programs, the name of the command that calls up that specific program must be entered. For example, if selection A is executed, the user is prompted to enter the command that executes the word processing program. Suppose that program is *MultiMate*; the user must enter the command that calls up the *MultiMate* program, which in this case is **wp**.

Depending on the speed of one's system, a few minutes may be required each time a menu selection is added to the main menu. During the process, various messages are displayed that provide information about the action being taken. The Menu/Directory Setup screen is redisplayed after a selection has been added. The process is then repeated for another selection. Finally, if there are no further menu additions, the main menu is installed by executing selection G.

Installing the New Menu

The second step in setting up the main menu is the installation. When the Installation routine is started (by entering **G** from the Setup menu), an information screen is displayed asking the user if the display of the main menu is to be automatic or manual. Figure 4.5 shows the contents of this information screen. An automatic display means that the menu will appear whenever the system is turned on or rebooted. Manual display means that the menu will be displayed only when the user enters the command **MENU** after a normal DOS prompt (e.g., the C> prompt).

Disk Organization Utilities 35

```
========================== INSTRUCTIONS ==========================

This routine installs your completed menu into your root directory.
   The Main Menu can be displayed one of two ways:
   - AUTOMATICALLY, whenever your system is turned on or a system
     reset is performed; or,
   - MANUALLY, by entering a command (called MENU) whenever you
     wish to call up the Main Menu.

For automatic menu display, it is necessary to create (or add to)
   an AUTOEXEC.BAT file.  If this file already exists, the
   necessary commands will be appended to the end of that file.

Enter the command AUTO to have the menu displayed automatically.
Enter the command MANUAL to have the menu displayed manually.

              <<<<< Press F1 to Return >>>>>
```

Figure 4.5. Information Screen for Installing New Menu

The command **MANUAL** must be entered to set up a manual display of the main menu; **AUTO** is used for automatic display. When **AUTO** is entered, the batch file creates an AUTOEXEC.BAT file, if one does not already exist. If this file does exist, then the contents of the file are displayed on the screen.

The user is then asked if additional commands may be added to the end of the file so that the main menu can be displayed. This is done through a confirmation prompt: "Continue (Y/N)?" A **Y** response adds the necessary commands to the end of the AUTOEXEC.BAT file and completes the installation process. **N** aborts the AUTO routine and the screen informs the user that the MANUAL option should be used to install the main menu.

When either the MANUAL or AUTO routines are finished, the user is informed that the installation is complete. In both cases, the user is placed in the DOS environment, with the standard DOS prompt (C>). Users who have chosen the AUTO option must reboot their system to see the main menu. If the MANUAL option has been executed, only the command **MENU** must be entered to see the new menu.

The Menu/Directory Setup Program Files

The batch files that run the Menu/Directory Setup utility are some of the longer routines contained in *Hard Disk Manager*. The utility begins when selection **1** is entered from the Disk/Directory menu. This activates the 1.BAT file in the \HDU\DISK directory; it contains the following commands:

```
        1.BAT
1: echo off
2: cls
3: type setup.scr
4: echo ENTER SELECTION:
5: prompt $e[22;18H
```

The function of this file is to display the Menu/Directory Setup screen (SETUP.SCR, shown in Figure 4.4).

Almost all the files shown in Figure 4.1 are used by the Menu/Directory Setup utility. The files used by this utility can be grouped as follows:

1. The letter batch files (A.BAT through F.BAT) in the \HDU\DISK directory; these are used for adding selections to the main menu.
2. The .TXT files, which are used by the letter batch files as input files for EDLIN routines executed in those files; they also are files that are combined with other files.
3. The files in the \HDU\DISK\MP directory, which are used when the Miscellaneous Programs choice is added to the main menu.
4. The G.BAT file and all of the screen and batch files located in the \HDU\DISK\AUTO directory; these files are used during menu installation.

The first three categories relate to the addition of individual menu items to the main menu. The last category involves the installation of the newly completed menu into the system. These are described in detail below.

The Program Files for Adding Menu Selections

The letter batch files add the individual menu items to the main menu. Although some of these files tend to be quite lengthy (some are over 100 lines), the functions they perform are fairly simple and there is a great deal of repetition.

The A.BAT file and the four files to which it passes control (DOCOPYC1.BAT, WPMORE.BAT, DOCOPYC2.BAT, and WPSTART.BAT) are reproduced in their entirety at the end of this chapter in Figure 4.11. An understanding of the workings of these files will apply to all the other letter files. It should be noted that the program files for selections A, B, and C are more complicated than the other selections because the user is specifying a directory; this is not the case in selections D, E, and F.

Five batch files are executed when A.BAT is selected:

- A.BAT, which calls a subroutine batch file DOCOPYC1.BAT
- A.BAT then calls WPMORE.BAT
- WPMORE.BAT executes WPSTART.BAT
- WPSTART.BAT calls a subroutine batch file, DOCOPYC2.BAT

The flow of these files is as follows:

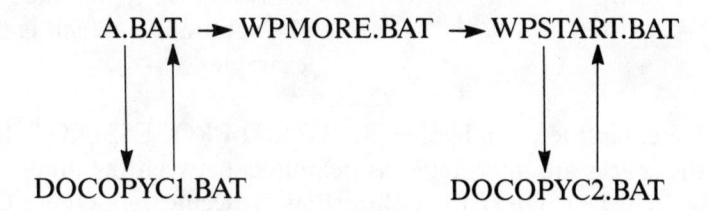

```
      A.BAT  →  WPMORE.BAT  →  WPSTART.BAT
        ↓↑                          ↓↑
   DOCOPYC1.BAT                DOCOPYC2.BAT
```

The subroutine files DOCOPYC1.BAT and DOCOPYC2.BAT are COPY CON routines for: 1) user input of the directory names, and 2) command execution names for the Word Processing program. The same files are also used by the batch files for Selections B and C.

How the Program Files Work

The A.BAT file begins by immediately passing control to the DOCOPYC1.BAT file, where the user is prompted to input the name of the directory containing the word processing program. The first three lines of A.BAT are shown below:

```
   A.BAT (beginning)
1: echo off
2: cls
3: command /c docopyc1 WORD-PROCESSING wpdir.tmp c:\wp
```

The call is made to the DOCOPYC1.BAT subroutine batch file in line 3 above. There are a number of arguments following the command: the name of the batch file (DOCOPYC1), and three replaceable parameters that are used by DOCOPYC1. The breakdown of components in line 3 is as follows:

Component:	Function:
command /c	Invokes secondary command processor
docopyc1	This is the batch file subroutine
WORD-PROCESSING	This is the %1 replaceable parameter in the subroutine, indicating the directory name
wpdir.tmp	This is the %2 parameter in the subroutine for a temporary file that holds the user's input
c:\wp	This is the %3 replaceable parameter in the subroutine, which is the text of the example

Note that there is a hyphen in "WORD-PROCESSING." This is because the spaces are interpreted as delimiters between the arguments.

The DOCOPYC1.BAT functions to execute the COPY CON routine for the user input of the directory name. It is structured in a subroutine context so that, should <Ctrl><Break> be pressed, the user is not left out in DOS somewhere with no menu and no prompt. It contains the following commands:

```
     DOCOPYC1.BAT
1 : echo off
2 : cls
3 : echo First, you must specify the name of the %1
           directory.
4 : echo Use the format shown in the example below. (If
           you make a
5 : echo mistake, press [Ctrl][Break], and start
           over.)
6 : echo (Example: %3)
7 : echo Please ENTER the directory name, PRESS the F6
           key and then PRESS Enter
8 : copy con:%2
9 : exit
```

In line 3, the %1 variable is replaced by "WORD-PROCESSING." The %3 variable in line 6 is replaced by "c:\wp." In line 8, using the COPY CON command, the batch file becomes user-interactive. (This process is described in detail in Appendix B.) The %2 variable is replaced by "wpdir.tmp." The COPY CON command takes the user's input (which is the directory name)

Disk Organization Utilities

and stores it in a file called WPDIR.TMP. In line 9, the EXIT command returns control to the file that made the subroutine call, which in this case is A.BAT. Command execution resumes in A.BAT at line 4. The entire contents of A.BAT are listed as follows:

```
   A.BAT
 1: echo off
 2: cls
 3: command /c docopyc1 WORD-PROCESSING wpdir.tmp c:\wp
 4: echo off
 5: cls
 6: if not exist wpdir.tmp goto ABORT
 7: copy wpbegin.txt + wpdir.tmp + cr.txt  wpbegin2.txt
 8: copy wpstart.txt + wpdir.tmp wpmore.bat
 9: del wpdir.tmp
10: wpmore
11: :ABORT
12: echo Program has been interrupted. Please  retry...
13: pause
14: cls
15: type setup.scr
16: echo ENTER SELECTION:
18: prompt $e[22;18H
```

Line 4 turns the echo off again, since DOS turns echo on when control moves from one batch file to another. In line 6, a check is made to determine if the subroutine was concluded without a <Ctrl><Break>. If this is not the case, control shifts to the ABORT section where an error message shown before the menu is redisplayed.

If WPDIR.TMP has been created without problems, in line 7 a text file is created around the user's directory name input. This file, WPBEGIN2.TXT, will be used later on for the batch file that runs the Word Processing menu choice. In line 8, the directory name input is added to a one-line text file, WPSTART.TXT; the result is the batch file WPMORE.BAT.

The contents of WPMORE.BAT are as follows:

```
   WPMORE.BAT
 1: wpstart <directory name as %1 variable>
```

Line 1 of WPMORE.BAT executes the WPSTART.BAT file, with the user's directory name input as a %1 variable. Thus, if the user specified his or her word processing directory as c:\wp, then line 1 of WPMORE.BAT would be:

```
wpstart c:\wp
```

From the WPMORE.BAT file, control is passed to the WPSTART.BAT file. The WPSTART.BAT file begins by displaying a message. Then, six IF commands check for the existence of the numbered batch files (1.BAT through 6.BAT) in the root directory. This is to determine what menu number to give the item that has been selected for addition to the main menu:

```
1:  if not exist 1.bat goto 1CHOICE
2:  if not exist 2.bat goto 2CHOICES
3:  if not exist 3.bat goto 3CHOICES
4:  if not exist 4.bat goto 4CHOICES
5:  if not exist 5.bat goto 5CHOICES
6:  if not exist 6.bat goto 6CHOICES
```

If a 1.BAT does not exist, then the new menu item will be number 1; control is then passed to the 1CHOICE section of the batch file. If it does exist, the test for the existence of 2.BAT is performed, and so on. (Note that the maximum number of menu choices that can be automatically added to the menu is 6: If a 6.BAT file is found to exist, the program will display an error message and return to the Setup menu.)

Next come the individual subsections for the installation of the selected menu item onto the specific location of the main menu (1CHOICE, 2CHOICES, etc.). These sections are similar to one another except for certain variables. The 1CHOICE section contains the following commands:

```
 1:  :1CHOICE
 2:  cd \hdu\disk
 3:  edlin mainmenu.tmp <1wpinput.txt
 4:  cd \
 5:  md %1
 6:  cd \hdu\disk
 7:  cls
 8:  command /c docopyc2 WORD-PROCESSING 1.tmp
 9:  echo off
10:  cls
11:  if not exist 1.tmp goto ABORT
```

Disk Organization Utilities

```
12:  copy \hdu\disk\wpbegin2.txt + 1.tmp +
     \hdu\disk\end.txt \1.bat
13:  go to END
```

In line 3 above, the menu item is added to the main menu, using EDLIN to edit the MAINMENU.TMP file. The input for the EDLIN routine comes from the redirected 1WPINPUT.TXT file. (See section 6.1 in Chapter 6 for a discussion of this technique.) In line 5, the directory is created, using as the %1 variable the directory name supplied by the user in A.BAT.

In line 8 above, control is passed to another batch file subroutine, DOCOPYC2.BAT. This subroutine batch file is exactly like DOCOPYC1.BAT except for the text of an ECHO command. In DOCOPYC2.BAT, the user supplies the command that executes the Word Processing program.

Control returns from DOCOPYC2.BAT to line 9 above. As in A.BAT, the IF NOT EXIST command in line 11 checks for successful completion of the DOCOPYC2 subroutine. The COPY command in line 12 sets up a batch file that will run the menu selection. The user's input is combined with WPBEGIN2.TXT and END.TXT, forming the 1.BAT file in the root directory.

In the 2CHOICES section, this combined file would be 2.BAT; for 3CHOICES, it is 3.BAT; and so on. If the user's input from the first COPY CON command was **c:\wp** and the input from the second COPY CON command was **wp**, the 1.BAT file would have the following contents.

```
                          1:  echo off
From WPBEGIN2.TXT         2:  cls
                          3:  cd c:\wp

User's input ─────────→   4:  wp          ── User's input (WPDIR.TMP)
(1.TMP)

                          5:  cd \
                          6:  cls
From END.TXT              7:  type mainmenu.scr
                          8:  echo ENTER SELECION:
                          9:  prompt $e[18;22H
```

At the end of each subsection (in this case, 1CHOICE), control is then passed to the END section, where the following message is displayed:

```
Be sure to
-install the menu (selection G) after adding all your
 menu choices
-copy the Word Processing program files into the
 c:\wp directory
```

This message is different when the Spreadsheet, Database, or other menu option has been added. A %1 variable is used for the directory name, so the user's directory name input is displayed in the message. The Setup screen is then redisplayed, and the user is ready to add another menu selection or to install the completed menu.

The Program Files for Installing the Menu

The batch files that make up the installation process include G.BAT in the \HDU\DISK directory, and all of the files in the \HDU\DISK\AUTO directory. The function of this routine is to copy the just-completed main menu into the root directory, and to create the process that makes this menu accessible. The process begins when a **G** is entered from the Setup menu. This activates the G.BAT file, which contains the following commands:

```
     G.BAT
1:   echo off
2:   cls
3:   cd auto
4:   type instruct.scr
5:   echo ENTER COMMAND:
6:   prompt $e[20;16H
```

After the current directory is changed to the \HDU\DISK\AUTO subdirectory (line 3), an instruction screen is displayed (shown in Figure 4.5). This instruction screen describes the automatic versus manual option for displaying the main menu. The following diagram illustrates the path of the various files involved in the installation:

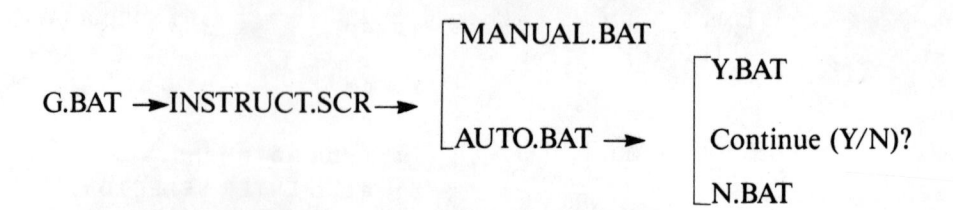

```
                              ⎡MANUAL.BAT
                              ⎢                         ⎡Y.BAT
G.BAT →INSTRUCT.SCR→          ⎢                         ⎢
                              ⎣AUTO.BAT  →              ⎢Continue (Y/N)?
                                                        ⎢
                                                        ⎣N.BAT
```

When the user enters the MANUAL command, the following batch file is activated:

```
     MANUAL.BAT
1:   echo off
2:   cls
3:   echo Copying main menu to root directory...
4:   copy \hdu\disk\mainmenu.tmp \mainmenu.scr
```

```
    5: copy \hdu\disk\menu.bat
    6: cd \
    7: cls
    8: echo Your menu system has now been installed. To
          display your
    9: echo menu at any time, simply enter the command
          MENU.
   10: prompt $n$g
```

The above batch file simply copies to the root directory the two files critical to the Manual process: MAINMENU.SCR and MENU.BAT. The AUTO.BAT file, in contrast, is somewhat more complicated. Figure 4.6 shows the contents of this file.

```
     AUTO.BAT
 1: echo off
 2: cls
 3: echo Copying main menu to root directory ...
 4: copy \hdu\disk\mainmenu.tmp \mainmenu.scr
 5: cd \
 6: if not exist autoexec.bat goto NOAUTO
 7: goto AUTO
 8: :NOAUTO
 9: echo Making AUTOEXEC.BAT file ...
10: cd \hdu\disk\auto
11: copy \hdu\dospath.txt + autoexec.tmp \autoexec.bat
12: cls
13: echo Your menu system has now been installed.  Reboot your computer
14: echo    (by pressing [Ctrl] [Alt] [Del]) to display the main menu.
15: prompt $n$g
16: goto END
17: :AUTO
18: cd \hdu\disk\auto
19: if exist flag.txt goto HAVEDONE
20: cls
21: echo There already is an AUTOEXEC.BAT file in your root directory.
22: echo    It contains the following commands:
23: type \autoexec.bat
24: type makeauto.scr
25: prompt Continue (Y/N)?
26: goto END
27: :HAVEDONE
28: echo Your new main menu has now been installed.  To continue,
29: pause
30: cd \
31: cls
32: type mainmenu.scr
33: echo ENTER SELECTION:
34: prompt $e[22;18H
35: :END
```

Figure 4.6. Contents of AUTO.BAT for Menu Installation

The AUTO.BAT file copies the MAINMENU.SCR file to the root directory, and then uses an IF command to determine if the system contains an AUTOEXEC.BAT file. This file is used to automatically display the main menu. If it does not exist, the AUTO.BAT file creates one with the command:

```
copy \hdu\dospath.txt + autoexec.tmp \autoexec.bat
```

The path specified by the user when the *Hard Disk Manager* was installed was stored in a file called DOSPATH.TXT. This is combined with some other commands to form the AUTOEXEC.BAT file.

If an AUTOEXEC.BAT file already exists, the authors assume that the user may not wish to have the existing one obliterated. A "Continue (Y/N)?" prompt asks permission to append some specific commands to the end of the existing AUTOEXEC.BAT file. The N.BAT file aborts the installation with instructions to install the menu manually. The Y.BAT file is as follows:

```
     Y.BAT
 1:  echo off
 2:  cls
 3:  echo Adding commands to your AUTOEXEC.BAT file...
 4:  cd \
 5:  copy \autoexec.bat + \hdu\dospath.txt +
     \hdu\disk\auto\autoexec.tmp
 6:  copy \hdu\disk\auto\nureturn.tmp \return.bat
 7:  copy \hdu\disk\auto\dospath2.txt
     \hdu\disk\auto\flag.txt
 8:  cls
 9:  echo Your menu system has now been installed.
         Reboot your computer by
10:  echo pressing [Ctrl] [Alt] [Del], to display the
         main menu.
11:  prompt $n$g
```

The long COPY command in line 5 above appends the contents of DOSPATH.TXT and AUTOEXEC.TMP to the existing AUTOEXEC.BAT file. Suppose the DOS path specified by the user was C:\DOS and the existing AUTOEXEC.BAT file simply ran the clock program for an AST board (ASTCLOCK). The resulting batch file after installation would have the following commands:

Disk Organization Utilities

```
From existing AUTOEXEC.BAT ──▶  1:  astclock
            From DOSPATH.TXT ──▶  2:  path c:\;\dos
                                  3:  echo off
                                  4:  cls
         From AUTOEXEC.TMP ────▶  5:  type mainmenu.scr
                                  6:  echo ENTER SELECTION:
                                  7:  prompt $e[22;18H
```

The COPY command in line 6 places a new RETURN.BAT file in the root directory. This will cause the new main menu to be displayed when the <F1> key is pressed, instead of the *Hard Disk Manager* menu. The COPY command in line 7 creates a file called FLAG.TXT; its existence simply serves to indicate that the necessary commands have been appended to the AUTOEXEC.BAT file. The AUTO.BAT file checks for the presence of this file to prevent the same commands from being added to the AUTOEXEC.BAT file again if a new main menu is installed.

The Miscellaneous Programs Option

When the Miscellaneous Programs selection is installed on the main menu, a submenu is displayed when this menu choice is selected. This submenu, in its initial state, is shown in Figure 4.7. The first item on this submenu,

---

MISCELLANEOUS PROGRAMS SUBMENU

---

1. Add A Selection To This Menu Screen

<<<<< Press F1 to Return to Main Menu >>>>>

Figure 4.7. Miscellaneous Programs Submenu

"Add A Selection To This Menu," does exactly what its description says. All of the files associated with the Miscellaneous Programs submenu are contained in the directory \HDU\DISK\MP.

Program Files for the Miscellaneous Programs Option

When selection 1 on the menu is entered, the following batch file is executed:

```
   1.BAT
1: echo off
2: cls
3: type mpinstru.scr
4: echo Continue (Y/N)?
5: prompt $e[17;18H
```

The instruction screen displayed by the above batch file is shown in Figure 4.8. If the user responds with **N** to the "Continue (Y/N)?" prompt, the Miscellaneous Programs menu is redisplayed. The Y.BAT file adds the new menu item to that menu. This is a long batch file similar to the WPSTART.BAT file described earlier. It is reproduced in its entirety in at the end of this chapter in Figure 4.12. It performs the following operations:

1. Using a subroutine batch File (DOCOPYC3.BAT), the user is prompted to enter the name of the menu item that is to appear on the Miscellaneous Programs menu screen. This file is similar to DOCOPYC1.BAT described earlier. Using a COPY CON command, the user's input is placed in TEMP.TXT.
2. A check is made of the number of menu items that already exist, using the Exist condition of multiple IF commands:

```
cd \misc
if not exist 2.bat goto 2CHOICES
if not exist 3.bat goto 3CHOICES
if not exist 4.bat goto 4CHOICES
if not exist 5.bat goto 5CHOICES
if not exist 6.bat goto 6CHOICES
goto OTHEREND
```

   For example, if a 2.BAT file does not exist, control is passed to 2CHOICES where the new menu item will be labeled "2."
3. In the subsections (2choices, 3choices, etc.), three COPY commands remake the Miscellaneous Programs screen with the new menu pick.

Disk Organization Utilities 47

The first COPY command adds a menu number to the user's input, and the second COPY command adds this combination to the menu. The last of the three prepares the menu for the next time a selection is added.

```
copy mp2begin.txt + temp.txt temp2.txt
copy mp1.scr + temp2.txt + mp2.scr miscprog.scr
copy mp1.scr + temp2.txt + mpline.scr
goto CONTINUE
```

4. Control then passes to CONTINUE. A subroutine batch file (DOCOPYC2.BAT) is executed that prompts the user for the name of the command that runs the program. The COPY CON command again is used to make this a user-interactive batch file. COPY CON places the input in TEMP.TXT:

```
echo ENTER the command, PRESS the F6 key, and
     then PRESS Enter:
copy con:temp.txt
```

Using the same IF command procedure as before, a batch file is written to run the new menu choice. Depending on what numbered batch files already exist, control is passed to 2BAT, 3BAT, 4BAT, etc.

5. In the 2BAT through 6BAT subsections, the TEMP.TXT input is combined into an appropriate numbered batch file. In the 2BAT subsection, for example:

```
copy mpbegin.txt + temp.txt + mpend.txt 2.bat
goto FIRSTEND
```

6. Control passes to FIRSTEND where completion messages are displayed. After a pause, the Miscellaneous Programs menu is redisplayed, containing the new menu pick.

=============================== INSTRUCTIONS ===============================

```
This routine allows you to add menu selections to the MISCELLANEOUS
   PROGRAMS SUBMENU Screen.  As many as five new menu selections
   may be added to the menu.  (If you need more than five, refer to
   chapter 4 of "Hard Disk Manager.")

You will be prompted for the following input:
   - The name of the program selection that will appear on the
     MISCELLANEOUS PROGRAMS SUBMENU Screen.  The menu number will
     will be supplied automatically.
   - The command that executes the menu selection.

                    <<<<< Press F1 to Return >>>>>
```

Figure 4.8. Instruction Screen for Miscellaneous Programs Option

Resetting the Menu

The Menu/Directory Setup utility allows the user to add up to six menu items automatically. On the seventh try, the following error message is displayed:

```
A total of six items has already been installed...
program ABORTED.
```

The only time this should happen is if there have been some repetitions, since there are only six choices, A–F. To find out what has gone wrong, the user must do the following:

1. First, examine the temporary main menu. This is done by selecting the Exit To DOS on the *Hard Disk Manager* menu, and then entering the following command:

    ```
    type \hdu\disk\mainmenu.tmp
    ```

2. Decide which of the menu items is superfluous. Unless a menu item has been placed on the menu manually, there should be some duplications. (Proceed to the next step even if the menu looks all right.)
3. Make note of the numbered items that should be on the menu and then enter the following command:

    ```
    dir \?.bat
    ```

    This should produce a listing of numbered batch files in the root directory (1.BAT, 2.BAT, and so on).
4. Erase the numbered batch file for every menu item that does not belong. For example, to erase the 4.BAT file, the command is

    ```
    erase \4.BAT
    ```

6. Return to *Hard Disk Manager* (by entering the command HDU) and run the Disk/Directory Setup routine again for the desired menu item. Be sure to install the menu when done (selection G).

To start a main menu again from scratch, select Exit To DOS, and erase *all* the numbered batch files (see steps 3 and 4 above). Then, copy the file MAINMENU.TMP from the *Hard Disk Manager* program disk back onto the C drive. This is done by entering the command:

```
copy a:\hdu\disk\mainmenu.tmp c:\hdu\disk
```

Disk Organization Utilities

Now run the Disk/Directory Setup utility from the beginning. When the completed menu is installed, it will replace any existing main menu previously created.

The Disk & Directory View/Print Utilities

These routines allow the user to view or print the contents of a disk or directory. When **2** is entered from the Disk/Directory menu, a submenu containing the View/Print options is displayed. This submenu is shown in Figure 4.9 (see page 50). The operations performed by the three menu selections are fairly simple.

The View/Print Contents of a Directory Utility

The first selection, View/Print Contents of a Directory, when executed, brings up the instruction screen shown in Figure 4.10 (see page 50). To view the contents of a particular directory, the user must enter the command **VIEW** followed by the directory path. To print a directory, the user must enter the command **PRINT**, again followed by the directory path. The flow of the files in this utility is as follows:

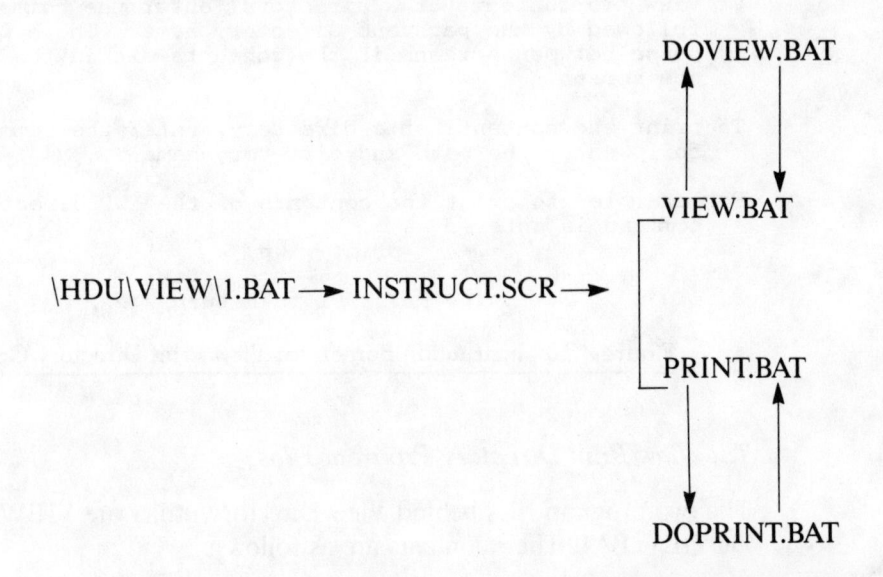

```
                                              DOVIEW.BAT
                                                 ↑ ↓
                                              VIEW.BAT
  \HDU\VIEW\1.BAT → INSTRUCT.SCR →         ┌─
                                           └─ PRINT.BAT
                                                 ↓ ↑
                                              DOPRINT.BAT
```

```
┌─────────────────────────────────────────────────┐
│ ══════════ DISK & DIRECTORY VIEW/PRINT MENU ════ │
│                                                 │
│      1.   View/Print Contents Of A Directory    │
│                                                 │
│      2.   View Contents Of All Directories      │
│                                                 │
│      3.   Print Contents Of All Directories     │
│                                                 │
│             <<<<< Press F1 to Return >>>>>      │
│                                                 │
└─────────────────────────────────────────────────┘
```

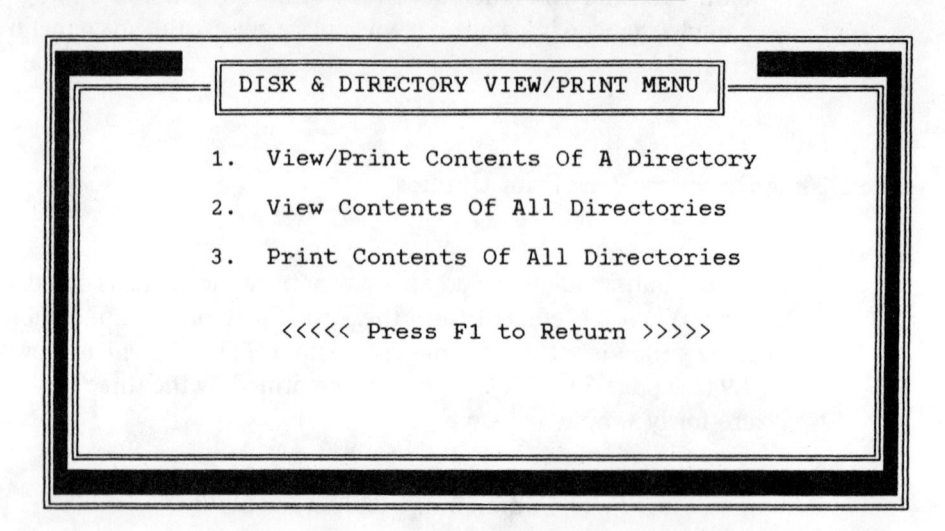

Figure 4.9. View/Print Options Menu

══════════════════ INSTRUCTIONS ══════════════════

This routine allows you to view or print the contents of a
   specific directory.

To view the contents of a directory, enter the command VIEW
   followed by the path and directory name. There will be a
   pause between screens if the contents exceed the size of
   one screen.

To print the contents of a directory, enter the command PRINT
   followed by the path and directory name.

For example, to print the contents of the \WP directory, the
   command is entered as
                        print   \wp

             <<<<< Press F1 to Return >>>>>

Figure 4.10. Instruction Screen for View/Print Directory Contents

The View/Print Directory Program Files

The two program files behind View Directory utility are VIEW.BAT and DOVIEW.BAT. Their contents are as follows:

Disk Organization Utilities

```
     VIEW.BAT
1:   echo off
2:   cls
3:   command /c doview %1
4:   echo off
5:   cls
6:   type view.scr
7:   echo ENTER SELECTION:
8:   prompt $e[22;18H
9:   setscrn

     DOVIEW.BAT
1:   echo off
2:   cls
3:   echo Here are the contents of the %1 directory:
4:   dir %1 /p
5:   echo End of directory listing.
6:   pause
7:   exit
```

In the above batch files, DOVIEW.BAT is a subroutine batch file called by the VIEW.BAT file. In line 3 of VIEW.BAT, the call is made to the DOVIEW.BAT file; the EXIT command at the end of the DOVIEW.BAT file returns control to line 4 in VIEW.BAT. This technique is used to ensure the redisplay of a menu should <Ctrl><Break> be pressed during program execution. Line 9 of both VIEW.BAT and PRINT.BAT executes the batch file SETSCRN.BAT. Refer to the heading "Use of the SETSCRN Command" in Chapter 5 for an explanation of this command.

The two program files behind Print Directory utility are PRINT.BAT and DOPRINT.BAT. Their contents are as follows:

```
     PRINT.BAT
1:   echo off
2:   cls
3:   command /c doprint %1
4:   echo off
5:   cls
6:   type view.scr
7:   echo ENTER SELECTION:
8:   prompt $e[22;18H
9:   setscrn
```

```
        DOPRINT.BAT
1:   echo off
2:   cls
3:   echo          PLEASE MAKE SURE THAT
4:   echo          -YOUR PRINTER IS TURNED ON
5:   echo          -AND THAT IT IS "ON-LINE"
6:   pause
7:   dir %1 >prn
8:   exit
```

As in the View Directory utility, the DOPRINT.BAT file is a subroutine of the PRINT.BAT file. Line 3 of PRINT.BAT makes the call to DOPRINT.BAT; control is returned to PRINT.BAT with the EXIT command at the end of DOPRINT.BAT.

In the above batch files, the DIR command is the key component. The directory name specified by the user when the PRINT and VIEW commands are entered is substituted for the %1 replaceable parameter. In the DOPRINT.BAT file, a reminder to turn on the printer is displayed with the ECHO commands. The output of the DIR command is redirected to the printer with the ">prn" specification.

The View Contents of All Directories Utility

The second utility on the Disk & Directory View/Print menu allows the user to get a screen listing of the directory files contained on the hard disk. This is a simple, two-file routine. When the user enters **2**, the 2.BAT file in the \HDU\VIEW directory is executed.

The View Contents Program File

The two program files behind the View Contents of All Directories utility are 2.BAT and DOTREE.BAT. Their contents are as follows:

```
        2.BAT
1:   echo off
2:   cls
3:   command /c dotree2
4:   echo off
5:   cls
```

Disk Organization Utilities

```
6: type view.scr
7: echo ENTER SELECTION:
8: prompt $e[22;18H
9: setscrn
```

DOTREE2.BAT
```
1: echo off
2: echo The disk contents will be displayed in a few
   moments...
3: echo (Press any key to continue when "More" is
   displayed in lower corner.)
4: tree /f | more
5: echo End of disk listing.
6: pause
7: exit
```

The DOTREE.BAT file functions as a subroutine of 2.BAT. Line 3 in 2.BAT makes the call to DOTREE.BAT. In line 7 of DOTREE2.BAT, the EXIT command returns control to 2.BAT.

The central command in the above batch files is the TREE command, with the /F option (line 4 of DOTREE2.BAT). This command displays a listing of all directories on a disk; the /F option includes the files in each directory. The | **more** specification causes the scrolling to pause after each screen of information.

The View/Print submenu is redisplayed when the listing is completed. Line 9 in 2.BAT executes the SETSCRN batch file. Refer to Chapter 5, "Use of the SETSCRN Command," for an explanation of this command.

The Print Contents of All Directories Utility

The third utility on the Disk & Directory View/Print menu permits the user to generate a printout of all the directories and files on the hard disk. It is executed when the user enters **3** from the Disk & Directory View/Print menu.

The Print Contents Program File

There are only two files associated with this utility: 3.BAT and DOTREE3.BAT. The contents of these files are as follows:

```
        3.BAT
1:  echo off
2:  cls
3:  command /c dotree3
4:  echo off
5:  cls
6:  type view.scr
7:  echo ENTER SELECTION:
8:  prompt $e[22;18H
9:  setscrn

        DOTREE3.BAT
1:  echo off
2:  cls
3:  echo        PLEASE MAKE SURE THAT
4:  echo        -YOUR PRINTER IS TURNED ON
5:  echo        -AND THAT IT IS "ON-LINE"
6:  pause
7:  echo Printing will begin in a few moments...
8:  tree /f >prn
9:  exit
```

The call is made to the DOTREE3.BAT subroutine in line 3 of 3.BAT. As before, this technique is used to ensure that a menu is redisplayed in the event the user presses <Ctrl><Break> during program execution.

Like the 2.BAT file, the key command is the TREE command, with the /F option (line 8 of DOTREE3.BAT). The ">prn" specification redirects the output of the command to the printer.

The Format Utilities

There are two reasons for the presence of these utilities in this package. The first reason is security. It really requires very little effort for an inexperienced user to enter the command **FORMAT** and inadvertently obliterate everything on a hard disk. Since the hard disk is rarely formatted, these utilities are set up to format floppy disks only. The second reason for the format utilities is convenience. Particularly when high-capacity or system disks are being formatted, it is easy to forget the various switches that must be used with the FORMAT command.

Disk Organization Utilities

The Format a Data Disk Utility

The first of the format utilities, Format a Floppy (Data Disk), will format a 360-KB or high-capacity floppy disk for normal usage as a data disk. When a **3** is entered from the Disk/Directory menu, the 3.BAT file in the \HDU\DISK is activated.

The Format a Data Disk Program File

The Format a Floppy (Data Disk) utility consists of two program files: 3.BAT and DOFORM3.BAT. The second batch file is a subroutine that is called by 3.BAT. By placing the FORMAT command in the subroutine, a menu will be displayed should the user press <Ctrl><Break> before the utility is completed.

The contents of these batch files are as follows:

```
   3.BAT
1: echo off
2: cls
3: command /c doform3
4: echo off
5: cls
6: type diskmenu.scr
7: echo ENTER SELECTION:
8: prompt $e[22;18H
9: setscrn

   DOFORM3.BAT
1: echo off
2: cls
3: echo This prepares 360 KB or High-Capacity flop-
        pies for use as data disks.
4: format a: /v
5: exit
```

The DOFORM3.BAT file is called as a subroutine in line 3 of the 3.BAT file. Note that the FORMAT command in line 4 in DOFORM3.BAT is written to format a disk in drive A. The /V switch will cause DOS to prompt the user for a volume label. The EXIT command at the end of DOFORM3.BAT returns control to line 4 of the 3.BAT file. The Disk/Directory menu is then redisplayed. Line 9 executes the batch file SETSCRN.BAT. See Chapter 5 for an explanation of this command.

The Format a System Disk Utility

The second format utility, Format a Floppy (System Disk), performs the same operation as the first, except that the disk can be used as a boot (system) disk. This means the computer can be started using this disk because all of the operating system files required for a system startup will be copied onto the disk during formatting.

The Format a System Disk Program File

Two program files are executed when the user selects this menu pick: 4.BAT and DOFORM4.BAT. The difference in these batch files and the 3.BAT and DOFORM3.BAT files described above is only the message that is displayed and the use of an additional switch in the FORMAT command. The message indicates a system disk is being formatted; the FORMAT command includes the /S option:

```
format a:/s /v
```

The /S switch indicates to DOS that the disk is to be formatted as a system disk. It should be noted that a disk should not be formatted in this way unless it really will be used as a boot disk. This is because an unnecessary amount of disk space will be occupied by the system files.

The Format a 360-KB/High-Capacity Disk Utility

The third format utility on the Disk/Directory menu is useful only if the user's system includes a high-capacity disk drive. This utility allows a user to format a 360 KB floppy disk in the high-capacity drive. This disk can then be used by that drive. (In certain situations, the reliability of these disks may be an issue; the reader should refer to "The Compatibility of Storage Media" in section 4.3 later in this chapter for a discussion of these circumstances.) When the user enters **5** from the Disk/Directory menu, the 5.BAT file in \HDU\DISK is executed.

Disk Organization Utilities

The Format a 360-KB/High-Capacity Disk Program File

Like the two other Format utilities, there are two program files associated with this menu choice: 5.BAT and DOFORM5.BAT. The commands in the 5.BAT and DOFORM5.BAT files are the same as the commands in the above utilities, with two exceptions: The message that is displayed refers to the high-capacity drive, and the format command is written as

```
format a:/v /4
```

The /4 option puts the high-capacity drive into the 360-KB formatting mode.

4.2 MODIFYING THE DISK/DIRECTORY UTILITIES

Although the Disk/Directory utilities cover many aspects of disk and directory management, the authors believe that many users will have requirements that will not be met by a generic package such as this. There are some operations that were intentionally not included. For example, there is no provision for use of the MD (Make Directory) or RD (Remove Directory). These commands are fairly easy operations for DOS. Experienced users will probably find it easier to execute these commands outside a menu or batch-file environment. The "Exit to DOS" menu choice can be useful for such situations.

However, if the system is to used by PC novices, it may be necessary or desirable to totally structure all aspects of disk and directory management. This section describes how to add, delete, or modify the Disk/Directory utilities.

Some Points to Keep in Mind

Here are a few general suggestions and reminders for commands and operations that may be involved in modifying or creating disk organization utilities. Most of these tricks were used in the Disk/Directory utilities.

1. The COPY CON command can be used in a batch file as a way of obtaining user input without interrupting the execution of the batch file. The command is preceded by instructions, and the user presses

<F6> and <Enter> when finished. The input is stored in the filename that follows the COPY CON command. Appendix B describes this process in detail.
2. User input obtained with the COPY CON technique can be combined into batch files or menu screens using the COPY command to append files to one another.
3. Using the EDLIN program with a redirected input file is a technique for automatically remaking a menu screen in a batch file. The input file must contain all the commands and data that would be entered if EDLIN were used manually for the same editing process.
4. The EXIST and NOT EXIST conditions of the IF command are useful for checking the validity of filename parameters entered by the user. Pathnames cannot be used in this command for DOS versions earlier than 3.0; it is necessary to change the directory to the current directory containing the file before the IF command is executed.
5. The MORE command is a useful way of controlling the scrolling of the screen displays exceeding the size of one screen. Piping is used to pass the output of a command through MORE, as in:

```
type info.scr | more
```

6. In circumstances where it is possible that the user may press <Ctrl><Break> before a utility is completed, it may be useful to call the main body of the batch-file program as a subroutine batch file. This is done through the use of the command

```
COMMAND /C <batch filename>
```

If the commands following COMMAND redisplay a menu, these commands will be executed if the user presses <Ctrl><Break> while the subroutine is executed. This technique is discussed in more detail in Appendix B.

Adding and Deleting Menu Items

Adding or deleting menu items in the Disk/Directory menu will not present many difficulties. The only area where the task may be a bit more complicated is in the Menu/Directory Setup utility, mainly because of the number of files involved. The reader should consult Chapter 10 for a step-by-step approach to adding and deleting menu items.

Disk Organization Utilities

Some Possible Modifications and Enhancements

There are any number of changes and modifications in the Disk/Directory utilities that can be made. The user may modify, delete, or add menu selections to the existing routines. This section describes these procedures and provides some suggestions for possible modifications and new additions. These are utilities that use DOS features or commands not covered in the existing utilities. The descriptions basically cover only the actual program files.

A Directory Sort Utility

This is an easy utility to add to the Disk & Directory View/Print menu. It allows the user to see or print directory listings sorted by date, size, or filename. It uses the VIEW.BAT and DOVIEW.BAT files from the View/Print Directory Contents utility, almost intact. Here are the two original files:

```
   VIEW.BAT
1: echo off
2: cls
3: command /c doview %1
4: echo off
5: cls
6: type view.scr
7: echo ENTER SELECTION:
8: prompt $e[22;18H
9: setscrn
```

```
   DOVIEW.BAT
1: echo off
2: cls
3: echo Here are the contents of the %1 directory:
4: dir %1 /p
5: echo End of directory listing.
6: pause
7: exit
```

The files could perhaps be renamed DIRSORT.BAT and DOSORT.BAT. (The filename in line 3 of VIEW.BAT would have to be changed to whatever filename replaces DOVIEW.BAT.)

The DIR command (line 4) in the DOVIEW.BAT file is the key component that must be modified. First, the SORT command is added to the end of the DIR command:

```
dir %1 /p | sort
```

This allows the user to alphabetize the directory listing by passing the directory information through the SORT filter in the above command. To sort directory listings by date or file size, the /+n switch is added to the end of the SORT command. (The "n" represents the screen column number that is to be the primary sort key; the default is column 1.) For example, to sort by file size, the switch would be set as /+14:

```
dir %1 /p | sort /+14
```

For a sort by date, one has to choose between a sort by month, day, or year, since only one column number can be entered. To sort by month, for example, the switch setting is /+24.

It should be noted that the use of the SORT command in the above examples does not permanently alter the order of the directory listing. Subsequent issuance of the DIR command alone would produce an unsorted directory listing.

A Remove Directory Utility

This utility is for users who wish to structure the removal of directories in a batch-file and menu environment. The RD command requires that a directory be empty of any files or subdirectories before it is removed. Thus, before a specified directory can be removed, it may be necessary to erase files or remove any subdirectories.

Before executing the RD command, it would probably be a good idea to precede the operation with some instructions indicating that an empty directory will have files listed. Suppose the specified directory was TEST. The listing for that directory would appear as follows:

```
Directory of C:\test
.          <DIR>      8-30-86   2:14p
..         <DIR>      8-30-86   2:14p
    2 File(s)    1052672 bytes free
```

Disk Organization Utilities

The instruction screen might contain directions for issuing a command that displayed the contents of the specified file and then returned the user to the Remove screen. The ERASEDIR.BAT file would use a replaceable parameter for the specified directory. It could contain the following commands:

```
      ERASEDIR.BAT
 1:   echo off
 2:   cls
 3:   rd %1
 4:   echo The %1 directory has been removed.
 5:   pause
 6:   cls
 7:   cd \hdu
 8:   type hdu.scr
 9:   echo ENTER SELECTION:
10:   prompt $e[22;18H
11:   setscrn
```

Various checks and error messages could be added to the above batch file.

4.3 SOME BACKGROUND INFORMATION ON DATA STORAGE AND DIRECTORIES

When using an AT, XT, or other IBM compatible fixed-disk system, the user has a number of choices to make concerning both the physical and logical storage of data. Data can be physically stored on the fixed disk, on floppy disks, or in some cases on high-capacity floppy disks. Logically, data can be stored in one or more subdirectories, organized by type, subject, frequency of use, or any other category of relevance to the user.

This section provides the user with background information on data storage, compatibility of storage media, and the logical organization of data through the use of hierarchical subdirectories.

Data Storage

Before a disk can be used for data storage, it must be formatted with DOS. The formatting process initializes the disk; in doing so, a number of important functions are performed. The FORMAT command analyzes the disk for any defective areas. At the same time, it prepares the disk for file storage by setting up a directory and the File Allocation Table. As an option, FORMAT also will copy onto the target disk the DOS files necessary for a system startup.

During the formatting process, DOS installs markings that divide the disk into a series of concentric circles called tracks. Each track is further divided into sectors, each of which holds 512 bytes of information. Using these physical location markers, DOS keeps track of where each file is stored. The directory is the index; the FAT contains pointers to the location of each directory entry.

The Compatibility of Storage Media

For the most part, data can be stored and retrieved interchangeably between fixed- and floppy-disk systems. However, 360-KB and high-capacity floppy-disk drives are not fully compatible. This incompatibility is particularly of concern to AT users with a single high-capacity floppy-disk drive.

360-KB disk drives cannot format, read from, or write to high-capacity disks because these disks require a higher write current. Only a high-capacity drive may use the high-capacity disks. However, the high-capacity disk drive can be used to format a 360-KB disk. This is done by using the "/4" option in the FORMAT command or by using the Disk/Directory utility selection number five:

5. Format a 360-KB Floppy in High Capacity Drive

TABLE 4.1. Formatting Compatibility.

Drive Type	360-KB Floppy Disk	High-Capacity Disk
360-KB Floppy Drive	YES Format A:	NO Error message: Invalid media or Track 0 bad—disk unusable Format Failure*
High-Capacity Drive	YES Format A:/4	YES Format A:

*The same error message appears when a high-capacity drive is used to format a 360-KB disk without specifying the /4 parameter in the FORMAT command.

Disk Organization Utilities

TABLE 4.2. High-Capacity and 360-KB Drives: Read/Write Compatibility.

Drive Type	Storage Media	
	360-KB Floppy Disk	*High-Capacity Disk*
360-KB Floppy Drive	YES	NO Error message: Disk error reading drive ...
High-Capacity Drive	YES	YES

This disk then can be used by both the high-capacity drive and the 360-KB drives on the XT and PC. Using this technique, data can be transferred from the AT's high-capacity drive to an XT or a PC.

It should be noted that the DOS manual cautions the user about the "/4" option. It states that 360-KB disks formatted with a high-capacity drive may not be *reliably* read or written to with a 360-KB drive. However, many users report no problems with this practice when the following procedures are followed:

1. Start with a new disk.
2. Format the disk in the high-capacity drive with the "/4" option.
3. *Write* to that disk only with the high-capacity drive.
4. *Read* from that disk only with the 360-KB drive.

Tables 4.1 and 4.2 summarize the formatting and read/write compatibilities between different types of drives and different storage media.

Logical Data Storage: DOS's Hierarchical Directories

A master directory or index is initialized when the hard disk is set up and the FORMAT command is issued. This master directory is referred to as the Root Directory. The Root Directory contains entries for each of the files located in it. In addition, the Root Directory can contain entries for other subdirectories. These subdirectories can, in turn, contain additional subdirectory entries or sub-subdirectory entries and so on. This downward branching of the Root Directory is referred to as a hierarchical or tree-structured directory.

Advantages

Hierarchical directories have many advantages. These include the ability to logically organize a hard disk system, the ability to expedite search and access times, and the ability to maximize the use of a hard disk's capacity.

Related groups of files can be placed together in the same directory. This could be useful feature, for example, when several individuals share the same XT or AT and want to segregate their data files. Similarly, data files associated with different programs (e.g., *Lotus 1-2-3* data files and *MultiMate* word processing files) can be organized by subdirectory.

Hierarchical directory structures also allow the user to circumvent capacity limitations of the Root Directory. Although the hard disk may not be filled to capacity, the size of the Root Directory is fixed. That is, it can only hold a limited number of entries.

Subdirectory entries, however, are treated as files and can hold an unlimited number of entries. DOS can quickly locate a file when it is located in a subdirectory. This is because DOS confines its search to only those files contained in the specified subdirectory. The system is able to do this by using a pathname preceding the filename. The pathname specifies each directory level through which DOS must move in order to access the specified file. It should be noted, however, that access time could actually be slowed if a file is located in a subdirectory too many layers below that of the Root Directory. That would be a case in which over-organization of the disk could unnecessarily complicate routine tasks.

Hierarchical Directories and Menu Access

Although hierarchical directories add a great deal of organization to a hard disk system, the degree of their complexity needs to be managed. A tree-structured directory that is obvious to one person can be truly perplexing to another. In order to provide easy access to any subdirectory level, a menu system can be developed that automatically changes the directories when a category is selected. Such a system allows users of all levels to navigate through the directory hierarchy. It also ensures that files are saved in the appropriate subdirectory; i.e., a menu system keeps a hard disk system organized.

Disk Organization Utilities

```
    A.BAT
 1: echo off
 2: cls
 3: command /c docopyc1 WORD-PROCESSING wpdir.tmp c:\wp
 4: echo off
 5: cls
 6: if not exist wpdir.tmp goto ABORT
 7: copy wpbegin.txt + wpdir.tmp + cr.txt wpbegin2.txt
 8: copy wpstart.txt + wpdir.tmp wpmore.bat
 9: del wpdir.tmp
10: wpmore
11: :ABORT
12: echo Program has been interrupted.  Please retry...
13: pause
14: cls
15: type setup.scr
16: echo ENTER SELECTION:
17: prompt $e[22;18H

    DOCOPYC1.BAT
 1: echo off
 2: cls
 3: echo First, you must specify the name of the %1 directory.
 4: echo    Use the format shown in the example below.  (If you make a
 5: echo    mistake, press [Ctrl] [Break], and start over.)
 6: echo          (Example:  %3 )
 7: echo Please ENTER the directory name, PRESS the F6 key and then
            PRESS Enter:
 8: copy con:%2
 9: exit

    WPMORE.BAT
 1: wpstart  (User input of directory name added here as %1 in A.BAT)

    WPSTART.BAT
 1: echo off
 2: cls
 3: echo Adding WORD PROCESSING to Main Menu screen...
 4: cd\
 5: if not exist 1.bat goto 1CHOICE
 6: if not exist 2.bat goto 2CHOICES
 7: if not exist 3.bat goto 3CHOICES
 8: if not exist 4.bat goto 4CHOICES
 9: if not exist 5.bat goto 5CHOICES
10: if not exist 6.bat goto 6CHOICES
11: cls
12: echo A total of six items has already been added...program ABORTED.
13: echo    Please refer to "Resetting The Menu" in Chapter 4 for details.
14: goto FINAL
15: :1CHOICE
16: cd \hdu\disk
```

(continued)

```
17: edlin mainmenu.tmp <1wpinput.txt
18: cd \
19: md %1
20: cd \hdu\disk
21: cls
22: command /c docopyc2 WORD-PROCESSING 1.tmp
23: echo off
24: cls
25: if not exist 1.tmp goto ABORT
26: copy \hdu\disk\wpbegin2.txt + 1.tmp + \hdu\disk\end.txt \1.bat
27: goto END
28: :2CHOICES
29: cd \hdu\disk
30: edlin mainmenu.tmp <2wpinput.txt
31: cd \
32: md %1
33: cd \hdu\disk
34: cls
35: command /c docopyc2 WORD-PROCESSING 2.tmp
36: echo off
37: cls
38: if not exist 2.tmp goto ABORT
39: copy \hdu\disk\wpbegin2.txt + 2.tmp + \hdu\disk\end.txt \2.bat
40: goto END
41: :3CHOICES
42: cd \hdu\disk
43: edlin mainmenu.tmp <3wpinput.txt
44: cd \
45: md %1
46: cd \hdu\disk
47: cls
48: command /c docopyc2 WORD-PROCESSING 3.tmp
49: echo off
50: cls
51: if not exist 3.tmp goto ABORT
52: copy \hdu\disk\wpbegin2.txt + 3.tmp + \hdu\disk\end.txt \3.bat
53: goto END
54: :4CHOICES
55: cd \hdu\disk
56: edlin mainmenu.tmp <4wpinput.txt
57: cd \
58: md %1
59: cd \hdu\disk
60: cls
61: command /c docopyc2 WORD-PROCESSING 4.tmp
62: echo off
63: cls
64: if not exist 4.tmp goto ABORT
65: copy \hdu\disk\wpbegin2.txt + 4.tmp + \hdu\disk\end.txt \4.bat
66: goto END
67: :5CHOICES
68: cd \hdu\disk
69: edlin mainmenu.tmp <5wpinput.txt
70: cd \
```

(continued)

```
71: md %1
72: cd \hdu\disk
73: cls
74: command /c docopyc2 WORD-PROCESSING 5.tmp
75: echo off
76: cls
77: if not exist 5.tmp goto ABORT
78: copy \hdu\disk\wpbegin2.txt + 5.tmp + \hdu\disk\end.txt \5.bat
79: goto END
80: :6CHOICES
81: cd \hdu\disk
82: edlin mainmenu.tmp <6wpinput.txt
83: cd \
84: md %1
85: cd \hdu\disk
86: cls
87: command /c docopyc2 WORD-PROCESSING 6.tmp
88: echo off
89: cls
90: if not exist 6.tmp goto ABORT
91: copy \hdu\disk\wpbegin2.txt + 6.tmp + \hdu\disk\end.txt \6.bat
92: :END
93: del \*.tmp
94: cls
95: echo WORD PROCESSING has now been added to your menu.
96: echo Be sure to
97: echo    - Install the menu (selection G) after adding all your menu
                choices;
98: echo    - Copy the Word Processing program files into the %1 directory.
99: goto FINAL
100: :ABORT
101: echo Program interrupted, menu item not added.  Please retry.
102: :FINAL
103: pause
104: cd \hdu\disk
105: cls
106: type setup.scr
107: echo ENTER SELECTION:
108: prompt $e[22;18H
```

Figure 4.11. Program Files for Adding Menu Selections to Miscellaneous Programs Menu: A.BAT; DOCOPY1.BAT; WPMORE.BAT; WPSTART.BAT

```
        Y.BAT
 1: echo off
 2: cls
 3: cd \misc
 4: command /c docopyc3
 5: echo off
 6: cls
 7: if not exist temp.txt goto ABORT
 8: echo Remaking submenu screen...
 9: if not exist 2.bat goto 2CHOICES
10: if not exist 3.bat goto 3CHOICES
11: if not exist 4.bat goto 4CHOICES
12: if not exist 5.bat goto 5CHOICES
13: if not exist 6.bat goto 6CHOICES
14: goto OTHEREND
15: :2CHOICES
16: copy mp2begin.txt + temp.txt temp2.txt
17: copy mp1.scr + temp2.txt + mp2.scr miscprog.scr
18: copy mp1.scr + temp2.txt + mpline.scr
19: goto CONTINUE
20: :3CHOICES
21: copy mp3begin.txt + temp.txt temp2.txt
22: copy mp1.scr + temp2.txt + mp3.scr miscprog.scr
23: copy mp1.scr + temp2.txt + mpline.scr
24: goto CONTINUE
25: :4CHOICES
26: copy mp4begin.txt + temp.txt temp2.txt
27: copy mp1.scr + temp2.txt + mp4.scr miscprog.scr
28: copy mp1.scr + temp2.txt + mpline.scr
29: goto CONTINUE
30: :5CHOICES
31: copy mp5begin.txt + temp.txt temp2.txt
32: copy mp1.scr + temp2.txt + mp5.scr miscprog.scr
33: copy mp1.scr + temp2.txt + mpline.scr
34: goto CONTINUE
35: :6CHOICES
36: copy mp6begin.txt + temp.txt temp2.txt
37: copy mp1.scr + temp2.txt + mp6.scr miscprog.scr
38: copy mp1.scr + temp2.txt + mpline.scr
39: :CONTINUE
40: del temp.txt
41: cls
42: command /c docopyc2 new temp.txt
43: echo off
44: cls
45: if not exist temp.txt goto ABORT
46: echo Writing batch file...
47: if not exist 2.bat goto 2BAT
48: if not exist 3.bat goto 3BAT
49: if not exist 4.bat goto 4BAT
50: if not exist 5.bat goto 5BAT
51: if not exist 6.bat goto 6BAT
52: :2BAT
53: copy mpbegin.txt + temp.txt + mpend.txt 2.bat
```

(continued)

Disk Organization Utilities

```
54: goto FIRSTEND
55: :3BAT
56: copy mpbegin.txt + temp.txt + mpend.txt 3.bat
57: goto FIRSTEND
58: :4BAT
59: copy mpbegin.txt + temp.txt + mpend.txt 4.bat
60: goto FIRSTEND
61: :5BAT
62: copy mpbegin.txt + temp.txt + mpend.txt 5.bat
63: goto FIRSTEND
64: :6BAT
65: copy mpbegin.txt + temp.txt + mpend.txt 6.bat
66: goto FIRSTEND
67: :FIRSTEND
68: del temp.txt
69: cls
70: echo The new selection has been added to the MISCELLANEOUS PROGRAMS
        SUB MENU
71: echo Only six menu choices can be placed on this menu automatically.
72: echo    To add more, or to change or remove menu items, please refer
            to chapter 4.
73: echo To continue,
74: goto END
75: :ABORT
76: echo Program has been interupted... Menu item not added.
77: goto END
78: :OTHEREND
79: del temp.txt
80: cls
81: echo Only six menu choices can be placed on this menu automatically.
82: echo    To add more, or to change or remove menu items, please refer
            to chapter 4.
83: echo To continue,
84: :END
85: pause
86: cls
87: type miscprog.scr
88: echo ENTER SELECTION:
89: prompt $e[22;18H
```

Figure 4.12. The Y.BAT Program File That Adds New Menu Items

c·h·a·p·t·e·r 5

Customized Display Utilities

There are many aspects of the screen and keyboard over which the user can exert control using the operating system. The user has the ability to customize the appearance of the display screen. This includes the screen colors, the appearance of the system prompt, and the positioning of the cursor. Further control over the screen and keyboard can be achieved through the use of input and output redirection. DOS also permits the user to reassign keys on the computer's keyboard. That is, the characters or operations generated by specific keys can be changed.

Individuals not familiar with DOS techniques for extended screen and keyboard control should refer to the background information on these topics in section 5.3 of this chapter.

The Customized Display utilities are menu-driven programs that can be used to change many attributes of the display screen.

What Are the Customized Display Utilities?

There are three categories of Customized Display utilities. They include routines for:

- changing the foreground color of the display screen
- changing the background color of the display screen
- changing various attributes of characters on the display screen (e.g., highlighting characters, underscoring characters, etc.)

Why Are They Used?

Often when setting up a menu-driven hard disk management system, it is desirable to highlight portions of those menus. For example, accentuation of certain characters or messages can increase a user's understanding of an instruction or can ensure that a user recognizes a warning message.

The Customized Display utilities can be used several ways. These include temporarily altering display attributes; including these same program files in batch routines that permanently alter display attributes (e.g., changing the AUTOEXEC.BAT so that the background screen color is always blue); and placing these program files in screen files to "paint" various aspects of a display screen.

How to Use the Utilities

The Customized Display utilities are accessed when selection 2 is chosen from the *Hard Disk Manager* menu. This selection changes the directory to \HDU\DISPLAY and displays the Customized Display menu. Any of the three selections on the screen can be chosen simply by typing the number of the desired utility. After the selection is made, the user is prompted for any required input; informational screens guide the user, when necessary, through the utility. If at any time the user chooses not to proceed with a utility, the <F1> key can be pressed to return to the first menu.

For the user who would like additional information on display and keyboard control, overviews of these topics can be found at the end of this chapter.

Organization of the Customized Display Utilities

The Customized Display utility is made up of three directories and a subdirectory. All are located in the main utility directory (HDU). The Customized Display utility directories include:

\HDU\DISPLAY	Contains the main display screen.
\HDU\FOREGRND	Contains the foreground color menu and the foreground color batch files.
\HDU\BACKGRND	Contains the background color menu and the background color batch files.

72 HARD DISK MANAGER

\HDU\DISPLAY\SCREEN   Contains the screen attributes/ design menu and the batch files to alter display attributes.

The directory and file structure is presented in Figure 5.1.

Activation of the Utilities

Choosing selection 2 on the main utility menu accesses the Customized Display utilities by activating the 2.BAT file in the \HDU directory. It contains the following commands:

```
   2.BAT
1: echo off
2: cls
3: cd display
4: type display.scr
5: echo ENTER SELECTION:
6: prompt $e[22;18H
7: setscrn
```

```
            \HDU <DIR>

              HDU.SCR

            \HDU\DISPLAY <DIR>

              DISPLAY.SCR
              1.BAT
              2.BAT
              3.BAT
              4.BAT

              \HDU\DISPLAY\SCREEN <DIR>

                SCREEN. SCR
                1.BAT ... 5.BAT

            \HDU\FOREGRND <DIR>

              FOREGRND.SCR
              1.BAT ... 9.BAT

            \HDU\BACKGRND <DIR>

              BACKGRND.SCR
              1.BAT ... 9.BAT
```

Figure 5.1. Directory and File Structure for the Customized Display Utility

Customized Display Utilities 73

```
┌─────────────────────────────────────────────────┐
│          ┌─────────────────────────┐            │
│          │   DISPLAY DESIGN MENU   │            │
│          └─────────────────────────┘            │
│                                                 │
│         1.   Change Foreground Color            │
│                                                 │
│         2.   Change Background Color            │
│                                                 │
│         3.   Change Screen Attributes           │
│                                                 │
│                                                 │
│         <<<<<  Press F1 to Return  >>>>>        │
│                                                 │
└─────────────────────────────────────────────────┘
```

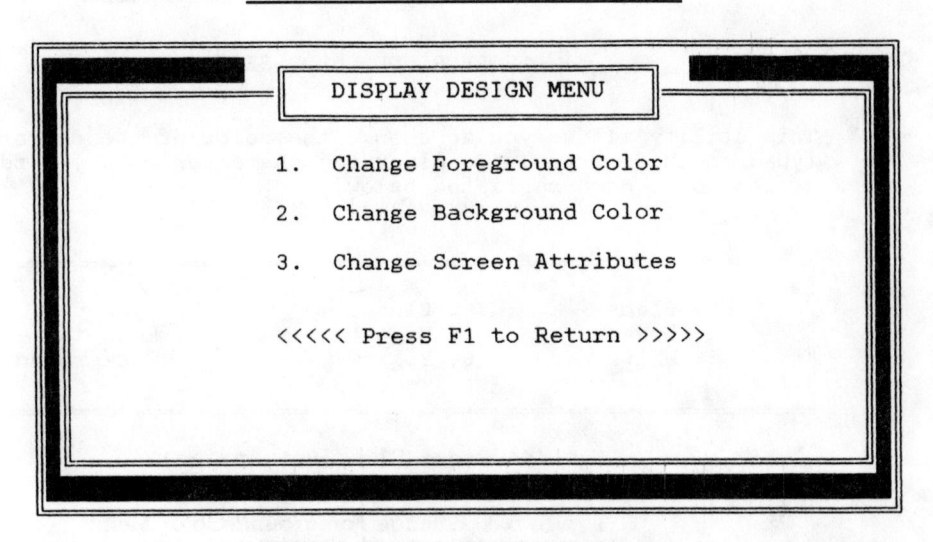

Figure 5.2. Customized Display Menu

The functions of this file are to change the current directory to \HDU\DISPLAY, display the Customized Display menu (DISPLAY.SCR), position the cursor at the end of the ENTER SELECTION: prompt, and reset the display attributes with SETSCRN.BAT. Figure 5.2 shows the Display Design menu screen.

5.1
THE CUSTOMIZED DISPLAY UTILITIES

The Change Foreground Color Utility

The Change Foreground Color utility (selection 1 on the Screen Display menu) produces the display shown in Figure 5.3. The user has nine options to choose from: eight color possibilities and an option to shift to the background color screen. The utility has separate screens for setting foreground and background colors. This is because DOS has a separate set of control codes for background and foreground colors rather than a single color-specific code.

HARD DISK MANAGER

```
                    FOREGROUND COLOR SELECTOR

This utility allows you to change the color of the characters
typed on this screen.  To alter the character color, enter any
of the color numbers listed below:
```

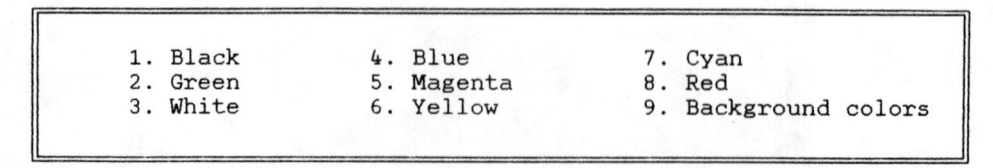

```
    ┌─────────────────────────────────────────────────────────┐
    │   1. Black        4. Blue         7. Cyan               │
    │   2. Green        5. Magenta      8. Red                │
    │   3. White        6. Yellow       9. Background colors  │
    └─────────────────────────────────────────────────────────┘
```

```
              <<<<< Press F1 to Return >>>>>
```

Figure 5.3. Change Foreground Color Menu

Once a color choice is selected, the color of all characters typed after that point will be altered. For example, if **4** (Blue) is selected, the screen is redisplayed with blue characters. All typed characters thereafter will appear blue until either the system is rebooted (reinitialized) or control is passed to another software package. In the latter case, most software packages employ their own color control sequences. For example, *Lotus 1-2-3*'s screen design utilizes cyan, white, and green as foreground and background colors. Similarly, *DisplayWrite3* contains its own utilities for setting screen and character color while in DW3. If, however, the foreground color is set using this DOS-based utility, the foreground color is retained when the user exits a particular software package.

It should be noted as a caution that changing the foreground color to match the background color (e.g., blue foreground, blue background) will produce a screen with invisible characters. An alternative color choice must be typed to make the characters visible again.

The last selection on the foreground color menu is 9, Background Colors. This selection permits the user to switch over to the background color screen to assess the aesthetics or visibility of a newly chosen foreground color against a background color option. Choosing this selection produces a similar selection screen for the background color.

Users who wish to make the foreground color appear whenever the system is booted should refer to the discussion of **AUTOEXEC.BAT** in section 5.2.

Customized Display Utilities   75

The Change Foreground Color Program Files

Nine batch files and one informational screen make up the components of the Change Foreground Color utility. Its execution begins when the user enters **1** from the Customized Display menu. This causes the 1.BAT file in the \HDU\DISPLAY directory to be executed. The commands in this file are as follows:

```
   1.BAT
1: echo off
2: cls
3: cd..\foregrnd
4: type foregrnd.scr
5: echo ENTER SELECTION:
6: prompt $e[20;18H
```

The above batch file changes the directory to \HDU\FOREGRND, displays an informational screen (FOREGRND.SCR), and positions the cursor for the ENTER SELECTION: prompt.

The foreground color screen utility contains nine batch files, one for each color selection and one to shift to background color settings. Each of the foreground color batch files has the same construction; only the color code parameter varies in each. 1.BAT is displayed below as an example:

```
   1.BAT
1: echo ^[[30m
2: echo off
3: echo echo ^[[30m >\setscrn.bat
4: cls
5: type foregrnd.scr
6: echo ENTER SELECTION:
7: prompt $e[20;18H
```

In this example, the codes used to set the display color are as follows:

^[[The escape character as it appears in a batch file followed by a left bracket ([). This is the same as the $e character used with the PROMPT command.

30   The numeric code sets the foreground or background color. Eight different background and foreground colors may be set. In this case, the number "30" sets a black foreground.

m   The "m" is the alpha code used to specify a background or foreground color.

NOTE: *The screen attribute code precedes the ECHO OFF command because ECHO OFF inhibits the action of the code until the batch file is ended.*

In Line 3, the first echo command outputs the command line "echo ^[[30m" to the batch file \SETSCRN.BAT (hence, the use of two echo commands). The SETSCRN.BAT file, the use of which is described in the next section, saves the user's attribute settings. The last four lines of all the color batch files are the same as the batch files described above. The command

```
type foregrnd.scr
```

redisplays the foreground screen once a new color is selected. The prompt is then set with the last two lines of the batch file as described above.

The batch file used to shift from the foreground color to background color screen is shown below:

```
9.BAT
1:   echo off
2:   cls
3:   cd ..\backgrnd
4:   type backgrnd.scr
5:   echo ENTER SELECTION:
6:   prompt $e[20;18
```

Use of the SETSCRN Command

The SETSCRN command is used to ensure that the user's foreground color selections and certain attribute settings (high intensity, return to normal, and reverse video) are saved. This command is necessary because control codes are used in the *Hard Disk Manager* menu screens to create colored borders. If SETSCRN were not used, some *Hard Disk Manager* screens would alter the user's foreground color settings.

For example, in the *Hard Disk Manager* menu, the codes:

```
||^[[31m■ ^[[37m||
```

type out a border screen that looks like:

▌█▐

First a vertical line border character is typed. Then the foreground (character) color is changed to red with the control codes:

    ^[[31m

Next, a solid border character is typed. It appears in red because the foreground color has been altered. After the solid block is typed, the foreground color is returned to normal (white) with the control codes:

    ^[[37m

Finally, the inner vertical line border is typed. If, for example, the user had set the foreground color to cyan, the codes ^[[37m (reset to white) would overwrite the cyan color setting.

The file SETSCRN.BAT initially contains a single line:

    echo ^[[0m

This is the control code setting for restoring the display attributes to normal. Whenever the foreground color is altered using any of the menu selections listed above, the ECHO command outputs the control code command (ECHO plus the specific control code) to the SETSCRN.BAT file. Thus, the user's color setting is "saved" by overwriting the contents of SETSCRN.BAT with the new default color setting.

For example, if the user decided to change the foreground color to cyan, the initial contents of SETSCRN.BAT would be:

    echo ^[[0m

Once the menu selection was chosen, the contents of SETSCRN.BAT would then be:

    echo ^[[36m

in which 36m is the code for a cyan foreground. If the user then decided to set the foreground color to blue, the contents of SETSCRN.BAT would be as shown on page 78.

```
echo ^[[34m
```

in which 34m is the code for blue foreground, and so on.

The Change Background Color Utility

The Change Background Color selection 2 produces the display shown in Figure 5.4. This screen is a mirror image of the foreground color selection screen (see description and cautions for foreground colors). It contains eight color options and a ninth option that allows the user to switch to the foreground color screen.

Once a screen color is selected, the screen is redisplayed with that color. Thereafter, the entire screen color will be altered. As with foreground colors, the screen color is retained until either the system is rebooted or control is passed from DOS to another software program. Users who wish to make the background color appear whenever the system is booted should refer to the discussion of AUTOEXEC.BAT in section 5.2.

The Change Background Color Program Files

Nine batch files and one informational screen make up the components of the Change Background Color utility. Its execution begins when the user enters **2** from the Customized display menu. This causes the 2.BAT file in

---

BACKGROUND COLOR SELECTOR

This utility allows you to change the color of this screen.
To alter the screen color, enter any of the color numbers
listed below:

```
1. Black       4. Blue        7. Cyan
2. Green       5. Magenta     8. Red
3. White       6. Yellow      9. Foreground colors
```

<<<<< Press F1 to Return >>>>>

Figure 5.4. Change Background Color Menu

Customized Display Utilities

the \HDU\DISPLAY directory to be executed. The commands in this file are as follows:

```
   2.BAT
1: echo off
2: cls
3: cd..\backgrnd
4: type backgrnd.scr
5: echo ENTER SELECTION:
6: prompt $e[20;18H
```

The above batch file changes the directory to \HDU\BACKGRND, displays an informational screen (BACKGRND.SCR), and positions the cursor for the ENTER SELECTION: prompt.

The background color screen, BACKGRND.SCR, is located in the \HDU\BACKGRND directory. The files located in this directory are constructed in exactly the same way as the foreground color batch files, with two exceptions. The numeric color control codes differ from the foreground batch files. Also, the redirected ECHO command that resets the SETSCRN.BAT file is not found in the background batch files. This is because the control codes for background colors are not affected by the control codes in the *Hard Disk Manager* menu screens. See Chapter 6 for more information.

The Change Screen Attributes Utility

The Change Screen Attributes on the Display Design menu produces the display shown in Figure 5.5. This screen contains five options; its primary function is to set various character attributes to enhance the display. Once a selection is chosen, the attribute screen is redisplayed with the changed attribute.

For each selection, the changes produced on the screen remain until either the system is rebooted, control is passed to another software package, or until the attribute is reset to normal. Selection 5 on this menu restores the display to normal. Note that the attributes for normal display, reverse video, and high-intensity foreground are saved in the SETSCRN.BAT file; blinking and invisible attribute settings are not.

More than one attribute can be changed at a time. For example, if characters are set to blink and then the reverse video attribute is set, the result will be a reverse video blinking screen. The attribute that was activated

```
┌─────────────────────────────────────────────┐
│          ╔═══════════════════════╗          │
│          ║ SCREEN ATTRIBUTES MENU ║         │
│          ╚═══════════════════════╝          │
│                                             │
│       1.   Increase Character Intensity     │
│                                             │
│       2.   Set Blinking Characters          │
│                                             │
│       3.   Reverse Video Image              │
│                                             │
│       4.   Set Invisible Characters         │
│                                             │
│       5.   Restore Display Characters to Normal │
│                                             │
│           <<<<< Press F1 to Return >>>>>    │
│                                             │
└─────────────────────────────────────────────┘
```

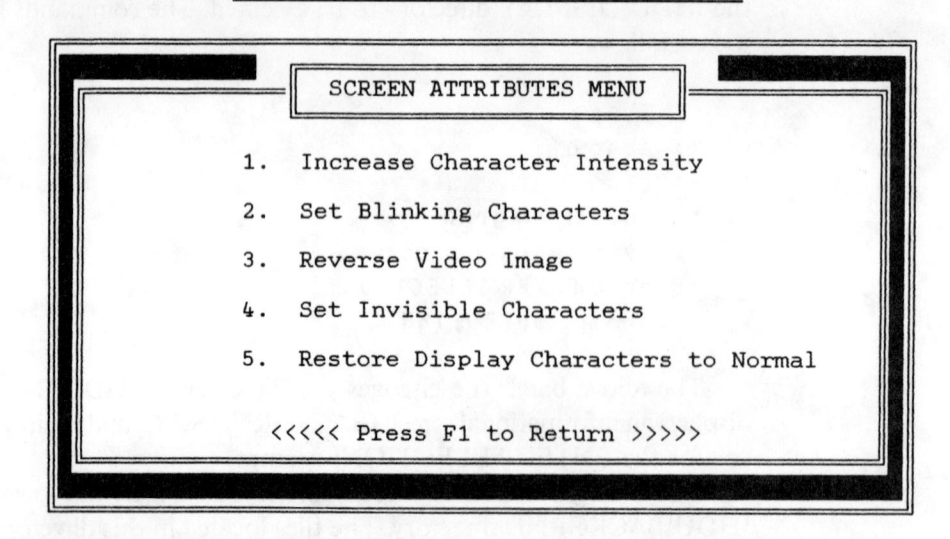

Figure 5.5. Change Screen Attributes Menu

will remain despite the selection of additional attributes until selection 5, Restore Display Characters to Normal, is selected.

Users who wish to make the screen attributes appear whenever the system is booted should refer to the discussion of AUTOEXEC.BAT in section 5.2.

The five individual display attribute menu choices are described below.

Increase Character Intensity

This selection increases the intensity of characters typed on the screen. It can be used to produce a brighter display under high-glare situations. It also can be used to highlight a line or set of lines on a display screen to draw the viewer's attention to certain information.

Set Blinking Characters

This selection makes characters typed on the screen blink. This attribute can also be used to draw the viewer's attention to a particular area of the screen. This is an attribute that one will want to use sparingly—a full screen of blinking characters can be difficult to focus on. It can be useful for displaying error message screens.

Customized Display Utilities 81

Reverse Video Image

This selection reverses the normal foreground/background color configuration on the display screen. On an IBM Color Display, characters appear black on a white display. On a monochrome screen, characters appear black on green or black on amber, depending on the type of monochrome screen. This attribute is particularly useful to highlight information on a monochrome display when other color choices are not available.

Set Invisible Characters

This selection masks the display of characters on the screen, in effect making any characters typed at the terminal invisible. It can be used to mask the display of characters when typing a password in a password protection routine.

Restore Display Characters to Normal

This selection restores the display to normal. It is used following any of the attribute changes listed on the Change Screen Attributes menu to return the display to a normal foreground/background configuration.

The Change Screen Attributes Program Files

Five batch files and one informational screen make up the components of the Change Screen Attributes utilty. Its execution begins when the user enters a **3** from the Customized Display menu. This causes the 3.BAT file in the \HDU\DISPLAY directory to be executed. The commands in this file are as follows:

```
   3.BAT
1: echo off
2: cls
3: cd screen
4: type screen.scr
5: echo ENTER SELECTION:
6: prompt $e[20;18H
```

The display attributes screen, SCREEN.SCR, is located in the \HDU\DISPLAY\SCREEN directory. Unlike the color utilities, the display attribute utilities are located in a subdirectory in the \HDU\DISPLAY directory screen; the directory contains five batch files.

File construction for these utility batch files is identical to that used for the color utilities. This is because the same sequence of numeric control codes is used for display attributes and display colors. In addition, the same alpha character (a lowercase "m") is used to set any attribute of the display, including color.

5.2
MODIFYING THE CUSTOMIZED DISPLAY UTILITIES

The screen display utilities can be modified in many ways. Individual batch files may be used to create other menus and utilities; or the three utilities—foreground color, background color, and screen attributes—can be combined into a single utility screen. This section describes how one might make modifications such as these.

Some Points to Keep in Mind

When considering modification alternatives, it is useful to keep several points in mind about the customized display utilities. Each attribute, whether it be screen color or some aspect of the display screen, has a unique control code attached to it. This control code, when preceded by an escape character, is intercepted by the device driver, ANSI.SYS, in order to change the screen display.

Most application software programs exercise their own control over attributes of the display screen. When in DOS, however, attributes of the display screen can be changed at any time. Although these utilities rely on batch files to change screen attributes, similar commands can be issued from the keyboard using the PROMPT command. For example, one might issue the command:

```
C>prompt $e[44m
```

This command would turn the background blue as each character is typed. Note that the PROMPT command contains the escape character "$e" followed by a left-hand bracket ([). To wash the entire screen with a blue

Customized Display Utilities 83

background, the Clear Screen (CLS) command must be issued. The only problem with using the PROMPT method is that one would have to know the control codes for each of the attributes.

Since the Customized Display utilities are located in three separate directories (\HDU\FOREGRND; \HDU\BACKGRND; and \HDU\DISPLAY\ SCREEN), this adds another factor that must be considered when modifying or combining the utilities. Newly created batch files would have to include commands that changed the directory so that files in each of these three subdirectories could be accessed. If utilities from two of the directories were combined, they first would have to be copied into the same directory.

Adding and Deleting Menu Items

Menu choices can be either added to the Customized Display utilities or deleted with ease. The sections that describe adding and deleting menu items in Chapter 10 should be consulted for users who wish to follow a step-by-step approach.

The Customized Display utilities are located in three directories: \HDU\DISPLAY, \HDU\FOREGRND, and \HDU\BACKGRND. All batch and screen files are located in those directories. The user must determine which directory is most appropriate to use when adding screen and batch files.

Permanently Setting Screen Attributes with the AUTOEXEC.BAT File

The Customized Display utilities can be used at any time to set attributes of the display. However, those setting are not permanent; each time that the system is turned on, the display attributes must be set. An alternative to this situation is to automatically set a predefined foreground/background color and attribute scheme by including the appropriate control codes in the system's AUTOEXEC.BAT file.

The AUTOEXEC.BAT is a user-created file that DOS automatically executes when the the system is initialized or reinitialized. This file resides in the root (C:\) directory and contains all of the commands that need to be executed at system startup. As such, it is the ideal vehicle for automatically setting default display attributes. Thereafter, if different attributes are desired, they may be reset using the Customized Display utilities.

For example, the following AUTOEXEC.BAT file could be written for a color monitor. When the system is initialized, a main menu (called MAIN.SCR) with a red foreground and blue background is automatically displayed.

```
   AUTOEXEC.BAT
1: echo^[[31m
2: echo^[[44m
3: echo off
4: cls
5: type main.scr
6: echo ENTER SELECTION:
7: prompt $e[22;18H
```

In this example, the control codes have the following meaning:

   ^[[The escape character followed by a left bracket ([).
   31m   Set foreground (character) color to red.
   44m   Set background (screen) color to blue.

One must check to see if an AUTOEXEC.BAT file already exists. If one exists, the best idea is to add the attribute-specific commands to the appropriate lines of the file. Any text editor or EDLIN can be used to do this modification (see EDLIN Help in the HELP utilities or refer to Appendix C). Once altered, the system must be rebooted so that the new AUTOEXEC.BAT file is read. Note that when a main menu is created using the Disk/Directory utilities, the user has the option of creating an AUTOEXEC.BAT file automatically.

Combining Utility Attributes

Although the utilities permit the user to set any possible attribute combination, some attribute and color settings don't make sense; some are downright ugly. For example, setting the foreground and the background for the same color functionally blanks the screen and makes it impossible to work with the display. A full screen of blinking characters can truly unnerve most anyone. And certain color combinations (for example, red foreground/yellow background) could better be done without.

In fact, one might be able to come up with several combinations of colors and attributes that are used most of the time. In this case, it might make

Customized Display Utilities

sense to combine all of those combinations into one utility screen. A new screen can be designed and created using the Screen Design utility (see Chapter 6). Or using EDLIN, one of the existing attribute screens can be modified. Combination attribute files will contain two or more control code sequences. The procedure below demonstrates how a batch file for a menu selection that changes three display attributes can be created. This example would produce a high-intensity, magenta character on a green background. It is assumed that the selection is called 1.BAT.

1. The EDLIN command is issued to create a file called 1.BAT:

   ```
   C>edlin 1.bat
   New file
   *i
         1:
   ```

2. In lines 1-3, the attribute codes are entered following the ECHO command and an escape character. The escape character is created by holding down the <Ctrl> key and typing **V**. The following is displayed:

   ```
   1:*echo^V
   ```

3. Then a left-hand bracket is typed followed by another left hand bracket and the control code for high intensity characters (**1m**).

   ```
   1:*echo^V[[1m
   ```

4. Line 1 is then entered, and a prompt appears for line 2. The control code sequence for magenta foreground is entered, as in the previous step.

   ```
   1:*echo ^V[[1m
   2:*echo ^V[[35m
   ```

5. The final batch file, which changes the attributes and displays a screen called MENU.SCR might appear as follows when listed with the EDLIN List Lines (L) command:

   ```
   1: echo ^[[1m
   2: echo ^[[35m
   3: echo ^[[42m
   4: cls
   5: type menu.scr
   6: echo ENTER SELECTION:
   7: prompt $e[22;18H
   ```

Creating a Menu Screen with Multiple Foreground/Background Colors

Although it is a little more complicated, it is possible to generate multiple colors on a display screen. One may create a single text file in which all attribute characteristics—foreground colors, background colors, and display attributes—are specified line-by-line or character-by-character. This is done by entering the control codes for the display directly preceding and/or following different components of the text. The screen can be "painted" so that different sections have different colors.

For example, to create a multicolor Main Menu screen in which each menu selection appears in a different color band (background color), the text of the .SCR file would appear as shown in Figure 5.6. Suppose the screen file in Figure 5.6 is called MENU.SCR. The multiple-color screen is displayed by simply entering the command

```
type menu.scr
```

The different colors are activated as each component of the screen is displayed.

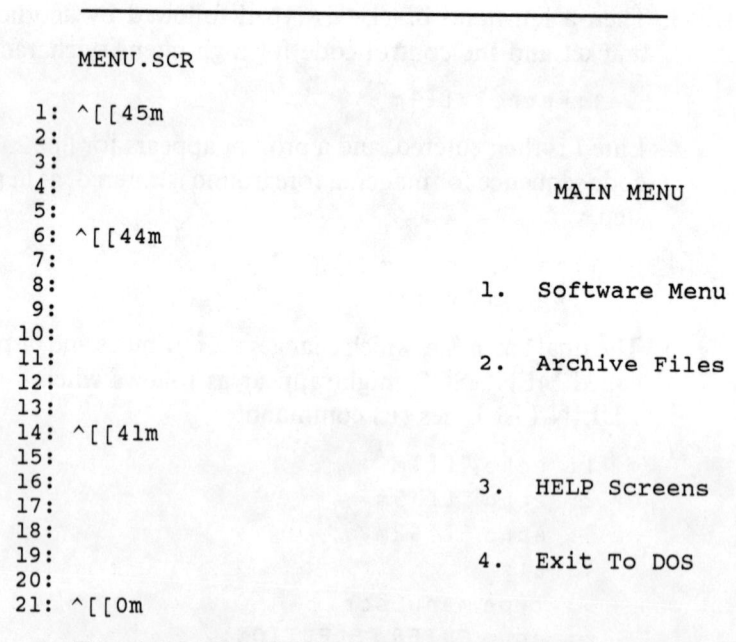

```
MENU.SCR

 1:  ^[[45m
 2:
 3:
 4:                              MAIN MENU
 5:
 6:  ^[[44m
 7:
 8:                       1.  Software Menu
 9:
10:
11:                       2.  Archive Files
12:
13:
14:  ^[[41m
15:
16:                       3.  HELP Screens
17:
18:
19:                       4.  Exit To DOS
20:
21:  ^[[0m
```

Figure 5.6. Text File for a Multiple-Colored Screen

Customized Display Utilities

This technique was used in generating the two-color borders for the *Hard Disk Manager* menus. The section in Chapter 6 entitled "Using Color in Screen Designs" describes this process in detail.

5.3
SOME BACKGROUND INFORMATION ON DISPLAY AND KEYBOARD CONTROL

Recent versions of DOS allow the user to control various aspects of the video display and keyboard through inclusion of the file ANSI.SYS. This ANSI.SYS file is included in the DOS program files. It is a loadable device driver, a hardware-specific program to which DOS transfers control whenever it must access the display. It contains the American National Standards Institute set of terminal codes.

How ANSI.SYS Works

In order for DOS to recognize ANSI.SYS, it must be placed in a user-created configuration file that is resident in the root directory. This configuration file, which must be called CONFIG.SYS, is read by DOS and remains in memory along with COMMAND.COM. Whenever DOS must access the video display, for example, it passes control to ANSI.SYS.

The CONFIG.SYS file is a text file, and it can be created using EDLIN or the COPY CON command. When *Hard Disk Manager* is installed on a system, a CONFIG.SYS file is automatically created if one does not exist. If such a file already exists, the command **device=ansi.sys** is appended to the existing file. It is this command that activates the ANSI.SYS device driver.

Controlling Attributes of the Display Screen

ANSI.SYS can be used to alter various attributes of the display because it allows the user to specify control codes that determine how characters appear on the screen. For example, the user can specify background and foreground colors, reverse video displays, and so on. In order to alter various attributes of the display, ANSI.SYS intercepts those control codes that begin with an escape character (ASCII 27). The escape character signals that all characters following it should be interpreted as commands. Another character also must follow the escape character in order to define the ANSI.SYS set of escape sequences that are specific to the PC. This character is the left bracket ([).

To incorporate various screen attributes into the design of a screen, the user must be familiar with DOS's extended screen and keyboard control codes. Appendix D lists the various control codes for the display screen. The escape character followed by a control code is the key to performing all kinds of tricks with the video screen. Control codes can be activated via a text (EDLIN) file, or they can be activated by the PROMPT command. A discussion of both methods follows.

Screen and Keyboard Control Using Text (EDLIN) Files

A control code can be specified in a text file, and then activated whenever the file is displayed with the TYPE command. The text file may be created using EDLIN or any other text editor. Control codes in text files always begin with the escape character, which is generated by typing <Ctrl> V followed by the left-hand bracket (the [character).

To demonstrate how a control code is placed in a text file, EDLIN will be used to create a simple file called RED.SCR. The purpose of this file when displayed by the TYPE command is to change the screen background color to red. Here is the process:

1. The user enters the following commands:
    ```
    edlin red.scr
    ```
    Then, in EDLIN:
    ```
    i
    ```
    This causes EDLIN to display the prompt for line 1.
2. First, the escape character is generated. This is done by:
    - Holding down the <Ctrl> key and typing **V**
    - Typing the left bracket character ([). This causes the symbols ^V to be displayed.
3. Next, another left bracket is typed. This is followed by the control-code value for a red background screen (41) and the letter "m"; now <Enter> is pressed. The symbols displayed are:
    ```
    ^V[41m
    ```
4. Finally, to end the EDLIN routine, the <Ctrl><Break> is pressed to end Insert Lines, followed by the command:
    ```
    E
    ```
    This ends the EDLIN session.

Customized Display Utilities

The above procedure creates a file that will change the screen background color to red. This is done by executing the command:

```
type red.scr
```

One may immediately observe the effects of this file by issuing a Clear Screen (CLS) command.

> NOTE: *After a control code is entered, the ^V characters are always subsequently displayed as ^[. This is normal.*

Single-purpose control code files of this type are called attribute-specific files. They are a handy way to activate control codes since their filenames match their functions. Similar files can be created for foreground colors (e.g., RED.FRG, BLUE.FRG) or other display attributes (e.g., BLINK.SCR, REVERSE.SCR). Once they have been created, the user can change screen attributes without the necessity of looking up the required control codes.

The technique of entering control codes directly into a text file can be used in screen files that use multiple display attributes, such as multiple colors, high intensity, and so on. For example, the following screen file (DEMO.SCR) will display each of the three lines of text in three different colors:

```
   DEMO.SCR
1: ^[[32m This is green foreground.
2: ^[[35m This is magenta foreground.
3: ^[[33m This is yellow foreground.
```

(Remember that the ^V character is displayed as ^[.) When the above file is displayed via the TYPE command, each of the three lines appears in a different color. These attribute files then can be activated at the system level or in batch files. This is the procedure followed in screen attribute files for the *Hard Disk Manager*.

Screen and Keyboard Control Using the PROMPT Command

Using the PROMPT command, an escape character followed by a control code can be placed in a batch file or entered directly at the system prompt. The PROMPT command causes a string of characters to be sent to the display. Typically, its purpose is to change the system prompt on the screen.

For example, if the user enters

```
prompt ENTER COMMAND $g
```

the C> prompt disappears and ENTER COMMAND appears.

A less well understood function of the PROMPT command is its ability to activate metastrings. *Metastrings* are groups of characters that are assigned a specific meaning in DOS. They always follow the word PROMPT and begin with a dollar sign ($). They allow the user to generate diverse types of system prompts. The user should consult Appendix A for further details on this aspect of PROMPT.

The one metastring of particular relevance here is the escape character ($e). This escape character is recognized by ANSI.SYS. As described above, ANSI.SYS interprets characters that follow the escape sequence as commands. Therefore, those strings that begin with the sequence $e are intercepted by ANSI.SYS and can be used to control many aspects of the display screen. The left bracket symbol ([) also must follow the $e metastring. For example, to change the background color to red using the PROMPT command, the command is entered as

```
PROMPT $e[41m
```

Following this command, all subsequent screen displays will have a red background. Entering Clear Screen (CLS), for example, will wash the screen in red.

Text File Versus the PROMPT Method

It has been the authors' experience that certain circumstances dictate which of these two methods should be used for screen and keyboard control. The following observations can be made about these two methods:

1. The PROMPT command, when used to send escape sequences to ANSI.SYS to control screen colors, does not work well with the ECHO OFF batch file command. ECHO OFF inhibits the screen display of DOS commands. When placed in a batch file preceding a PROMPT $e commmand, ECHO OFF blocks execution of the escape sequence until the batch routine ends. This peculiarity prevents the user from producing a color menu screen using the PROMPT command while inhibiting the display of DOS commands.

2. Screen colors and display attributes are best activated by attribute-specific text files. These files contain the desired control codes for altering the display characteristics. They are files created using the EDLIN method described above. To activate that attribute-specific file, one may simply execute the command **TYPE** followed by the filename.
3. For cursor control and keyboard reassignment, either method can be used, but the *Hard Disk Manager* uses the PROMPT command exclusively.

Keyboard Reassignment

ANSI.SYS also can be used to alter the characters and functions assigned to the computer's keyboard. For example, instead of producing the letter "Z," this letter key could produce the word "ZEBRA" when typed. Reassigning the alpha-numeric keys is probably of limited value. However, there are unlimited possibilities for the function keys.

Key reassignment is accomplished using the same two methods described previously: in a text (EDLIN) file, or via the PROMPT command. In either case, one may specify new characters for the key, or the key can execute a specific command or batch file. The format for assigning new characters to a key is:

```
^[[#;#;...#p  (in an EDLIN file)
```

or

```
PROMPT $e[#;#;...#p
```

The first # represents the ASCII value of the key to be changed; the second # (and subsequent ones, if necessary) represent the ASCII values of the character(s) that are replacing the first #. For example, suppose it is desired to have the "Z" key produce the word "ZEBRA." The command would be:

```
^[[90;90;69;66;82;65p  (in an EDLIN file)
```

or

```
PROMPT $e[90;90;69;66;82;65p
```

More useful is the assignment of a command or batch file to a key. The format for this operation is shown on page 92.

```
^[[#;"string";p (in an EDLIN file)
```

or

```
PROMPT $e[#;"string";p
```

NOTE: *In all cases, the lowercase "p" ends the command sequence.*

The <F1> key reassignment in the *Hard Disk Manager* uses the batch file HDU.BAT to issue the prompt command to reassign that key. This is the batch file used to display the *Hard Disk Manager* menu. The key is given the new function of executing a batch file called RETURN.BAT when pressed. The last line of HDU.BAT contains the following command:

```
prompt $e[0;59;"return";13p $e[22;18H
```

The parameters of this command have the following meaning:

$e[	This is the escape character and left bracket combination required for activating control codes via the PROMPT command.
0;59;"return";	These characters assign the string "return" to the F1 key, which has an ASCII value of 0,59.
13p	The ENTER keystroke (ASCII value 13) is appended to the previous characters. All key reassignment commands must end with the lowercase "p."
$e[22;18H	These characters perform cursor positioning functions. (Refer to the "Cursor Control" section.)

All forty function-key combinations (10 for unshifted, 10 for <SHIFT> plus function key, 10 for <Crtl> plus function key, and 10 for <Alt> plus function key) are designated by two digits. The first digit is always zero. See Appendix F for a list of ASCII values for the forty function-key combinations.

Cursor Control

Another capability that ASNSI.SYS gives the user is the ability to control the position of the cursor. The two previously discussed methods for ex-

Customized Display Utilities

ecuting display attribute routines are used: the PROMPT command and text (EDLIN) file execution with the TYPE command. The authors use the former method exclusively in the *Hard Disk Manager* since cursor positioning is always used for in conjunction with a screen prompt.

Appendix D shows the various types of cursor control routines that can be used. For example, to move the cursor to a specific screen position, the command in an EDLIN file would be:

    ^[[#;#H

Redirection of Screen and Keyboard Input and Output

This DOS capability is not dependent on ANSI.SYS. It can be accomplished without the aid of this device driver. Redirection is accomplished using the symbols >, >>, and <. Output can be redirected to a file or a device using the > symbol, as in:

    DIR \WP>PRN

This command redirects the output of the DIR command to the printer instead of the display screen. To send the information to a file, the command is entered as:

    DIR \WP>LIST.TXT

In this case, the output is sent to a file called LIST.TXT. If the file already exists, the existing data in that file are overwritten. To append the information to an existing file, the >> symbols are used.

Keyboard input can be redirected so as to come from a file or device by using the < symbol. For example, input for the SORT filter could come from a file instead of the keyboard with this command:

    SORT <LIST.TXT

One interesting aspect of keyboard redirection is that input to a program (such as EDLIN) can be entirely defined from a file instead of the keyboard, as in:

    EDLIN < WPINPUT.TXT>NUL

In this command, the EDLIN program is executed, and the commands for running EDLIN come from the file WPINPUT.TXT. The screen display that would normally occur is suppressed by the redirection of output to NUL (a dummy device, i.e., the trash can). The only glitch is that the input file must pass control back to the keyboard at the end of the input file (that is, exit the EDLIN program). Otherwise, the EDLIN program is waiting for further input and the system is hung.

Redirection also can be performed using DOS filters (SORT, FIND, and MORE) and piping. *Piping* refers to the chaining together of DOS commands such that standard inputs and outputs are automatically redirected. The "¦" symbol is used in piping. Piping is frequently used with the DOS filters, as in:

```
DIR ¦ MORE
```

In this case, the output of the DIR command is redirected through the MORE filter. Appendix A describes these commands in more detail.

chapter 6

Screen Design Utility

Screen designs can be created using a text editor, the ASCII extended character set, and color control codes. These characters include ASCII values 128 to 255, which go beyond the upper- and lowercase alphabetic and numeric characters. Included in the extended character set are some 50 graphic characters that allow the user to create all kinds of border and screen designs. Although using a combination of the extended character set and color controls codes falls far short of being a screen painter, these features can be used to create rudimentary logo designs and professional quality menus.

What Is the Screen Design Utility?

The Screen Design utility is used with the DOS text editor, EDLIN. To use this utility, informational and instructional screens lead the user into a EDLIN-based design template. The utility places the user in EDLIN and provides row and column markers for centering and designing a screen.

Why Is It Used?

For the user who does not do enough text editing to justify purchasing a text editor program, EDLIN can be used to create program files and screen designs. Unfortunately, it is difficult to center and align graphic characters with EDLIN. This utility is simply a design template to be used like a ruler might be in creating screen designs.

The usefulness of this program lies not just in the template but also in how it is used with the EDLIN text editor. The template, itself, is an efficiency aid. Beyond pure efficiency are the aesthetics of a screen design. Therefore, unlike other utilities in this package, this chapter will devote equal attention to a description of the utility and a number of tips on how to use it successfully to create all types of screen designs.

How to Use the Utility

Choosing the Screen Design utility option on the *Hard Disk Manager* menu produces the display shown in Figure 6.1. This screen introduces the user to the utility: It tells the user that a template will be displayed and explains that a working knowledge of EDLIN is necessary to use this template. A confirmation (Y/N) prompt is displayed so that the user may terminate the session at this point. If the user does not have a sufficient knowledge of EDLIN and wishes to first review EDLIN's commands, he or she may refer to Appendix C or the EDLIN help screens included with *Hard Disk Manager*.

If the user responds with **N**, the main utilities menu is redisplayed and the Help utilities option may be chosen. If the user responds with **Y**, a second instructional screen is displayed. This screen is presented in Figure 6.2.

The instruction screen tells the user how to issue the DESIGN command and what he or she can expect as results. The user must enter the DESIGN command followed by a space and the desired screen name. Since this screen name will be saved as a file with the extension .SCR, the screen

```
                              DESIGN AID
===============================================================
DESIGN AID is a screen that is used with DOS's text editor,
   EDLIN, to center logo or screen designs.  It simply gives column
   numbers across the top and bottom.  The center of the screen is
   marked with the symbol, ^.  Row numbers (1-21) are listed
   down the left-hand side of the screen.

To use this facility, you must have a working knowledge of DOS's
   EDLIN text editor.  If you need EDLIN help, consult the DOS
   manual or the EDLIN help option under the Help utilities
   section of this program.
```

Figure 6.1. Screen Design Utility Information Screen

Screen Design Utility

```
                         INSTRUCTIONS
===============================================================
This utility creates a file with a name you specify and transfers in a
   design aid template. At the * prompt, EDLIN commands can be issued.

To use the design aid template to create a logo or screen design,
   type the command DESIGN followed by the name you wish to call the
   screen.  For example, to create a design called FLOWER, the
   command is entered as
                         DESIGN flower

The screen name can contain a maximum of eight characters and must
   adhere to the character restrictions for DOS filenames.  The
   extension of this design screen will automatically be .SCR.

To edit an existing screen, use the same command; the template will
   be found only in new screens.

               <<<<< Press F1 to Return >>>>>
```

Figure 6.2. Instruction Screen for Screen Design Utility

name must comply with DOS's rules for naming files. It should be noted that all screens created with this utility will be saved in the directory \HDU\DESIGN. Once created, this screen can be copied to any hard disk directory. If at any time the user wants to terminate this utility session, the <F1> key may be pressed to return the user to the *Hard Disk Manager* menu (or the main menu, if one is installed).

Once the DESIGN command is entered, a message is displayed on the screen to indicate that the screen file and template are being created. The screen name selected by the user is automatically included in the message.

After the screen file has been created, the user is placed in EDLIN and instructed to view the template with the EDLIN command LIST LINES command. This command transfers the template into the screen file specified and displays the template in EDLIN. It is a 21-line file with column numbers across the top and bottom. The second line of the template meters the column numbers in increments of ten. The template file as it appears in EDLIN is shown in Figure 6.3. This template is used to create screen designs by providing row and column number references for situating characters on the screen. The planning process for such a design is described later in this chapter.

When the design process is complete, the row numbers for the template can be deleted, and the screen file is saved by terminating the EDLIN session with the END EDIT command.

98   HARD DISK MANAGER

```
 1:*   1234567890123456789012345678901^345678901234567890123456789 0123
 2:    ========1=========2=========3=========4=========5=========6===
 3:
 4:
 5:
 6:
 7:
 8:
 9:
10:
11:
12:
13:
14:
15:
16:
17:
18:
19:
20:
21:    123456789012345678901234567890123456789012345678901234567890123
```

Figure 6.3. The Template File as It Appears in EDLIN

6.1
THE SCREEN DESIGN UTILITY

Organization of the Screen Utility

The screen design utility is located in a single directory: \HDU\DESIGN. It contains three screen files and four program files, and it is located in the main utility directory. The directory and file structure is shown in Figure 6.4.

```
            C:\HDU <DIR>

              HDU.SCR

           \HDU\DESIGN <DIR>

              DESIGN.SCR
              Y.BAT
              N.BAT
              INSTRUCT.SCR
              DESIGN.BAT
              DESIGNIN.TXT
              LOGOAID
```

Figure 6.4. Directory and File Structure for the Screen Design Utility

Screen Design Utility

The initial screen for this utility is the file DESIGN.SCR. DESIGN.SCR then gives the user two options, to continue or not to continue. These options are contained in the files Y.BAT and N.BAT. Selection of the negative alternative redisplays the *Hard Disk Manager* menu. Selection of the affirmative alternative ("Y") displays the file INSTRUCT.SCR. The user must then enter the command **DESIGN** followed by a screen name. This activates DESIGN.BAT. DESIGN.BAT reads input from a text file, DESIGNIN.TXT, calls the EDLIN program, and displays the design template, LOGOAID.

The Screen Design Program Files

The Screen Design utility contains three screen files:

DESIGN.SCR   This is the first screen that the user encounters with the Screen Design Utility. It defines the utility and displays a "Continue (Y/N)?" confirmation prompt.

INSTRUCT.SCR   This is an instruction screen for the utility.

LOGOAID   This screen is the template for the Screen Design utility. It is displayed on the screen whenever the utility is used for building screen files.

The initial screen, DESIGN.SCR gives the user two options, to continue or not to continue. These options are contained in the files Y.BAT and N.BAT. The contents of the these files are as follows:

```
    N.BAT
1:  echo off
2:  cls
3:  cd hdu
4:  type \hdu.scr
5:  echo ENTER SELECTION:
6:  prompt $e[22;18H
7:  setscrn
    Y.BAT
1:  echo off
2:  cls
3:  type instruct.scr
4:  echo ENTER COMMAND:
5:  prompt $e[22;16H
```

HARD DISK MANAGER

In both of the confirmation prompt batch files (N.BAT and Y.BAT), the last line of the batch file contains the prompt command. The prompt command is used here with parameters to set the cursor position.

Issuing the Screen Design utility command, DESIGN followed by a screen name, activates a batch file named DESIGN.BAT. The contents of DESIGN.BAT are shown below:

```
        DESIGN.BAT
 1:     echo off
 2:     cls
 3:     if "%1"=="" goto ERROR
 4:     if exist %1.scr goto NOTNEW
 5:     echo CREATING A TEMPLATE FOR A NEW SCREEN DESIGN
             CALLED %1.scr.
 6:     echo Enter the command L at the * prompt to view
             the template.
 7:     edlin %1.scr <designin.txt>nul
 8:     goto DOEDLIN
 9:     :NOTNEW
10:     echo The screen called %1.scr already exists...
11:     echo Enter the command L at the * prompt to view
             the screen.
12:     :DOEDLIN
13:     edlin %1.scr
14:     cd ..
15:     cls
16:     type hdu.scr
17:     echo ENTER SELECTION:
18:     prompt $e[22;18H
19:     setscrn
20:     goto END
21:     :ERROR
22:     echo You must supply the name of the design
             screen. Try again...
23:     pause
24:     cls
25:     type design.scr
26:     echo Continue (Y/N)?
27:     prompt $e[15;17H
28:     :END
```

How DESIGN.BAT Works

In line 3 of DESIGN.BAT, the program first checks if the user has supplied the name of the screen file; if not, control is passed to the ERROR section and the Screen Design utility screen is redisplayed. Line 4 then peforms a check for an existing file by that name; if one exists, control skips down to NOTNEW, where different messages are displayed and EDLIN is invoked. This is to prevent the LOGOAID template from being added to existing design screens that the user is editing.

For new screen design files, after appropriate messages in lines 5-6, the LOGOAID template is added to the new screen design file in line 7. The specified screen name is substituted for the %1 replaceable parameter. Using DOS redirection capabilities, two EDLIN commands are automatically issued as input from a text file called DESIGNIN.TXT. In other words, the **<designin.txt** portion of the command tells EDLIN to get its instructions from the file DESIGNIN.TXT instead of the keyboard. The contents of the DESIGNIN.TXT input file are:

```
DESIGNIN.TXT
1: Tlogoaid
2: E
```

The two EDLIN commands are TRANSFER LINES (**T** in line 1) and END EDIT (**E** in line 2). The TRANSFER LINES (**T**) command in the DESIGNIN.TXT file is used to transfer the design template (LOGOAID) into the first line of the EDLIN file. The END EDIT (**E**) command is then issued to save the newly created file with the design template. Note that all of the output from the EDLIN command is redirected away from the display screen by the inclusion of **>nul** at the end of line 7 of DESIGN.BAT.

Once DESIGNIN.TXT has completed its input, control is then passed back to the line 8 of the DESIGN.BAT file. Here, control is shifted to the DOEDLIN section where the EDLIN command is issued for the screen design file so that the user may now begin his or her screen design.

As can be seen, file input and output redirection can be quite useful. Readers unfamiliar with the redirection capabilities of DOS may wish to consult Chapter 2.

6.2 PLANNING A SCREEN FOR USE WITH THE DESIGN UTILITY

To efficiently create a screen design requires a little upfront planning as well as an understanding of the ASCII Extended Character Set's constraints.

A display of the most commonly used ASCII characters for screen design can be found in the Help Utilities section of *Hard Disk Manager*.

Screen Design Constraints with the ASCII Extended Character Set

The ASCII Extended Character Set allows the user to create block designs only—angled as well as curved characters are not available in the character set. This means that some logo designs must be an approximation of the actual design. For example, it is not possible to create a smooth oval design, but it is possible to create an approximation of such a shape using square or rectangular characters (see Figure 6.5). Similarly, curved portions of large block letters cannot be drawn and must be approximated using square or rectangular characters. The "A" and "N" characters in Figure 6.6 demonstrate this effect. However, a number of characters in the ASCII extended character set can be used to create some well-designed block designs. In particular, the ASCII extended character set includes 28 characters that are specific to the creation of border designs. These characters are shown in Appendix E.

These extended ASCII characters can be used to produce a number of variations on double and single border designs. One also can enhance these border characters with additional ASCII block characters. An example of such a design is shown in Figure 6.7. In the design in Figure 6.7, the double

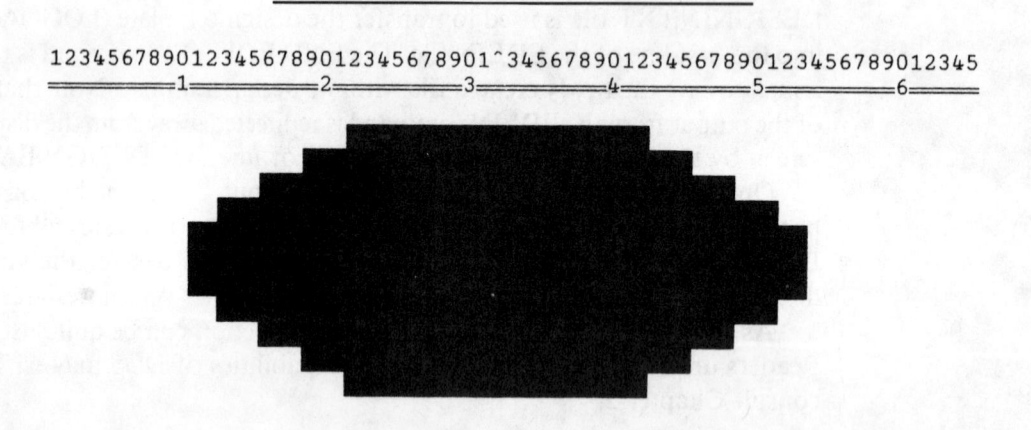

Figure 6.5. Approximation of Oval Shape

Screen Design Utility

```
123456789012345678901234567890^3456789012345678901234567890123 45
======1======2======3======4======5======6======
```

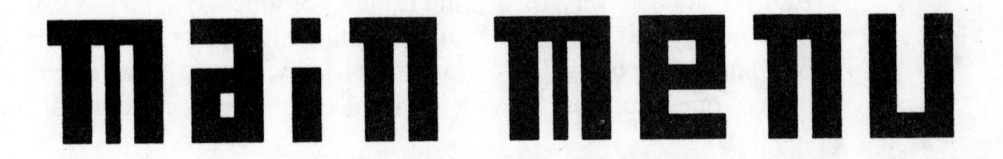

main menu

```
123456789012345678901234567890123456789012345678901234567890123 45
```

Figure 6.6. Large Block Letter Design

border characters (ASCII values 186, 187, 188, 200, 201, and 205) were combined with the ASCII solid block character, ASCII 219, to create a much thicker, more pronounced border.

Figure 6.7. Example of Border Design

HARD DISK MANAGER

Sketching Out a Screen Design

The row and column numberings on the utilities design template are intended to give the user a frame of reference for determining screen design, character centering, screen size, etc. Even with this utility, screen design with EDLIN can be a very frustrating experience unless one invests some time in planning. This is because EDLIN is a line editor; one must build a screen on a line-by-line basis. Thus, in addition to conceptualizing an overall screen design, one also must be able to visualize the design in terms of lines.

```
*1
      1:     12345678901234567890123456789012345678901234567890123456789012345
      2:*    ==========1==========2==========3==========4==========5==========6=====
      3:
      4:
      5:
      6:
      7:
      8:
      9:
     10:
     11:
     12:
     13:
     14:
     15:
     16:
     17:
     18:
     19:
     20:
     21:
     22:    123456789012345678901234567890123456789012345678901234567890112345
```

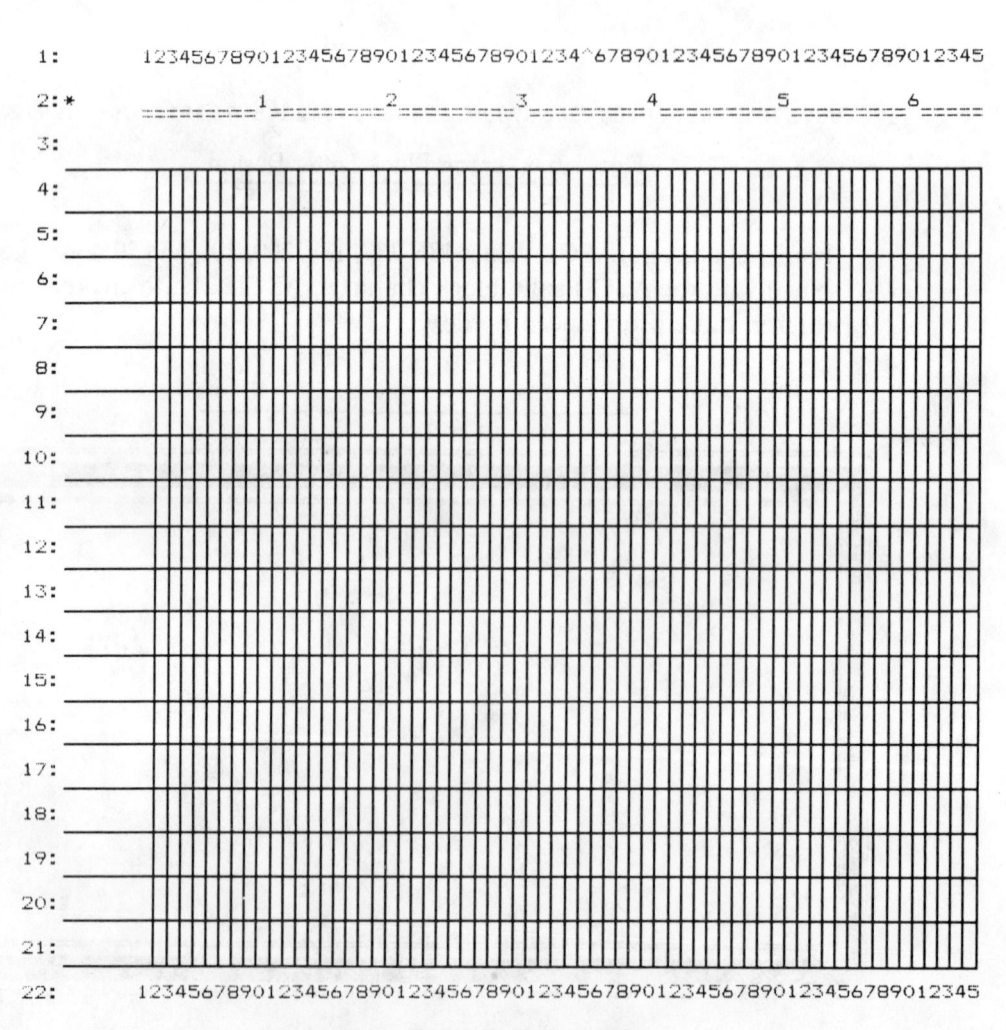

Figure 6.8. Grid for Screen Design

Screen Design Utility

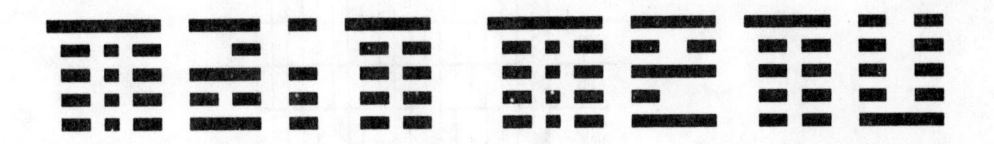

```
12345678901234567890123456789012345678901234567890123456789012345
========1=========2=========3========4=========5========6========
```

```
███ ███ ███   ███ ██  █ ███ ███
 █  ██  █ █   ██  █ █ █  █  █ █
 █  █   █ █   █   █ █ █  █  █ █
███ ███ ███   ███ █  ██  █  ███
```

```
12345678901234567890123456789012345678901234567890123456789012345
```

Figure 6.9. Large Block Letters Drawn with ASCII Character 220

Using a piece of graph paper or a grid such as that presented in Figure 6.8, one can plan out exactly how the design should appear.

It should be noted in Figure 6.8, and also with the design utility, that there is far greater spacing between rows than between columns. To produce continuous shaded areas as in Figure 6.7, one must use rectangular characters. All of the border characters shown in Figure 6.7 are rectangular and can be used to create continuous borders. However, a close examination of the ASCII solid-block characters indicates that not all are rectangles nor do they fill an entire cell of the grid. In fact, some are left-justified, some are right-justified, and some are either top- or bottom-justified. For example, consider the block letters shown in Figure 6.6. These letters were "drawn" using ASCII character 219, a solid rectangular character (█). If this figure were redisplayed using ASCII character 220, a solid square, bottom justified character (▄), the display would look like that shown in Figure 6.9. Figure 6.10 shows the ASCII solid block characters superimposed on a portion of the grid from Figure 6.8. Only one solid character (219) and three dotted characters (176, 177, 178) are full-sized rectangles.

Creating a Screen Design

The ASCII extended characters are drawn using the <Alt> key and the numeric keypad (on the right of the IBM keyboard). A character from the

ASCII VALUE

| 176 |
| 177 |
| 178 |
| 219 |
| 220 |
| 221 |
| 222 |
| 223 |

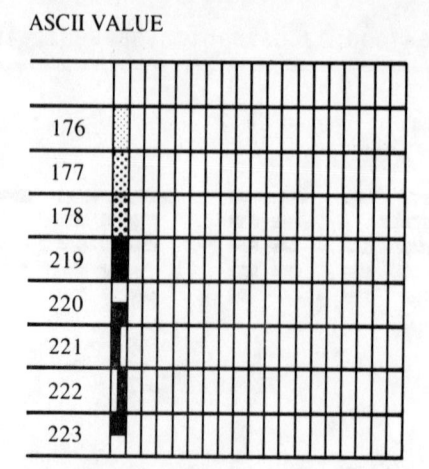

Figure 6.10. ASCII Block Characters Superimposed on Grid

ASCII extended character set is generated by:

- holding down the <Alt> key
- typing the ASCII code for the character on the numeric keypad
- releasing the <Alt> key

When the <Alt> key is released, the ASCII character is displayed on the screen. If the numeric sequence is interrupted or if one fails to hold down the <Alt> key, some other character, often a control character, will be displayed. (Note that these characters cannot be generated using the numbers along the top row of the keyboard; the numeric keypad numbers on the right side of the keyboard must be used.)

It can be very tedious drawing a border by depressing the <Alt> key, typing out the ASCII code, releasing the <Alt> key, and repeating this sequence over and over again. An alternative to these finger gymnastics is to use the EDLIN command REPLACE TEXT (or a Search and Replace function in any other text editor). The EDLIN REPLACE TEXT command allows the user to specify the range of lines to be searched, the character or string to be replaced, and the substitute character or string. Thus, one can replace any ASCII character with an ASCII extended character. This means that any convenient key can be used to draw the border; then it can be replaced globally by an ASCII border character. This process is described below.

Some Information on the EDLIN REPLACE TEXT Command

The EDLIN REPLACE TEXT command is issued at the EDLIN * prompt and has the following format:

```
[line][,line][?]R[string][<F6>string]
```

The lines specified in the first two line parameters are scanned for the occurrence of a text string (the first string parameter); the text of the first string is replaced by the text in the second string parameter. A confirmation prompt can be inserted before the replacement by including the [?] parameter. The range may be specified with the following line options:

First line only	The search begins with this line and ends with the last line in memory.
Second line only	The search begins following the current line and ends with this line.
Neither line	The search begins following the current line and ends with the last line in memory.

For example a border drawn in EDLIN with plus (+) signs in rows 1-10 can be replaced by a solid rectangular block character, ASCII 219. This can be done at the * prompt by entering the command:

```
1,R+<F6><Alt 219>
```

The < > symbols signify a key that is depressed: Depression of the <F6> key produces a <Ctrl> Z character (^Z); depression of the <Alt> key while typing NUMERIC KEYPAD values of 219 produces the ASCII block character ■. Thus, the actual characters displayed by this command would be

```
1,R+^Z■
```

Using the REPLACE TEXT Command in Screen Design

This section provides a step-by-step approach to using the REPLACE TEXT command to build screen designs. Learning these brief routines can save the user a great deal of frustration when EDLIN is employed to build logotype screens.

HARD DISK MANAGER

Setting Up the Screen

Consider the border design presented in Figure 6.7. This border was planned out using a grid similar to the one shown in Figure 6.8. Figure 6.11 shows the planning process using this grid. Suppose a user wishes to create a screen called MENU.SCR. From the instruction screen of the Design utility, the user enters the following command:

```
DESIGN menu
```

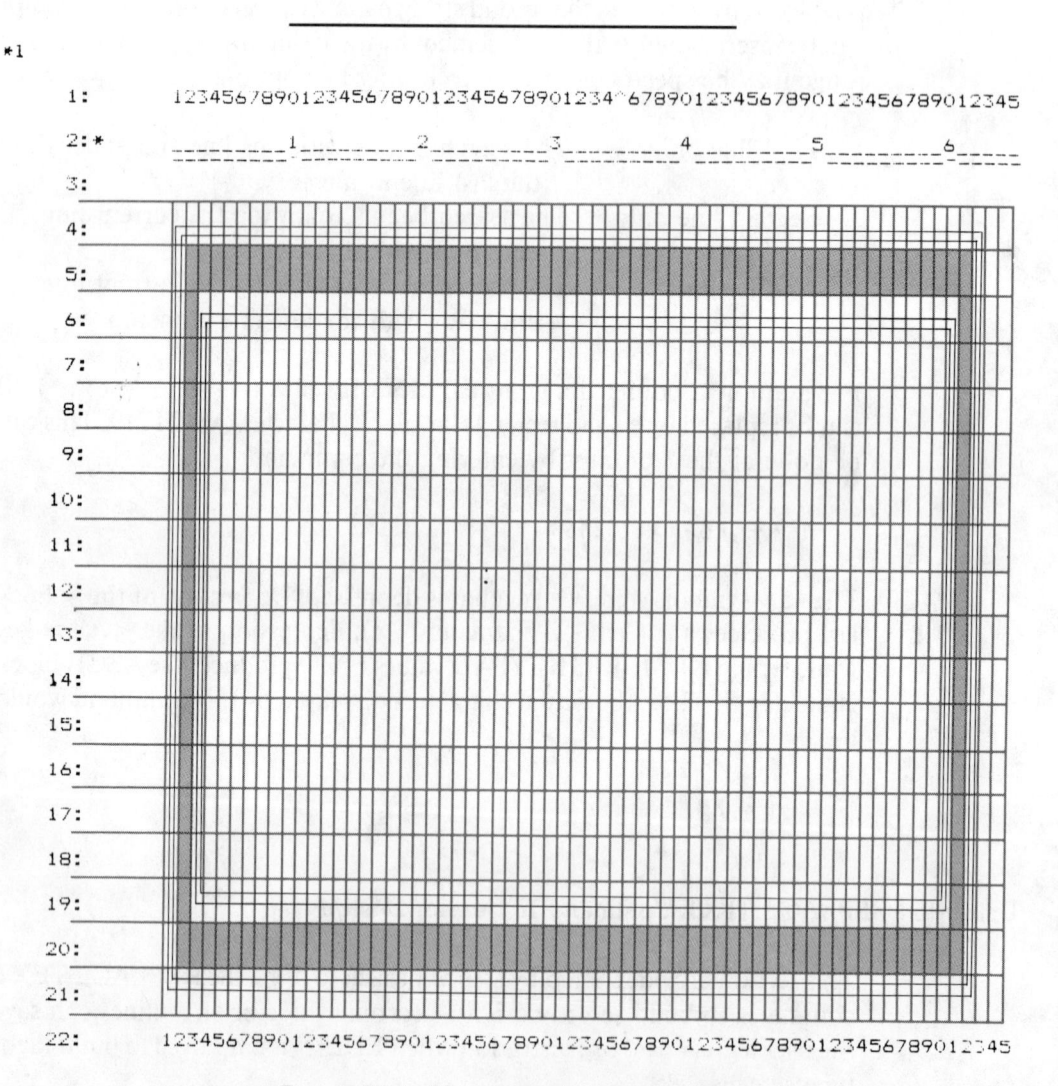

Figure 6.11. Planning a Border Design

This creates an EDLIN file and template called MENU.SCR.

Entering the LIST LINES command, the user can view the template. At Row 3 the border design can begin (the first two rows are temporarily occupied by the template column markers). Thus, the user enters a "3" at the asterisk prompt and obtains the display shown in Figure 6.12.

Referring to the grid, the user spaces over to type the character for the left corner of the border. In the case of this example, the user types <Alt> 201 to produce a double line left border corner. Then, instead of repetitively typing <Alt> 205 to produce a double-line border across the top, the user can type a plus sign (+). Finally the right corner of the border is created by typing <Alt> 187 for a double-line right border corner.

On the next line (line 4), an <Alt> 186 character is typed for the vertical border followed by an <Alt> 219 character for the inside solid border. Thereafter, a period (.) can be used to signify the ASCII 219 value. The solid border is completed using the period (.) and another <Alt> 186 character is typed for the right vertical border.

To complete the top of the design, three ASCII characters are typed on the next line (line 5): <Alt> 186, <Alt> 219, and <Alt> 201, for

```
*L
         1:*    12345678901234567890123456789012345^67890123456789012345678901 23
         2:     ===========1=========2=========3=========4=========5=========6===
         3:
         4:
         5:
         6:
         7:
         8:
         9:
        10:
        11:
        12:
        13:
        14:
        15:
        16:
        17:
        18:
        19:
        20:
        21:            123456789012345678901234567890123456789012345678901234567890123
*3
         3:*
         3:*
```

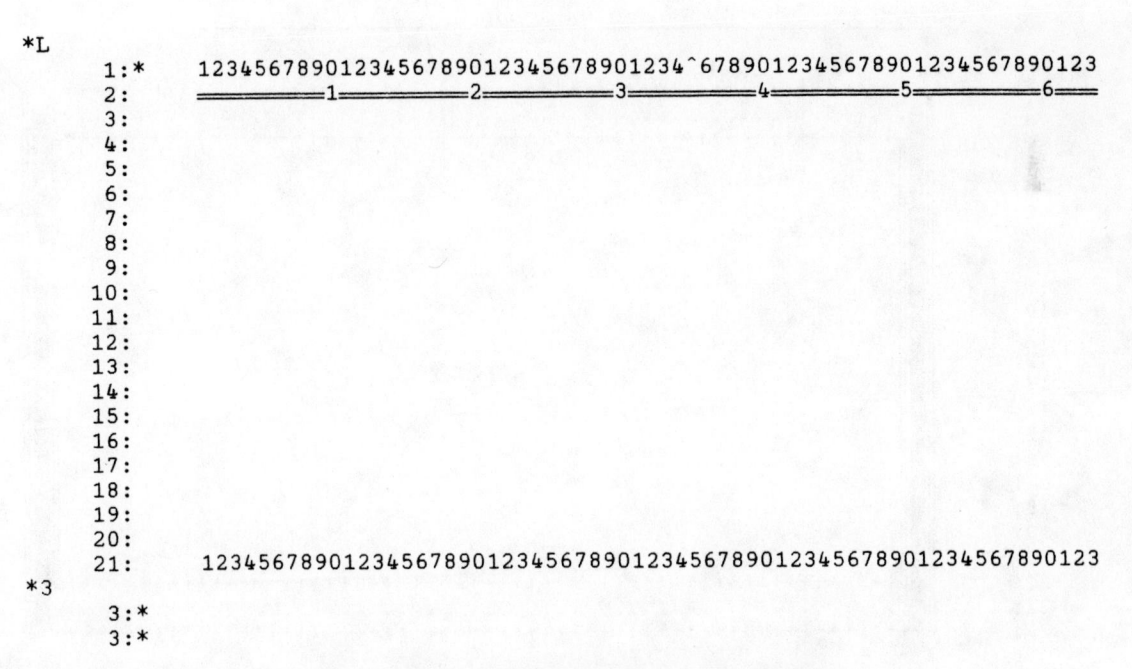

Figure 6.12. The Design Template in EDLIN

```
1:*     ┌++++++++++++++++++++++++++++++++++++++++++++++++++++++++++++++++++++┐
2:      ┃........................................................................┃
3:      ┃┌++++++++++++++++++++++++++++++++++++++++++++++++++++++++++++++++++┐┃
```

Figure 6.13. The Top Three Lines of the Border Design Using Temporary + and . Characters

the outside border, solid inner border, and left inner corner, respectively. Then the plus sign (+) is used to draw the inner horizontal border. At the right margin, a left inner border corner <Alt> 187, a solid inner border character <Alt> 219, and an outer border character <Alt> 186 are typed. This display of the top three lines of the design is shown in Figure 6.13.

Using the grid as an aid, the remainder of the design is "drawn," substituting plus (+) and period (.) characters for <Alt> 205 and <Alt> 219 characters, respectively. The full screen design is shown in Figure 6.14.

Running the REPLACE TEXT Command

Once the screen design is completed, the EDLIN REPLACE TEXT command can be used to fill in the correct ASCII characters. In this example,

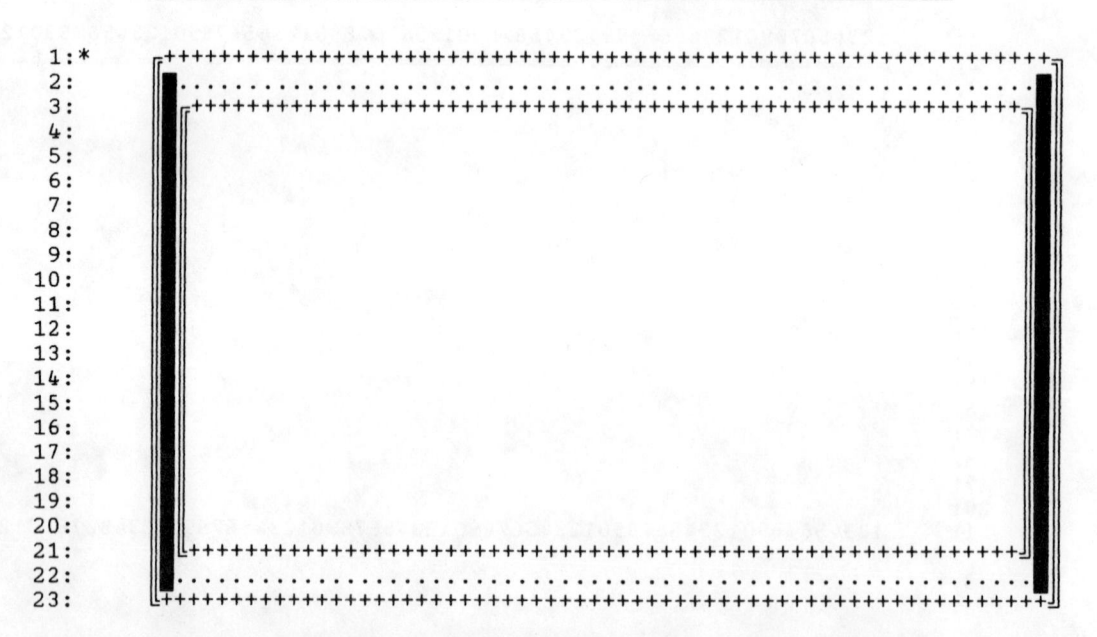

```
 1:*     ┌++++++++++++++++++++++++++++++++++++++++++++++++++++++++++++++++++++┐
 2:      ┃........................................................................┃
 3:      ┃┌++++++++++++++++++++++++++++++++++++++++++++++++++++++++++++++++++┐┃
 4:      ┃┃                                                                    ┃┃
 5:      ┃┃                                                                    ┃┃
 6:      ┃┃                                                                    ┃┃
 7:      ┃┃                                                                    ┃┃
 8:      ┃┃                                                                    ┃┃
 9:      ┃┃                                                                    ┃┃
10:      ┃┃                                                                    ┃┃
11:      ┃┃                                                                    ┃┃
12:      ┃┃                                                                    ┃┃
13:      ┃┃                                                                    ┃┃
14:      ┃┃                                                                    ┃┃
15:      ┃┃                                                                    ┃┃
16:      ┃┃                                                                    ┃┃
17:      ┃┃                                                                    ┃┃
18:      ┃┃                                                                    ┃┃
19:      ┃┃                                                                    ┃┃
20:      ┃┃                                                                    ┃┃
21:      ┃└++++++++++++++++++++++++++++++++++++++++++++++++++++++++++++++++++┘┃
22:      ┃........................................................................┃
23:      └++++++++++++++++++++++++++++++++++++++++++++++++++++++++++++++++++++┘
```

Figure 6.14. Full Border Design Using Temporary + and . Characters

Screen Design Utility 111

two replace text commands must be issued: One to replace the plus sign (+) with the ASCII double line border character (ASCII 205) and one to replace the period (.) with the ASCII solid block character.

The first command is entered at the * prompt to replace the "+" characters, starting with the third line of the screen through the last line in memory:

```
3,R+<F6><Alt 205>
```

The text editor then replaces each plus sign (+) on a line-by-line, character-by-character basis. During the replacement process, the user can actually see the new border design move across the screen as it is created. When the replace command is completed, the user is returned to the * prompt. At this point, it is a good idea to use the LIST LINES (L) command to view the results.

Assuming that the results of the first command are acceptable, the second command is entered, starting with line 4 through the last line in memory:

```
4,R.<F6><Alt 219>
```

When the second character replacement process is completed, the LIST LINES command is again issued. If the entire screen is acceptable, the user may choose to erase the template borders, using the DELETE LINES (D) command (See "Removing the Template Borders"). Finally, the file is saved by issuing the END EDIT (E) command.

Using Color in Screen Designs

The ASCII extended character set can be used in combination with control codes to create colored screen designs. In the previous chapter, it was noted that all control codes begin with an escape character (the ^[symbols), which is created by:

- depressing the <Ctrl> key
- typing the "V" key
- entering a left-bracket symbol (the [character)

This generates the escape character, which is represented by the ^[symbols. This control character is recognized by ANSI.SYS, which in turn activates various control codes. These control codes then change attributes of the display. To create colored border designs, the foreground and background color control characters are used.

For example, consider the side of a border design as follows:

║█║

This would be produced within EDLIN or a text editor by depressing the <Alt> key and by typing the following ASCII values on the numeric keypad:

<Alt>186<Alt>219<Alt>186

Using this sequence on a monochrome screen, a hollow and shaded border design is created.

The shaded portion of the border design could just as well be created in color. (If you are working with a color monitor, for example, you will note that such a technique has been used in the menus of the *Hard Disk Manager*.) The technique is a fairly straightforward one:

1. Turn on the foreground color using a control code.
2. Type the border (ASCII) character.
3. Restore the color to normal (or the default character color).

Thus, to produce the same border design with red shading, the following combination of ASCII characters and control codes is typed:

<Alt>186^[[31mm<Alt>219^[[37m<Alt>186

The results of typing this sequence produce the following:

1. The hollow border character, <Alt> 186, is created.
2. The character color attribute is changed to red, ^[[31m.
3. While the character color is red, the shaded border character, <Alt> 219, is created.
4. After producing a red shaded character, the character color attribute is changed back to white (the default color), ^[[37m.
5. The inside hollow border character, <Alt> 186, is created.

NOTE: *The escape character (^ [) must precede the attribute code (e.g., [31m). In this example, the default screen colors are white on a black background.*

Figure 6.15 shows the EDLIN screen file that displays the main menu for *Hard Disk Manager*. Use of both the extended ASCII character set and

Screen Design Utility 113

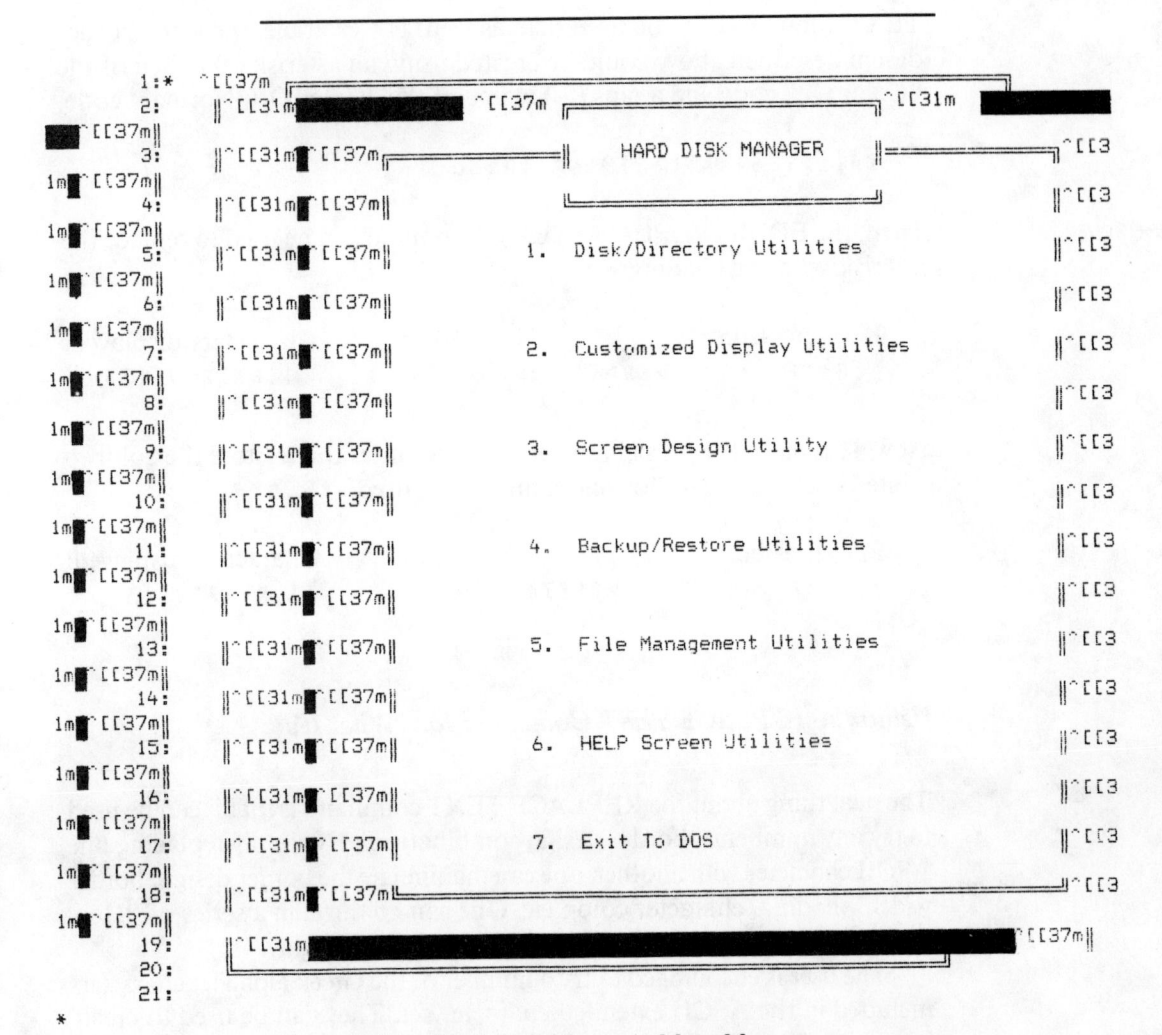

```
            1:*   ^[[37m
            2:    ||^[[31m                              ^[[37m                                  ^[[31m
  ^[[37m    3:    ||^[[31m^[[37m,----------------------||  HARD DISK MANAGER  ||----------------------,^[[3
1m^[[37m||   4:    ||^[[31m^[[37m||                      ||                     ||                      ||^[[3
1m^[[37m||   5:    ||^[[31m^[[37m||       1.   Disk/Directory Utilities                                 ||^[[3
1m^[[37m||   6:    ||^[[31m^[[37m||                                                                     ||^[[3
1m^[[37m||   7:    ||^[[31m^[[37m||       2.   Customized Display Utilities                             ||^[[3
1m^[[37m||   8:    ||^[[31m^[[37m||                                                                     ||^[[3
1m^[[37m||   9:    ||^[[31m^[[37m||       3.   Screen Design Utility                                    ||^[[3
1m^[[37m||  10:    ||^[[31m^[[37m||                                                                     ||^[[3
1m^[[37m||  11:    ||^[[31m^[[37m||       4.   Backup/Restore Utilities                                 ||^[[3
1m^[[37m||  12:    ||^[[31m^[[37m||                                                                     ||^[[3
1m^[[37m||  13:    ||^[[31m^[[37m||       5.   File Management Utilities                                ||^[[3
1m^[[37m||  14:    ||^[[31m^[[37m||                                                                     ||^[[3
1m^[[37m||  15:    ||^[[31m^[[37m||       6.   HELP Screen Utilities                                    ||^[[3
1m^[[37m||  16:    ||^[[31m^[[37m||                                                                     ||^[[3
1m^[[37m||  17:    ||^[[31m^[[37m||       7.   Exit To DOS                                              ||^[[3
1m^[[37m||  18:    ||^[[31m^[[37m'---------------------------------------------------------------------'^[[3
1m^[[37m||  19:    ||^[[31m                                                                       ^[[37m||
            20:
            21:
  *
```

Figure 6.15. *Hard Disk Manager* Main Menu
as Shown in EDLIN with Color Control Codes

the control characters is evident in the file. Although it may seem a bit overwhelming, note that there is a lot of repetition in the control codes. These can be embedded in the design using the EDLIN REPLACE TEXT command. This technique is described in the following section.

Using the REPLACE TEXT Command with Color Designs

Just as was the case with creating a full screen of ASCII values, typing out a number of control codes can be a tedious process. The EDLIN REPLACE

TEXT command can be used here as well. For example, the same border design described above could be created using an asterisk (*) in lieu of the "Color On" code and a plus (+) in lieu of the "Color Off/Normal" code:

```
<Alt>186*<Alt>219+<Alt>186
```

Then, the EDLIN REPLACE TEXT command can be used to replace the asterisk with red shading:

Keys pressed: Characters displayed:
`1,R*<F6><Ctrl><V>[[31m`   `1,R*^Z^V[[31m`

Now, to replace the plus character with the codes that restore the color to white on black, the following command is used:

Keys pressed: Characters displayed:
`1,R+<F6><Ctrl><V>[[37m`   `1,R+^Z^V[[37m`

Using the REPLACE TEXT Command for "What If's"

The neat thing about the REPLACE TEXT command is that it can be used to try any number of border design combinations. By simply replacing one ASCII character with another, one can manipulate the border design, border width, shading, character color, etc. One can go through a series of "How does this look?" combinations until the design is right.

The user is encouraged to try a number of the Greek alphabet characters included in the ASCII extended character set. They can be used to create interesting filagree-like designs. For example, the (Φ) character was used to change the design shown in Figure 6.7 to the design shown in Figure 6.16. The user is also encouraged to use the REPLACE TEXT command to create any number of color/design combinations. As long as the REPLACE TEXT command is used, no border design must be permanent!

Removing the Template Borders

Since the template lines are located in Lines 1-2 and Line 22, the DELETE LINES (D) command must be issued twice. At the * prompt, the following

Screen Design Utility 115

```
 1:
 2:   ΦΦΦΦΦΦΦΦΦΦΦΦΦΦΦΦΦΦΦΦΦΦΦΦΦΦΦΦΦΦΦΦΦΦΦΦΦΦΦΦΦΦΦΦΦΦ
 3:   Φ                                              Φ
 4:   Φ                                              Φ
 5:   Φ                                              Φ
 6:   Φ                                              Φ
 7:   Φ                                              Φ
 8:   Φ                                              Φ
 9:   Φ                                              Φ
10:   Φ                                              Φ
11:   Φ                                              Φ
12:   Φ                                              Φ
13:   Φ                                              Φ
14:   Φ                                              Φ
15:   Φ                                              Φ
16:   Φ                                              Φ
17:   Φ                                              Φ
18:   Φ                                              Φ
19:   Φ                                              Φ
20:   Φ                                              Φ
21:*  Φ
22:   ΦΦΦΦΦΦΦΦΦΦΦΦΦΦΦΦΦΦΦΦΦΦΦΦΦΦΦΦΦΦΦΦΦΦΦΦΦΦΦΦΦΦΦΦΦΦ
23:
```

Figure 6.16. Border Design with Φ Character

command is issued:

   1,2D

This deletes the first two lines and now adjusts the last template line up to Line 20. Again, the DELETE LINES (D) command must be issued to remove Line 20:

   20D

With the finished screen design, the user can now add up to three rows in the middle to compensate for lines lost to the previous three template rows. Or, the user can save the border as is.

If additional rows (i.e., more depth) are desired, rows may be added with the INSERT LINES (I) command. Then the border design on the line above the insert can be copied down using the COPY LINES (C) command. For example, consider the border example shown in Figure 6.7. An additional line may be added around line 6. This would be accomplished using the INSERT LINES COMMAND (I). At the * prompt, the following command is issued:

```
 1:
 2:
 3:
 4:
 5:
 6:
 7:*
 8:
 9:
10:
11:
12:
13:
14:
15:
16:
17:
18:
19:
20:
21:
22:
23:
```

Figure 6.17. Border Design with Row Insert

Then, when the full screen is displayed with the LIST LINES (L) command, a blank row appears at line 6. The remainder of the border rows have been adjusted down one row (see Figure 6.17).

To copy down the right and left border from the previous line, the COPY LINES (C) command is issued:

```
5,5,6C
```

This command tells EDLIN to copy line 5 (indicated as line 5 through line 5) to line 6. The border then appears as continuous. Two additional lines can be added by repeating the same procedure.

6.3 MODIFYING THE SCREEN DESIGN UTILITY

Unlike the other utilities included on the accompanying disk, the Screen Design utility is a single utility—it is just an EDLIN-based screen design template. Even so, this utility can be modified slightly and other screen design utilities can be added. This section describes how one might modify the Screen Design utility and/or create new utilities.

Several Points to Keep in Mind

The ASCII Extended Character Set is used to create screen designs. These characters are produced by depressing the <Alt> key and typing the appropriate ASCII sequence on the numeric keypad. This is an extraordinarily awkward way to create extensive screen designs. An alternative is to use the EDLIN REPLACE TEXT command described previously.

It also should be remembered that EDLIN can accept input from a text file. This is a more streamlined way to incorporate EDLIN into a Screen Design utility. In addition, elimination of a number of EDLIN steps is a less confusing way for the novice user to use such utilities.

The following structure is built into the Screen Design utility. The addition of new utilities should follow the same format for ease of use.

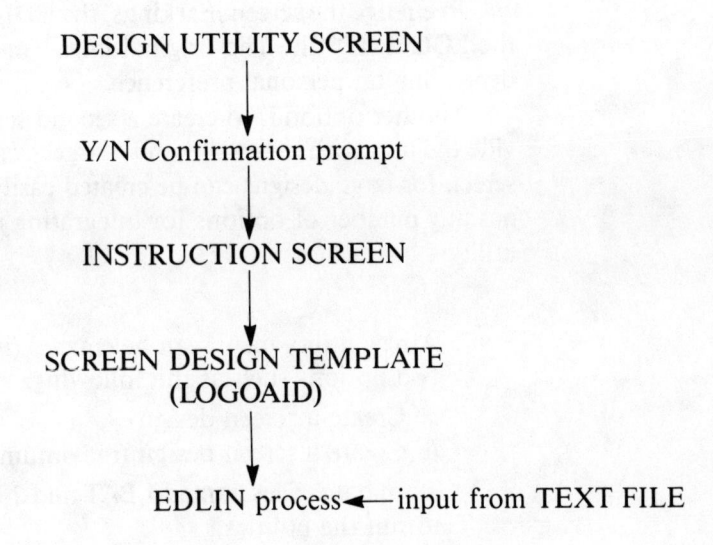

DESIGN UTILITY SCREEN
↓
Y/N Confirmation prompt
↓
INSTRUCTION SCREEN
↓
SCREEN DESIGN TEMPLATE
(LOGOAID)
↓
EDLIN process ← input from TEXT FILE

Adding and Deleting Menu Selections

Menu choices can be added to the Screen Design utility to create a utility with several design options. Or, the design template can be deleted. The sections that describe adding and deleting menu items in Chapter 10 should be consulted for users who wish to follow a step-by-step approach.

The Screen Design utility is located in the \HDU\DESIGN directory. All batch and screen files are located in those directories. When adding new menu choices, all batch and screen files should be placed in the \HDU\DESIGN directory.

Changing the Template Spacing

The Screen Design template contains spacing markers for each character position as well as spacing markers for each ten characters and the center of the screen. These markings are based on a screen width of 75 characters. In actuality, it is possible to create screen designs that are wider. However, when doing so, individual lines wrap around; i.e., the portion of the character string that does not fit on a single line appears on the next line below. It can be very confusing visually to work with this. With a little trial and error, the center of the screen as well as the left and right margins can be determined and marked for reference purposes.

To change the screen markings, the EDLIN commands can be used on the LOGOAID file. The original lines can be either retained or deleted, depending on personal preference.

Another option is to create a second screen design template and provide the user with a "small" and "large" screen option. A new design-aid screen for large designs can be created easily with EDLIN. Then the user has any number of options for integrating this screen design aid into the utility:

1. A new utility menu can be created (in lieu of DESIGN.SCR) with two options such as the following:
   a. Create a screen design
   b. Create a screen design (maximum size)
   Then batch files named 1.BAT and 2.BAT would have to be created to run the utilities.
2. The current DESIGN.SCR screen can be modified to include both options. The regular and full size screen options can be either activated by numeric batch files (as in option *a* above) or by mnemonic commands (e.g., DESIGN).
3. The INSTRUCT.SCR screen can be altered to instruct the user to type one of two mnemonics:

DESIGN or WDESIGN

Screen Design Utility 119

In this case, DESIGN produces the template included in the original utility. WDESIGN stands for WIDE DESIGN for the new wider template. If this alternative is chosen, only one new batch file, WDESIGN, needs to be created. It would be identical to the DESIGN.BAT file except that it would call a template of a different name. To create the WDESIGN batch file, EDLIN can be used. Then the EDLIN TRANSFER command can be used to bring in the entire DESIGN.BAT file for modification:

```
C>edlin wdesign.bat
New file
*tdesign.bat
```

When the WDESIGN.BAT file is then listed with the L command, the entire DESIGN.BAT contents will be displayed. At this point the file can be edited. Of course, in this example, the instructional screens must be changed to reflect the addition of a new option.

Creating Prefabricated Designs

Instead of starting with a blank screen template, utilities also may be designed that permit the user to choose between several preexisting menu or screen designs. The construction of such a utility could take many forms.

By way of illustration, the user could begin with a menu screen that displayed each major type of border character (e.g., double border, solid border, single border, etc.) as a menu selection. When the border selection is made, a batch file could then create the corresponding menu design. One also could make the utility a bit more elaborate by allowing the user to choose the size of the border, the shape of the border, etc. For example, the screen might contain some of the following selections.

```
Select Border Size:

1. 21x75, no dividers
2. 21x75, top divider
3. 10x60, no dividers
4. 10x60, top dividers

Select Border Character:

5. Single border ( | )
```

```
6. Double hollow border ( ‖ ‖ )

7. Double filled border ( ▌ )

8. Solid border ( ▌ )

ENTER SIZE AND CHARACTER CHOICES >
```

If batch files were created for selections 1-8, then the user could respond to the prompt by typing the size and character choices. For example:

```
ENTER SIZE AND CHARACTER CHOICES >3,8
```

This would produce a half-screen, rectangular, solid border. In this particular example, selection 3 activates the file 3.BAT. 3.BAT would in turn contain a replaceable parameter for the character choice (8.BAT, in this example).

The size choices would, in effect, be generic borders constructed out of any combination of characters such as plus signs, asterisks, etc. The character choices could activate batch files that use the EDLIN REPLACE TEXT command. Input for the EDLIN processes would be entered from a text file that contained the appropriate data and commands. This technique was used in the Screen Design utility discussed previously.

The same techniques could be used to transfer some prefabricated geometric designs into a screen template.

chapter 7

Backup/Restore Utilities

The information stored on a hard disk is always vulnerable. Files may become unavailable due to system failure or lost as a result of hard disk failure. Or, they may be inadvertently erased, over-written, or altered as a result of inexperience or carelessness.

Perhaps the most important DOS commands are those that protect the user from inadvertent data loss. These are the BACKUP and RESTORE commands. Too often, however, these commands are not used or are not used effectively because they require a working knowledge of DOS.

The Backup/Restore utilities guide users through several menu-driven file Backup and Restore options.

What Are the Backup/Restore Utilities?

There are six Backup/Restore utilities. They include routines for:

- performing full disk backups and restorations
- performing partial disk backups and restorations, including backups by date, selective backups of modified-only files, and partial restorations of subdirectories

Why Are They Used?

The utilities described in this chapter are designed to provide the user with an array of backup and restore possibilities. Using the DOS command

BACKUP, the backup routines copy the files in a special format that allows a single file to occupy more than one floppy disk. Files copied with the Backup utilities must be placed back on a hard disk using the Restore utilities (or by manually using the DOS command **RESTORE**).

These utilities can be used for full backups or for selective backups or restorations. They provide the user with a backup facility that is both efficient and reliable. In addition, installation of these facilities encourages users of all levels to recognize the importance of performing backups as a part of their daily routines.

How to Use the Utilities

The Backup/Restore utilities are accessed when selection 4 is chosen from the *Hard Disk Manager* main menu. This selection changes the directory to HDUBACKUP and displays the Backup/Restore Menu. Any of the six selections on the screen can be chosen simply by typing the number of the desired utility. After the selection is made, the utilities prompt the user for any required input; informational screens guide the user through the process. If at any time the user chooses not to proceed with a utility, the <F1> key can be pressed to return to the first menu.

For the user who would like additional information on data security with electronic media, some background information on this topic can be found at the end of this chapter.

Organization of the Backup/Restore Utilities

The Backup/Restore utilities are located in one directory and five subdirectories. All are found as subdirectories of the main utility directory (\HDU). The directory and file structure is shown in Figure 7.1.

The functions performed by these directories and their contents are as follows:

\HDU\BACKUP   This contains the Backup/Restore menu screen, the batch files and menu screens that run the menu choices on that menu, and subdirectories for the various Backup/Restore menu options. The files for Full Backup also are contained in this directory.

Backup/Restore Utilities

\HDU\BACKUP\PARTIAL   This subdirectory contains several batch files and an instruction screen for the partial backup routine.

\HDU\BACKUP\DATEBACK   This subdirectory contains several batch files and an instruction screen for the routine that backs up files by date.

\HDU\BACKUP\MODIFY   This subdirectory contains batch files and an instruction screen that are used for backing up only files that have been modified or created since the last backup.

\HDU\BACKUP\FULLREST   This subdirectory contains two batch files that run the full-restore menu option.

\HDU\BACKUP\PARTREST   This subdirectory contains several batch files and an instruction screen for a routine that allows the user to selectively restore backed-up files to the hard disk.

```
C:\HDU\BACKUP    <DIR>

    1.BAT        PARTIAL.SCR
    2.BAT        BACKMENU.SCR
    3.BAT        PARTREST.SCR
    4.BAT        FULLREST.SCR
    5.BAT        FULLBACK.SCR
    6.BAT        DATEBACK.SCR
    Y.BAT        MODIFY.SCR           C:\HDU\BACKUP\PARTIAL    <DIR>
    N.BAT
                                          Y.BAT        PARTIAL.BAT
                                          N.BAT        INSTRUCT.SCR


C:\HDU\BACKUP\DATEBACK    <DIR>       C:\HDU\BACKUP\MODIFY     <DIR>

    Y.BAT        BYDATE.BAT               Y.BAT        MODIFY.BAT
    N.BAT        INSTRUCT.SCR             N.BAT        INSTRUCT.SCR


C:\HDU\BACKUP\FULLREST    <DIR>       C:\HDU\BACKUP\PARTREST   <DIR>

    Y.BAT                                 Y.BAT        PARTIAL.BAT
    N.BAT                                 N.BAT        INSTRUCT.SCR
```

Figure 7.1. Directory and File Structure for the Backup/Restore Utilities

Activation of the Utilities

Selection 4 on the main utility menu accesses the Backup/Restore utilities by activating the 4.BAT file in the \HDU directory. It contains the following commands:

```
   4.BAT
1: echo off
2: cls
3: cd backup
4: type backmenu.scr
5: echo ENTER SELECTION:
6: prompt $e[22;18H
7: setscrn
```

The functions of this file are to change the current directory to \HDU\BACKUP, display the Backup/Restore menu (BACKMENU.SCR), position the prompt at the end of the ENTER SELECTION prompt, and reset the display attributes with the SETSCRN.BAT file. Figure 7.2 shows the Backup/Restore screen.

Each menu choice on the Backup/Restore menu has two or three batch files that run the routine. For the Backup routines, the central command

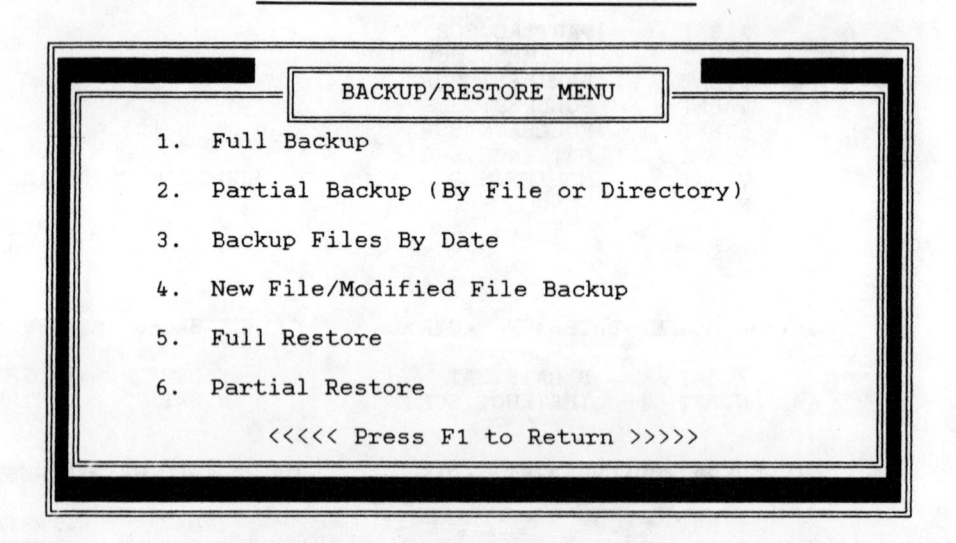

```
              BACKUP/RESTORE MENU

     1.  Full Backup

     2.  Partial Backup (By File or Directory)

     3.  Backup Files By Date

     4.  New File/Modified File Backup

     5.  Full Restore

     6.  Partial Restore

              <<<<< Press F1 to Return >>>>>
```

Figure 7.2. The Backup/Restore Menu

Backup/Restore Utilities

in the operation is the DOS command BACKUP. In the restore utilities, the DOS command RESTORE is the basis of the utilities.

All of the utilities on this menu are generally structured the same way. The numbered batch files (1.BAT, 2.BAT, and so on) in the \HDU\BACKUP directory start the utility. Each menu selection brings up an information screen that describes the individual operation. The "Continue (Y/N)?" prompt allows the user to continue or abort the operation. A **Y** entry by the user executes a Y.BAT file, and a response of **N** executes an N.BAT file. The N.BAT file, which always returns the user to the Backup/Restore menu, contains the following commands:

```
  N.BAT
1: echo off
2: cls
3: cd ..
4: type backmenu.scr
5: echo ENTER SELECTION:
6: prompt $e[22;18H
7: setscrn
```

The CD command in line 3 changes the directory to the parent directory, which in this case is \HDU\BACKUP.

The action taken by the Y.BAT file varies with the utility: In some cases, this actually starts the operation; in others, it may produce an instruction screen. If instructions follow the **Y** response, the user must enter a specific command to start the operation. For example, the Partial Backup utility requires the user to enter the command PARTIAL.

Specific batch files for each utility are described in the sections on each utility.

7.1 THE BACKUP/RESTORE UTILITIES

The Full Backup Utility

This utility is used when it is necessary to perform a complete backup of the hard disk. The backup medium may be either 360-KB floppy disks or high-capacity floppy disks. In either case, the disks must first be formatted; the backup must be done from the hard disk to floppy disks in drive

A. A disk error message is displayed if an attempt is made to backup data to an unformatted floppy disk.

The number of disks required for a full backup is a function of the amount of data stored on the disk. A fully loaded, 10-megabyte hard disk requires approximately twenty-eight 360-KB floppy disks. To determine roughly how many disks will be needed, the DOS command CHKDSK (Check Disk) can be used to find out how many bytes of disk space the hard disk is using. This value is then divided by either 360,000 (if 360-KB disks are used) or 1,200,000 (if high-capacity disks are used). This result should roughly equal the number of floppy disks that will be used during the backup.

It is important to note that any files that are already stored on the floppy disks will be erased. A DOS message to this effect is displayed during the backup process.

Running the Utility

When Full Backup is selected from the Backup/Restore menu, a message screen is displayed that describes the procedure (Figure 7.3). If the user responds to the "Continue Y/N?" prompt with **Y** the backup then begins. In this routine, all subdirectory files are copied as well as root directory files. If the first disk cannot hold all of the files on the hard disk, DOS prompts the user to insert another floppy. This process continues until all files have been copied. The disks should be numbered in the order that they are used. As each file is backed up, its filename is displayed on the screen.

A message is displayed informing the user of the success or failure of the backup. The failure message includes possible causes. When the backup is completed, the user is returned to the *Hard Disk Manager* menu.

```
                              FULL BACKUP


This routine will back up ALL files on your hard disk to floppy
    diskettes in drive A.  Before you continue, make sure that:

        1.  You have enough FORMATTED floppy diskettes available.
        2.  You have "Uninstalled" any application software such
                as 1-2-3 or dBASE that should not be duplicated.

You should not continue if you need to perform either of these tasks.

                    <<<<< Press F1 to Return >>>>>
```

Figure 7.3. Full Backup Message Screen

Backup/Restore Utilities

The information screen that is displayed when the user selects the Full Backup option contains some references to the backup of copy-protected software. This topic is discussed in more detail in the following section.

The Backup of Copy-Protected Software

One issue that can be exceedingly annoying and frustrating is that of how to deal with the backup of copy-protected software. Application software packages (such as *Lotus 1-2-3*) usually permit hard disk installation but frequently do not allow the program to be duplicated via the DOS BACKUP/RESTORE routines. A Backup operation will backup copy-protected software along with everything else; the Restore routines will attempt to write the copy-protected software back onto the hard disk but will not be successful. For the user with such programs on their hard disk, there are generally two options:

1. "Uninstall" the program prior to using any backup programs. "Uninstall" routines generally vary from one program to another. The user should consult the software documentation for details.
2. Proceed with the backup operation. However, when restoring files to the hard disk, the user should include the /P option; this causes DOS to display the prompt "Restore Read Only files (Y/N)?" (i.e., copy-protected), to which the user should respond with **N** for "No." The Partial Restore utility should be used for this purpose, and it describes the process in more detail.

The user should consult the software documentation for the recommended procedure.

The Full Backup Utility Program Files

There are three batch files that run this utility. The utility is initialized when the user enters **1** on the Backup/Restore menu. This executes the 1.BAT file in the \HDU\BACKUP directory:

```
   1.BAT
1: echo off
2: cls
3: type fullback.scr
```

```
          4: echo Continue (Y/N)?
          5: prompt $e[21;18H
```

The 1.BAT batch file displays the information screen (FULLBACK.SCR) shown in Figure 7.3 and ends with the "Continue (Y/N)?" prompt. The user is expected to respond by entering either **Y** or **N** after the prompt, thus executing either Y.BAT or N.BAT. The latter choice aborts the routine and the former begins the backup operation. Y.BAT contains the following commands:

```
      Y.BAT
  1: echo off
  2: cls
  3: backup c:\  a:/s
  4: if errorlevel 1 goto ABORT
  5: cls
  6: echo  Backup is now complete.
  7: echo  Use the Restore Utilities to copy files back
           onto hard disk.
  8: goto END
  9: :ABORT
 10: cls
 11: echo  Problems... Backup terminated!
 12: echo  Were your diskettes formatted?
 13: :END
 14: pause
 15: cls
 16: type backmenu.scr
 17: echo ENTER SELECTION:
 18: prompt $e[22;18H
 19: setscrn
```

The BACKUP command in the third line is the key to this utility. The addition of the /S parameter ensures that all subdirectory files are included in the process. Line 4 uses the IF command ERRORLEVEL parameter to test for a successful backup. If the error level indicates that the backup was not completed, then control is passed to the error message section (:ABORT in line 9). Otherwise, the "Backup is now complete" message is displayed (lines 6 and 7).

Lines 16 through 18 return the user to the Backup/Restore Utilities menu. Line 19 resets the display attributes with the SETSCRN.BAT file.

The Partial Backup Utility

This utility allows the user to back up only selected directories and/or files. This option can be used in addition to or as an alternative to full backups. The user may find this handy when he or she desires to back up only the relevant or current data on the hard disk. Like the Full Backup, however, a sufficient number of formatted floppy disks must be available to hold the information.

When this option is selected from the Backup/Restore menu, a message screen is displayed that describes the process. If the user responds to the "Continue (Y/N)?" prompt with **Y** an instruction screen is displayed. The user must enter the command **PARTIAL**, followed by the name of the directory or file to be backed up. For example, if the entire \DBASE directory is to be backed up, the command is entered as:

```
partial \dbase
```

To back up only a specific file, the PARTIAL command is followed by the path and the filename as in

```
partial \123data\chapter6.wks
```

NOTE: *The global filename characters ? and * can be very useful for partial backups. When several files with similar filenames must be backed up, global filename characters can be used instead of typing the command multiple times. For example, to back up chapters 1 through 9 (e.g., chapterX.wks), the following command could be issued:*

```
partial \123data\chapter?.wks
```

Just as in the Full Backup, DOS warns the user that any files already existing on the target disks will be erased. However, if the user wishes to add backup files to another disk without destroying its existing files, the BACKUP command has a special parameter (/A) that permits this process. (The user should consult the BACKUP command in Appendix A for a description of how this parameter may be used in manual execution of the BACKUP command.) During a partial backup, DOS prompts the user to insert floppy disks until all of the specified files have been copied. All filenames are displayed on the screen as they are backed up.

A "Backup Successful" message is displayed if no problems have been encountered during the backup. If problems have been encountered, the message will say "Backup terminated" and will include suggestions as to possible causes. The Backup/Restore menu is then redisplayed.

The Partial Backup Utility Program Files

The Partial Backup option consists of four batch files and two information screens. It is activated by the 2.BAT file:

```
   2.BAT
1: echo off
2: cls
3: type partial.scr
4: cd partial
5: echo Continue (Y/N)?
6: prompt $e[18;18H
```

The file 2.BAT displays the information screen shown in Figure 7.4, changes the directory to \HDU\BACKUP\PARTIAL, and positions the cursor at the end of a "Continue (Y/N)?" prompt. Entering **N** executes N.BAT and returns the user to the *Hard Disk Manager* menu. A response of **Y** executes Y.BAT, which contains the following commands:

```
   Y.BAT
1: echo off
2: cls
3: type instruct.scr
4: echo ENTER COMMAND:
5: prompt $e[21;17H
```

The principal function of the above batch file is to display an instruction screen and position the cursor after the ENTER COMMAND prompt. The instruction screen (INSTRUCT.SCR) is shown in Figure 7.5.

As indicated by the instructions, the user must enter the command PARTIAL followed by one or more parameters. The commands contained in the PARTIAL.BAT file are essentially the same as the Y.BAT file that runs the "Full Backup" routine (discussed previously), with one important difference: In this utility, the BACKUP command in line 3 is written as

```
backup c:%1 a:%2
```

Backup/Restore Utilities

FILE OR DIRECTORY BACKUP

This backs up a specified file or directory to one or more floppy
    disks in the A drive. Before you can continue, be sure that

  1. You have enough FORMATTED floppy diskettes available for
     the backup.
  2. You know the names of the directories and/or file(s) that
     are to be backed up, including the paths.

You should not continue if this is not the case.

        <<<<< Press F1 to Return >>>>>

Figure 7.4. The Partial Backup Screen

This command uses replaceable parameters (%1 and %2). The replaceable parameters are used for flexibility—to permit the user to enter variables (e.g., different directory names, etc.). The first replaceable parameter is the directory and/or file to be backed up. The second replaceable parameter is for the /S option, if the user elects to back up a directory as well as its subdirectories. If only one parameter is entered with the PARTIAL com-

---
===================== INSTRUCTIONS =====================

To backup a specific file or directory, you must enter the
    command PARTIAL followed by the filename or directory name,
    including the path (if any). For example, a file in the WP
    directory named MEMO1123.DOC would be entered as
                    partial \wp\memo1123.doc

To backup only the WP directory, the command is entered as
                    partial \wp

You may include subdirectories under the specified directory by
    entering a /S after the command, as in
                    partial \wp /s

        <<<<< Press F1 to Return >>>>>

Figure 7.5. Instructions for Partial Backup

mand, the %2 is ignored. The only other difference in PARTIAL.BAT from the Y.BAT of "Full Backup" is in the error message, which is somewhat more specific to this utility.

The Backup Files by Date Utility

Using this utility, partial backups of hard disk files can be performed in which the criterion for backup is the file's date. This means that the user can selectively back up all those files that have been modified or created since a particular date. During the backup, DOS examines each file's date stamp to see if it meets the specified criterion. For this reason, it is important to enter the date *each* time the system is turned on. By placing the DOS DATE and TIME commands in an AUTOEXEC.BAT file, this can be a relatively easy task. If the system contains a multifunction board with a clock calendar, the process can be even easier: The AUTOEXEC.BAT file should execute the board's program that sets the date and time automatically.

Running the Utility

When this menu choice is selected from the Backup/Restore menu, an information screen is displayed. If the user enters **Y** in response to the "Continue (Y/N)?" prompt, an instruction screen is displayed. The user must enter the command **BYDATE** followed the date from which files should be backed up. The date format is MM-DD-YY. For example, the following command would be entered to back up all hard disk files that have been created or modified since August 27, 1987:

```
bydate 08-27-87
```

NOTE: *If it is necessary to back up only files in a specific directory using the date parameter, the BACKUP command should be used manually.*

DOS will display a warning that files on the target disk will be erased. The user is then prompted to insert disks until all files have been backed up.

Like the other backup operations, a "Backup successful" message is displayed if the operation has been successful; otherwise, the message is "Backup terminated" with suggestions as to the possible causes of the problems. The Backup/Restore menu is displayed when the backup is complete.

Backup/Restore Utilities

The Backup Files by Date Program Files

The Backup Files by Date option is made up of four batch files and two information screens. The utility is started by entering **3** at the Backup/Restore menu, which executes the batch file 3.BAT:

```
  3.BAT
1: echo off
2: cls
3: cd dateback
4: type dateback.scr
5: echo Continue (Y/N)?
6: prompt $e[18;18H
```

The 3.BAT file displays the information screen shown in Figure 7.6, changes the directory from \HDU\BACKUP to \HDU\BACKUP\DATE-BACK, and positions the cursor at the end of the "Continue (Y/N)?" prompt. Entering **N** executes N.BAT and returns the user to the Backup/Restore menu. A response of **Y** executes Y.BAT, which contains the following commands:

```
  Y.BAT
1: echo off
2: cls
3: type instruct.scr
4: echo ENTER COMMAND:
5: prompt $e[16;17H
```

BACKUP FILES BY DATE
===

This backs up only those hard disk files to drive A that have
   been created or modified on or after a specified date.
   Before you continue, be sure that

   1. You have enough FORMATTED floppy diskettes available for
       the backup.
   2. You are certain of the dates of the files that are to be
       included in the backup.

You should not continue if this is not the case.

             <<<<< Press F1 to Return >>>>>

Figure 7.6. The Backup Files by Date Screen

```
                      ══════════ INSTRUCTIONS ══════════

     To backup files by date, you must enter the command BYDATE
          followed by that date.  The date format is MM-DD-YY.

     For example, to back up all hard disk files created or modified
          on or after June 27, 1986, the command would be entered as
                              bydate 6-27-86


                     <<<<< Press F1 to Return >>>>>
```

Figure 7.7. Instructions for Backup Files by Date

The object of the previous batch file is to display an instruction screen (IN-STRUCT.SCR in line 3) and position the cursor after the ENTER COMMAND prompt. The text of the INSTRUCT.SCR file is shown in Figure 7.7.

In response to the prompt on the INSTRUCT.SCR, the command **BYDATE** followed by a date in the format of DD-MM-YY must be entered. All hard disk files that have been modified after the specified date will be backed up. The BYDATE.BAT file is similar to the Y.BAT file that runs the Full Backup routine, with two exceptions. One difference is in the use of the BACKUP command in the line 3. In BYDATE.BAT, it is written in following manner:

```
backup c:\ a:/s/d:%1
```

The /S parameter includes all subdirectories in the backup operation. The date function is activated by the /D parameter. The user's date input is substituted for the replaceable parameter (%1) after the /D switch. One other minor difference in BYDATE.BAT and the Y.BAT of Full Backup is that the message that is displayed if the Errorlevel condition occurs is specific to this utility.

The New File/Modified File Backup Utility

With this utility, the user may back up only those files that have been created or modified since the last full backup was performed. DOS is able to tell whether a file has been created or modified since the last backup by examining a single bit in the file attribution byte. When a backup is made

Backup/Restore Utilities

of a file, this bit is given an "on" status. If this file is subsequently modified, this bit is changed to "off." In new files, it automatically carries an "off" status.

The advantage is this: The user can make a full backup of the hard disk and then, on subsequent backups, use this utility to back up only those files that have changed or have been added since the last backup. For a hard disk with many files, this can save a lot of time if only a limited number of files are involved. However, each subsequent Modify Backup requires its own backup disk(s). Depending on the number of disks involved, after three to four Modify Backups, it may be easier to start the process over again with a Full Backup. (See "The Full Restore Utility" section for the restoration process.)

Running the Utility

When New File/Modified File Backup is selected, the user is first presented with a description screen. If **Y** is entered in response to the "Continue (Y/N)?" prompt, an instruction screen is displayed. The user must enter the command **MODIFY**. All new or modified files on the hard disk are then backed up. If the modify routine is run on only one directory and its subdirectories, then the name of that directory along with the MODIFY command is entered:

```
modify \wp
```

The utility then backs up only the new or modified files found in the \WP directory and its subdirectories. Just as in the other backup utilities, the user must have enough formatted floppy disks available for all of the files that will be included in the backup. DOS prompts the user to insert diskettes until all the necessary files have been backed up.

When the backup has been completed successfully, a message is displayed to this effect. The Backup/Restore menu is displayed when the modify routine is completed.

Backup Files Created/Modified Program Files

There are two instruction screens and four batch files associated with the menu choice Backup Files Created/Modified Since Last Backup. The differences between this utility and the Backup Files By Date routine (described above) are slight. The utility is started by entering **4** at the Backup/Restore menu, which executes the batch file 4.BAT:

```
   4.BAT
1: echo off
2: cls
3: type modify.scr
4: cd modify
5: echo Continue (Y/N)?
6: prompt $e[18;18H
```

The two information screens used by this utility are specific to this application. They are shown in Figures 7.8 and 7.9. The command for this utility is **MODIFY**. If only a specific directory is to be backed up, then the name of that directory is included with the MODIFY command. The first four lines of MODIFY.BAT are as follows:

```
1: echo off
2: cls
3: cd \
4: backup c:%1 a:/s/m
```

There are only two differences between this command and the Backup Files By Date utility (BYDATE.BAT). In line 3 of MODIFY.BAT, the current directory is changed to the root directory so that the backup will start at that level should the user not enter the %1 parameter. The other difference

```
                    NEW/MODIFIED FILE BACKUP

This backs up only those files that have been created or modified
   since the last backup was performed.  Before you continue,
   be sure that

   1.  You have performed a full backup once before (use
       the Full Backup option).
   2.  You have enough FORMATTED floppy diskettes available for
       the backup.

You should not continue if this is not the case.

               <<<<< Press F1 to Return >>>>>
```

Figure 7.8. The Backup by Modified Programs Screen

Backup/Restore Utilities 137

```
============================ INSTRUCTIONS ============================
To use the modify-backup routine, you simply enter the command
   MODIFY.  If you only want files in a specific directory
   included in the backup, you should include the name of that
   directory after the MODIFY command.

For example, to backup all files modified or created in the \WP
   directory since the last backup, the command is entered as
                          modify wp

               <<<<< Press F1 to Return >>>>>
```

Figure 7.9. Instructions for Backup by Modified Programs

is in the use of the BACKUP command in line 4. The /S parameter includes all subdirectories in the backup. The /M parameter is the Modify switch; this parameter backs up only those files that are new or have been modified since the last backup. The %1 replaceable parameter is ignored if the user does not enter a specific directory; in this case, the backup begins at the root directory level.

The Full Restore Utility

The Full Restore utility is used to restore files copied by the Backup utilities back onto a hard disk. This utility restores all files on a backup disk to the hard disk, regardless of whether they were made with a full backup or a partial backup routine. If the user wishes to restore files more selectively, then the Partial Restore utility should be used.

It should be noted that the Full Restore utility restores all subdirectory files that are contained on the backup disks, but the subdirectories must already exist on the hard disk. Thus, if the user is restoring files to a hard disk that has been reformatted, it is necessary to first recreate the directory structure on the hard disk (using the Make Directory (MD) command).

Running the Utility

When Full Restore is selected from the Backup/Restore menu, an information screen is displayed. If the user responds to the "Continue (Y/N)?" prompt with **Y** the restore routine then begins. The user is prompted to place the first disk in the floppy drive. If the backup used more than one disk, the user is prompted to insert each numbered disk in turn. The disks must be restored in the proper sequence or an error message is displayed.

> NOTE: *If partial backups have been made since the last full backup, the full backup should be restored first. Then—beginning with the oldest—the partial backups should be restored.*

The Backup/Restore menu is redisplayed when the operation is finished.

The Full Restore Utility Program Files

The Full Restore utility is made up of three batch files and one information screen. When **5** is entered at the prompt on the Backup/Restore menu, the 5.BAT file in the \HDU\BACKUP directory is executed:

```
    5.BAT
1:  echo off
2:  cls
3:  type fullrest.scr
4:  cd fullrest
5:  echo Continue (Y/N)?
6:  prompt $e[22;18H
```

The 5.BAT file displays the information screen shown in Figure 7.10 and changes the current directory to \HDU\BACKUP\FULLREST. If **Y** is entered in response to the "Continue (Y/N)?" prompt, the restore process begins. The operation is entirely contained in the Y.BAT file. Its contents are as follows:

```
    Y.BAT
1:  echo off
2:  cls
3:  restore a: c:\ /s
4:  if errorlevel 1 goto ABORT
5:  cls
6:  echo Restore is now complete.
7:  goto END
8:  :ABORT
9:  echo Problems... Restore terminated!
10: :END
```

Backup/Restore Utilities 139

```
11: pause
12: cls
13: cd \hdu\backup
14: type backmenu.scr
15: echo ENTER SELECTION:
16: prompt $e[22;18H
17: setscrn
```

The RESTORE command in line 3 starts the restore process at the root directory level. The /S parameter includes all subdirectories. Like the backup routines, the Errorlevel condition is used in the IF command in line 4 to test for successful completion of the RESTORE command. Lines 12 through 16 return the user to the Backup/Restore menu. Line 17 resets the display attributes with SETSCRN.BAT.

The Partial Restore Utility

This utility is used to selectively restore to the hard disk files that have been backed up with the Backup utilities. There are a number of different options. The user can restore a single file, groups of files (using global filename characters), a single directory, or a directory and all of its subdirectories. Also, it is possible to have DOS display a prompt before restoring any files

---

FULL RESTORE
===

This restores all files to the fixed disk that have been backed up using the various Backup options. Subdirectories will be included. The following points should be kept in mind:

1. If any partial backups have been performed since the last full backup, you should restore the full backup first --then restore the partial backups, beginning with the oldest.

2. The subdirectories must already exist on the hard disk if subdirectory files are included in the backup.

3. All files on the backup diskettes will be restored. If you need to selectively restore only certain files, use the Partial Restore option.

       <<<<< Press F1 to Return >>>>>

Figure 7.10. The Full Restore Screen

that have been modified since the last backup. This is useful when the user wishes to avoid overwriting existing hard disk files and old backup versions, and when the backup has included copy-protected software.

Running the Utility

When Partial Restore is selected from the Backup/Restore menu, an information screen that describes the various options is displayed. If **Y** is entered in response to the "Continue (Y/N)?" prompt, an instruction screen is displayed. The user must enter the command **PARTIAL** followed by one or more parameters. For example, consider a situation in which partial file restorations are being done from a word processing subdirectory (\WP). The following examples show what commands would be used under different file restoration conditions.

CONDITION	EXAMPLE	COMMENTS
Single File	partial \wp\resume.doc	Path and filename is used.
Group of Files	partial \wp*.doc	Global filename character (*) signifies all files with a .DOC extension.
Single Directory	partial \wp	Directory is \WP.
With Subdirectories	partial \wp /s	The /S parameter includes all subdirectories.
Subdirectories with Prompt	partial \wp/s/p	Includes a DOS prompt before restoring any files that have been changed. The prompt is also displayed before Read-Only files are restored.

The Backup/Restore menu is redisplayed when the operation is finished.

Backup/Restore Utilities   141

The Partial Restore Utility Program Files

This choice on the Backup/Restore menu uses four batch files and two informations screens. The 6.BAT file starts the operation when the user enters **6** from the Backup/Restore menu:

```
   6.BAT
1: echo off
2: cls
3: type partrest.scr
4: cd partrest
5: echo Continue (Y/N)?
6: prompt $e[13;18H
```

The file 6.BAT displays the information screen shown in Figure 7.11, and changes the current directory to \HDU\BACKUP\PARTREST. A **Y** response to the "Continue (Y/N)?" prompt executes the Y.BAT file, which contains the following commands:

```
   Y.BAT
1: echo off
2: cls
3: type instruct.scr
4: echo ENTER COMMAND:
5: prompt $e[22;18H
```

The instruction screen (INSTRUCT.SCR) displayed by the TYPE command is shown in Figure 7.12. As indicated by the instructions, the command **PARTIAL**—followed by one, two, or three parameters—is entered.

PARTIAL RESTORE

This allows you to selectively restore files to the fixed disk that have been backed up using the various Backup options.

Subdirectories must already exist on the hard disk if subdirectory files to be included in the restore.

<<<<< Press F1 to Return >>>>>

Figure 7.11. The Partial Restore Screen

```
=========================== INSTRUCTIONS ===========================
To restore a specific file or directory, you must enter the command
    PARTIAL followed by the filename or directory name, including the
    path (if any).  For example, a file in the WP directory named
    MEMO1123.DOC would be entered as
                     partial \wp\memo1123.doc

To restore only the WP directory, the command is entered as
                     partial \wp

Subdirectories may be included by adding a /S after the command, as in
                     partial \wp /s

If you have made no partial backups since the last full backup, you may
    wish to use the /P parameter as well.  This will let you choose
    whether or not to restore a file that has been modified since
    the last backup.  The command may include other options, as in
                     partial \wp /s /p

             <<<<< Press F1 to Return >>>>>
```

Figure 7.12. Instructions for Partial Restore

This activates the PARTIAL.BAT file. With one exception, the commands in this file are the same as the commands in the Y.BAT file, the main program file for the Full Restore utility (described previously in this chapter). The only difference is in the RESTORE command. In the PARTIAL.BAT file, it is written as:

```
restore a: c:%1 %2 %3
```

The above command contains three replaceable parameters. The first, %1, accommodates the directory name or the pathname/filename specifications that are entered with the PARTIAL command. The second and third replaceable parameters are used for the /S and /P options, if the user elects to include them with the PARTIAL command. They are ignored by DOS if they are not used.

7.2

MODIFYING THE BACKUP/RESTORE UTILITIES

Although the Backup/Restore utilities cover most aspects of the DOS RESTORE and BACKUP commands, there are a few options of these commands that are not included. The user may wish to add to or modify the

Backup/Restore Utilities

existing utilities. On the other hand, the user may wish to remove infrequently used utilities, or add utilities for operations outside of the DOS commands, such as routines for tape backup and restore. Also, these utilities have been written for use with DOS version 2.0 or later. Subsequent versions of DOS provide some enhancements to the BACKUP and RESTORE commands that are not covered by these utilities. The user may wish to add these enhancements to the utilities.

This section describes in detail some of these possible enhancements and modifications.

Some Points to Keep in Mind

The PROMPT command is used to control the position of the cursor. It contains an escape character ($e), a left-hand bracket ([), and the line and column number parameters. If the length of the screen is increased, the first # parameter must be increased. If the prompt, ENTER SELECTION, is changed to a longer or shorter string, the second # parameter also will have to be changed accordingly.

Replaceable parameters are used in the Backup/Restore utilities to permit the user to enter variables such as directory and filenames. Some batch files may contain two replaceable parameters (e.g., to accept a drive and directory specification). If the user enters only one variable, the second replaceable parameter is ignored.

The following structure is built into the Backup/Restore Utilities. The addition of new utilities should follow the same format for ease of use.

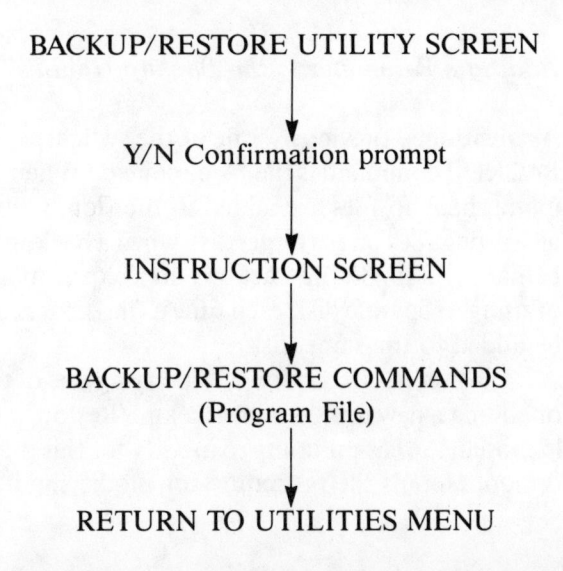

BACKUP/RESTORE UTILITY SCREEN
↓
Y/N Confirmation prompt
↓
INSTRUCTION SCREEN
↓
BACKUP/RESTORE COMMANDS
(Program File)
↓
RETURN TO UTILITIES MENU

Adding, Deleting, and Modifying Menu Items

The user may wish to remove unwanted menu choices from the Backup/Restore menu, or add new ones, or modify existing selections. All of this can be accomplished without any special forewarnings. The reader should consult Chapter 10 for a step-by-step approach to performing these tasks.

In adding new menu items, it may be desirable to create a separate subdirectory for the utility. If information screens are used with the "Continue (Y/N)?" prompt, this will be a requirement, since all of the existing backup directories already have Y.BAT and N.BAT files. Also, be sure to put the "Press F1 to Return" message at the bottom of any information screens. This facility activates the RETURN file and is always available. It is helpful for the user who sometimes gets lost in menus.

Whether adding, deleting, or modifying menu selections, it is important to test the utility thoroughly. This is an easily overlooked step. It is easy to assume that everything will work as expected, but it often doesn't. In debugging the new utility, observe the DOS error messages carefully as they will generally provide a clue as to the source of the problem. For example, a message like "Command or file not found" generally means that a batch file has not been created. Or, it could mean that a required Change Directory (CD) command is absent from the batch file.

The Backup/Restore utilities are critical to the integrity of one's system. If the utilities will be used by novices, it is important to try them out from their perspective. Make sure that all mistakes have been anticipated.

Adding a Parameter to the Backup Utilities

As mentioned previously, one of the switches that can be used in the DOS BACKUP command is the /A parameter. When this is included in the command, backup files are added to the floppy disk. Normally, DOS erases all existing files on the target disk when a backup is made. This option could be handy if single-file backups are frequently made. In this way, instead of using a separate disk each time a file is backed up, all backup files could be added to the same disk.

The user has the option of modifying one of the existing Backup utilities, or adding a new utility to the Backup/Restore menu. If the former method is chosen, the easiest utility to modify for this purpose is the Partial Backup option. Here is the procedure for modifying it.

1. The batch file that contains the principal component of the Partial Backup utility is PARTIAL.BAT in the \HDU\BACKUP\PARTIAL directory. Change the current directory to this directory and execute EDLIN on this file.
2. Edit line #3. The existing command is:

    backup c:%1 a:%2

    This should be changed to:

    backup c:%1 a:%2 %3

    The addition of the extra replaceable parameter will allow the user to add the /A option at the end of the PARTIAL command. This is the only change necessary for this file. End the EDLIN program.
3. It may be desirable to add some descriptive information to the two information screens that are used by this command. One of these is the INSTRUCT.SCR file, located in \HDU\BACKUP\PARTIAL; the other is PARTIAL.SCR, located in \HDU\BACKUP.
4. Use the EDLIN program to modify both of these files. Try to keep the file length (the number of lines) the same as the existing file. This will ensure that the cursor position of the PROMPT command in Y.BAT (in the same directory) does not have to be changed. The file length should not exceed 21 lines.

Once the changes have been made, be sure to test out the modified routine. The modification now allows the user to enter the PARTIAL command with up to three parameters: the directory and/or filename, the /S switch, and now the /A switch. DOS will ignore the last two if they are not entered with the PARTIAL command.

7.3 SOME BACKGROUND INFORMATION ON DATA SECURITY

Data backup and security can be some of the most important aspects of hard disk management. This is because all hard disk users will eventually discover that information stored on the fixed disk can be lost in a matter of seconds.

Sooner or later, hard disks will fail; without a proper backup system in place, data may be irreplaceable. Also, a user's critical or sensitive files may be susceptible to unauthorized access unless special precautions are taken. Situations such as these argue strongly for data-security controls.

These controls can range from simply performing daily backups of data files to the installation of sophisticated backup devices.

There are many ways to deal with these issues and minimize potential catastrophes. DOS commands can be used to back up and restore files and to change particular files to Read-Only access. More sophisticated security can be achieved through the use of various hardware and software products. These products give the user the ability to limit file and system access, to create audit trails, and to prevent illegal file duplication. Other products provide highly sophisticated methods for data backup.

DOS-Based System Security

For most users, DOS's BACKUP and RESTORE commands can provide adequate security against loss of data through fixed disk or system failure. However, this security is effective only when these routines are performed regularly.

The nature of the data on the fixed disk determines how often a system backup should be performed. For example, if several individuals use and update many files on a daily basis, then a system backup should be performed daily. However, in a situation such as this, it is not likely that regular backups will be performed unless *one* person has been given the responsibility for this task.

Thus, system backups must become a routine part of a user's day. In order to eliminate the need to remember the appropriate DOS commands and to standardize the procedure, a menu-based system is desirable. It is further necessary to determine how many backup disks are required on a typical day. The required number of disks must be formatted before the BACKUP command can be used.

It is also a good idea to have multiple sets of backup disks for three reasons:

1. Floppy disks, just like hard disks, have a finite lifespan and can wear out from repeated use.
2. A second backup copy should be secured away from the system site. Should a fire occur, both a hard disk system as well as a backup copy located nearby will be lost.
3. If a power or system failure occurs before the BACKUP routine is completed, all the backup files are useless. This is because BACKUP erases everything on the floppy disk. When the program is interrupted, the previous backup is destroyed before the new one is completed. The user should alternate between two sets of disks whenever a complete or partial backup is performed. This ensures that both sets are current.

Other Available Types of Security

In many areas of business, controlling system access and data duplication are equally important as protection against irreparable data loss. This section provides an overview of the types of security that may be obtained by special security-oriented packages.

Microcomputer security products are available in several different areas:

1. *Access Control:* Certain products allow a user to restrict data and system access. Using sophisticated password systems, an individual can be "locked out" of the system entirely. Or, a user may be permitted access to some programs and data files but not to others. Further, a user may be permitted to read particular data files but not to write to them. Each level of access in such a hierarchy is controlled through the use of passwords. Generally, there is a master password for the system manager that permits access to all levels.
2. *Audit Trails:* It also is possible to keep track of who has used a system. This is known as an audit trail. Security packages with highly developed access controls often have schemes that pair a password with a specific user. Each time the password is used, it may be recorded in a special file, together with the date and time of its use. Thus, a manager can keep track of both when and by whom the system and/or specific files have been used. This type of system can be particularly useful when many individuals must use a PC-XT that contains important or sensitive data.
3. *Copy Protection:* There are products available that prevent unauthorized duplication of programs or data stored on the fixed disk and floppy disks. Files or programs may be encrypted with a special code that prevents them from being copied. Other encryption programs may allow information to be copied, but only onto specially encrypted disks; the disks themselves may not be copied. This type of system can prevent illegal duplication of applications software that is not copy protected (such as *dBASE II*). In such cases, the programs are copied onto encrypted disks. The users are then given these disks to run the programs rather than the original program disks. For organizations concerned about their liability for illegal software duplication, security packages of this type may be worth considering.

chapter 8

File Management Utilities

Since a large number of files may be created and stored on a hard disk, these files must be organized and maintained. Unlike a manual filing system in which one can glance at documents for information, electronic storage of data means that files must be retrieved from disk and read into memory to review their contents. Thus, electronically stored files can be difficult to identify and access without some sort of file management system. Periodically, old or infrequently used files must be archived to make room for new ones. Such tasks are the "housekeeping" functions with which every user must contend.

The File Management utilities are basic functions used in the maintenance and "housekeeping" functions of a hard disk system.

What Are the File Management Utilities?

There are six File Management utilities. They include routines for:

- copying files
- moving files from one directory to another
- combining files and performing text searches for character strings
- locating a file on the hard disk
- assigning files as Read-Write or Read-Only access

Why Are They Used?

Although routine "housekeeping" functions are not difficult to perform, they require a working knowledge of many DOS commands. As a result,

File Management Utilities

some functions are not performed as often as they should be. The File Management utilities are designed to provide the user with a standard set of easy-to-use routines for maintaining a hard disk system.

How to Use the Utilities

The File Management utilities are accessed when selection 5 is chosen from the *Hard Disk Manager* main menu. This selection changes the directory to \HDU\FILE and displays the File Management menu. Any of the six selections on the screen can be chosen simply by typing the number of the desired utility. After the selection is made, the utilities prompt the user for any required input; informational screens, when necessary, guide the user through the utility. If at any time the user chooses not to proceed with a utility, the <F1> key can be pressed to return to the previous menu.

For the user who would like additional information on file management and hard disk maintenance, overviews of these topics can be found at the end of this chapter.

Organization of the File Management Utilities

The batch files and information screens for all of the File Management utilities are found in a single directory: \HDU\FILE. There are no subdirectories for any of the File Management utilities. Because there is no multiple usage of the "Continue (Y/N)?" prompt by these utilities, there is no need for separate directories for the corresponding Y.BAT and N.BAT files.

The contents of the \HDU\FILE directory are shown in Figure 8.1. As can be seen in Figure 8.1, there are only three types of files in the \HDU\FILE

```
C:\HDU\FILE    <DIR>

      1.BAT        ARCHIVE.BAT      ARCHIVE.SCR
      2.BAT        COMBINE.BAT      COMBINE.SCR
      3.BAT        MOVE.BAT         MOVE.SCR
      4.BAT        SEARCH.BAT       SEARCH.SCR
      5.BAT        LOCATE.BAT       FILEMENU.SCR
      6.BAT        DOLOCATE.BAT     LOCATE.SCR
      7.BAT        DODCOPY.BAT      NOINPUT.TXT

C:\HDU\PROTECT <DIR>

      PROTECT.BAT        PROTECT.SCR
      UNPROTEC.BAT       INSTRUCT.SCR
      Y.BAT              N.BAT
```

Figure 8.1. Directory and File Structure for the File Management Utilities

directory. The numbered batch files start the individual utilities. Each of these displays an appropriate instruction screen (the .SCR files). Finally, as indicated by the instruction screen, the user activates the specific utility by entering a command followed by any required parameters. This command is the name of a batch file that performs the given operation (e.g., ARCHIVE.BAT).

Activation of the Utilities

Selection 5 on the main menu accesses the File Management utilities by activating the 5.BAT file in the \HDU\FILE directory. It contains the following commands:

```
  5.BAT
1: echo off
2: cls
3: cd file
4: type filemenu.scr
5: echo ENTER SELECTION:
6: prompt $e[22;18H
7: setscrn
```

As can be seen from the above commands, the principal function of this batch file is to change the current directory to the \HDU\FILE directory

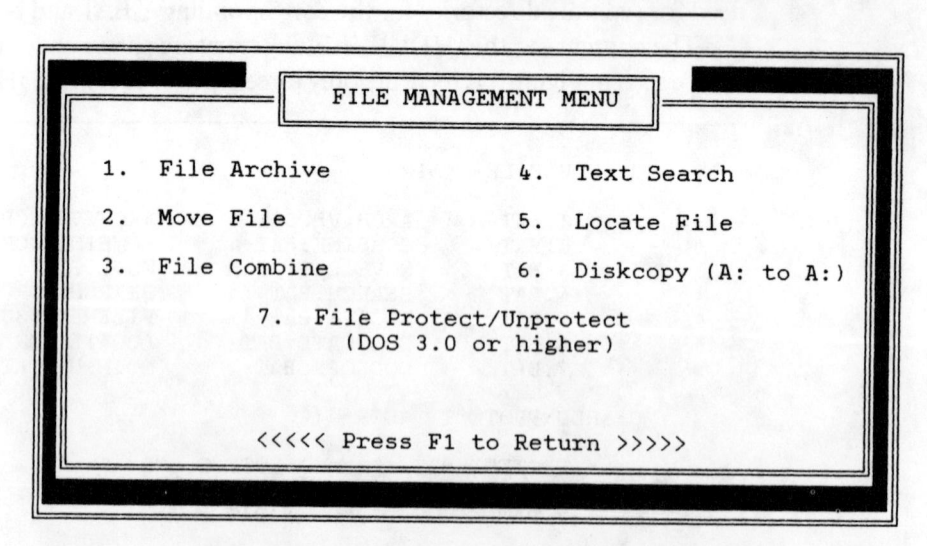

```
┌─────────────────────────────────────────────────────┐
│                 FILE MANAGEMENT MENU                │
│                                                     │
│   1.  File Archive        4.  Text Search           │
│                                                     │
│   2.  Move File           5.  Locate File           │
│                                                     │
│   3.  File Combine        6.  Diskcopy (A: to A:)   │
│                                                     │
│              7.  File Protect/Unprotect             │
│                  (DOS 3.0 or higher)                │
│                                                     │
│            <<<<< Press F1 to Return >>>>>           │
└─────────────────────────────────────────────────────┘
```

Figure 8.2. File Management Utilities Menu

File Management Utilities

and to display the File Management screen (FILEMENU.SCR). The last line resets the screen display attributes with SETSCRN.BAT. (See Chapter 5 for an explanation of this function.) The File Management menu screen is shown in Figure 8.2.

8.1
THE FILE MANAGEMENT UTILITIES

The File Archive Utility

The File Archive utility allows the user to copy hard disk files onto a floppy disk in drive A. It provides a structured approach to the DOS COPY command. When a **1** is entered by the user from the File Management screen, an information screen is displayed. Figure 8.3 shows the text of this screen.

As can be seen from Figure 8.3, the user is given instructions on how to enter the ARCHIVE command and directions and suggestions in the use of pathnames and global filename characters. The user must enter the command **ARCHIVE** followed by the pathname/filename of the file(s) to be archived. Before the copy is attempted, a message is displayed showing the user what filename was entered.

Normal DOS messages are displayed if the copy is successful or unsuccessful. The File Management menu is redisplayed regardless of the outcome.

FILE ARCHIVE
===

With this utility, you may copy one or more files from the
    hard disk to a floppy disk in drive A. If the file is too
    large for one floppy disk, or you wish to copy more files
    than will fit on the floppy, use the Partial Backup option
    under the Backup/Restore Utilities.

To archive a file, enter the command ARCHIVE followed by the path
    and filename. To archive more than one file, use global
    filename characters.

For example, to archive a file in the \WP directory called
    MEMO.DOC, the command is entered as
                    archive \wp\memo.doc

         <<<<< Press F1 to Return >>>>>

Figure 8.3. File Archive Information Screen

Undoubtedly, experienced users will find it easier to simply go straight into DOS to run the COPY command. However, for the less experienced, the information screen in the File Archive utility can be a useful reminder of the necessity of using directory paths, and of the convenience of using global filename characters.

The File Archive Program Files

Two batch files and one information screen make up the components of the File Archive utility. Its execution begins when the user enters **1** from the File Management menu. This causes the 1.BAT file in the \HDU\FILE directory to be executed. The commands in this file are as follows:

```
   1.BAT
1: echo off
2: cls
3: type archive.scr
4: echo ENTER COMMAND:
5: prompt $e[22;16H
```

The above batch file simply displays an information screen (AR-CHIVE.SCR) and positions the cursor after the ENTER COMMAND prompt. The information contained on ARCHIVE.SCR is shown in Figure 8.3.

When the user enters the command **ARCHIVE** along with the pathname/filename of the file to be archived, this executes the AR-CHIVE.BAT file. This file contains the following commands:

```
    ARCHIVE.BAT
 1: echo off
 2: cls
 3: if "%1"=="" goto ERROR
 4: echo Copying %1 to disk in drive A ...
 5: copy %1 a:
 6: goto DONE
 7: :ERROR
 8: echo  You must specify the name of the file with
          the ARCHIVE command. Try again.
 9: pause
10: cls
```

File Management Utilities 153

```
11: type archive.scr
12: echo ENTER COMMAND:
13: goto END
14: :DONE
15: pause
16: cd \hdu\file
17: cls
18: type filemenu.scr
19: echo ENTER SELECTION:
20: prompt $e[22;18H
21: setscrn
22: :END
```

The IF command in line 3 checks to see if the user has included the argument with the command. The ECHO command in line 4 is a confirmation of the filename the user is attempting to copy. The pathname/filename that is entered with the ARCHIVE command is substituted for the %1 replaceable parameter in this line as well as the COPY command in line 5.

There is no suppression of output so all DOS messages are displayed if the COPY is successful or unsuccessful. The last five lines redisplay the File Management menu.

The Move File Utility

Using the Move File utility, a user can copy a file from one location on the hard disk to another location, and then erase the file from the original location. This routine combines the DOS commands **COPY** and **ERASE** into one operation.

The process begins when **2** is entered at the File Management menu. This activates the display of an information screen. Figure 8.4 shows the text of this screen. The user must enter the command **MOVE** together with two arguments: the source directory/filename and the target directory. The filename is not allowed as a part of the target directory specification; a file automatically will be assigned the same filename in the new location.

Multiple files may be moved using global filename characters in the source information. For example, the following command would move all .WKS files from \123DATA to \NEW123:

```
move \123data\*.wks   \new123
```

FILE MOVE

```
With this utility, you may move one or more files from one
    directory to another.  The file is first copied into the
    target location and then erased from the source location.
    Multiple files may be moved by using global filename
    characters in the source filename designation.

To move files, enter the command MOVE followed by the path and
    filename of the source file, and then the target directory.

For example, to move a file in the \WP directory called
    REPORT.DOC to the \WP\DATA directory, the command is entered
    as
              move   \wp\report.doc   \wp\data


                <<<<< Press F1 to Return >>>>>
```

Figure 8.4. File Move Screen

After the MOVE command is entered, a confirmation message appears that displays the source and target arguments entered by the user. For example, the above command produces the following message:

```
Moving \123data\*.wks file(s) to \new123 ...
```

The user must enter the MOVE command with both arguments. If the first argument is absent or invalid, DOS error messages are displayed. If the second argument is absent or invalid, in addition to DOS error messages, the following additional message appears:

```
Target directory invalid or not specified. Try again.
```

The user is then returned to the Move Utility Instruction screen. When the file has been successfully moved, the File Management menu is redisplayed.

The Move Utility Program Files

The Move File utility is composed of two batch files and one instruction screen. The operation begins with the entry of **2** on the File Management menu. This executes the 2.BAT file in the \HDU\FILE directory. This file has the following commands:

File Management Utilities

```
   2.BAT
1: echo off
2: cls
3: type move.scr
4: echo ENTER COMMAND:
5: prompt $e[22;16H
```

The TYPE command (line 3) displays the instruction screen, MOVE.SCR, and positions the cursor after the ENTER COMMAND prompt. The text of MOVE.SCR is shown in Figure 8.4.

When the user enters the MOVE command, the MOVE.BAT file is executed. The commands in this file are as follows:

```
    MOVE.BAT
 1: echo off
 2: cls
 3: if "%2"=="" goto ERROR
 4: echo Moving %1 file(s) to %2 ...
 5: cd %2
 6: if exist move.bat goto ERROR
 7: copy %1 %2
 8: del %1
 9: pause
10: cls
11: cd \hdu\file
12: type filemenu.scr
13: echo ENTER SELECTION:
14: prompt $e[22;18H
15: setscrn
16: goto END
17: :ERROR
18: echo Target directory invalid or not specified.
        Try again.
19: pause
20: cls
21: type move.scr
22: echo ENTER COMMAND:
23: prompt $e[22;16H
24: :END
```

Line 3 uses the IF command to ensure that the user entered the second argument. This prevents the DEL command (line 8) from erasing the source file without it first being copied. Line 4 generates the confirmation prompt. The %1 and %2 replaceable parameters are obtained from the arguments that the user supplies when the MOVE command is entered.

The function of the CD and IF commands in lines 5-6 is to check that the user has entered a valid directory for the second argument. This prevents the disastrous course of events in which the DEL command (line 8) erases the source file without it first being copied. If the specified directory is not valid, the current directory remains \HDU\FILE. Then, if the MOVE.BAT file is found to exist in the current directory, this means that the current directory has not been changed and an error has occurred; control is then passed to the ERROR portion of the batch file. Otherwise, it can be assumed that the %2 parameter has been entered correctly; DOS thus executes the COPY and DEL commands in lines 7-8.

There are two different "endings": If the ERROR condition occurs, the error message is displayed and the user is returned to the Move File instruction screen. Note that this does not occur if there is a problem with the first argument: DOS error messages are displayed and the File Management menu is redisplayed. This menu is also displayed when the operation is completed successfully.

In all cases, a pause occurs with the message "Strike a key when ready" before the screen is cleared.

The File Combine Utility

This utility allows the user to utilize the file concatenation abilities of the DOS COPY command. A lesser known function of the COPY command is its file combination or concatenation facility. Using conventional file specifications, several of the COPY command switches, and "+" signs, any number of files may be linked together. With this utility, the user may combine two ASCII (text) files.

The utility is activated when **3** is entered on the File Management menu. This displays the information screen shown in Figure 8.5. As indicated in the instructions, the second file is appended to the first. The user must enter the command **COMBINE** followed by the two arguments: the source file and the file that is to be appended to it. Drive specifications and/or pathnames must be included with each filename.

When the file combine is complete, the following message is displayed:

```
File combine is now complete. Combined files are
stored in _____
```

File Management Utilities 157

FILE COMBINE

```
This routine will combine two ASCII (text) files.  The files
   will be combined in the first (source) file and stored under
   that filename.  If you wish to combine more than two files,
   repeat the process with the results of the first combination.

To combine the files, enter the command COMBINE followed by source
   file, and then the other file that is to be appended to the
   to the source file.  Include any necessary drives and/or paths.

   For example, to combine two files in the \123DATA directory
   called REPORT.PRN and SUMMARY.PRN, where the first file is added
   to the second, the command is entered as
            combine \123data\summary.prn \123data\report.prn


              <<<<< Press F1 to Return >>>>>
```

Figure 8.5. File Combine Screen

The blank space in the message at the bottom of page 156 contains the name of the source file. After a pause, the File Management menu is redisplayed.

The File Combine Program Files

The File Combine utility is comprised of two batch files and one information screen. It is activated by the 3.BAT file in the \HDU\FILE directory. This file contains the following commands:

```
   3.BAT
1: echo off
2: cls
3: type combine.scr
4: echo ENTER COMMAND:
5: prompt $e[22;16H
```

The above commands display the COMBINE.SCR information screen (line 3) and position the cursor after the ENTER COMMAND prompt (lines 4–5). The program continues when the user enters the COMBINE command with the two required arguments. This activates the COMBINE.BAT file, which is shown on page 158.

```
            COMBINE.BAT
         1: echo off
         2: cls
         3: if "%1"=="" goto ERROR
         4: if "%2"=="" goto ERROR
         5: copy %1+%2 %1
         6: echo  File combine is now complete. Combined files
               are stored in %1
         7: goto DONE
         8: :ERROR
         9: echo  You must specify both arguments after the
               command. Try again.
        10: pause
        11: cls
        12: type combine.scr
        13: echo ENTER COMMAND:
        14: goto END
        15: :DONE
        16: pause
        17: cd \hdu\file
        18: cls
        19: type filemenu.scr
        20: echo ENTER SELECTION:
        21: prompt $e[22;18H
        22: setscrn
        23: :END
```

The two IF commands in lines 3 and 4 check for inclusion of the two required arguments. The COPY operation in line 5 uses the two arguments entered by the user with the COMBINE command for the replaceable parameters %1 and %2. The last five lines redisplay the File Management menu. Line 22 resets the screen display attributes with the SETSCRN.BAT file.

The Text Search Utility

With the Text Search utility, the user may search ASCII files (text files) for specific character strings. It utilizes the DOS FIND filter. A filter is a command or program that transforms input data and outputs the results to a file or a device such as a printer. Through the use of global filename

File Management Utilities 159

TEXT SEARCH

```
This routine will search through one or more ASCII (text) files
    for the occurrence of a specified string.  To search more than
    one file, use global filename characters in the filename
    specification (e.g., *.prn).

The command is entered in the following format:
    SEARCH  <directory location> <filename> <string>

For example, to search all batch files (*.BAT) in the \UTILITY
    directory for the occurrence of the string "a:", the command
    would be entered as
                    search  \utility  *.bat  a:
String may not have spaces.  To print results, press [Ctrl] [PrtSc]
    before entering command; repeat when done to turn off printing.

         <<<<< Press F1 to Return >>>>>
```

Figure 8.6. Text Search Screen

characters and the FOR command, more than one file can be included in the search. It is important to note, however, that this routine is upper- and lowercase sensitive (e.g., the letters "a" and "A" are considered different characters).

The utility begins when **4** is entered from the File Management menu. This produces the information screen shown in Figure 8.6. The user must enter the command **SEARCH** followed by three arguments: the directory location of the file(s), the filename(s), and the character string that is the subject of the search.

The command is entered in the following format:

SEARCH <directory location> <filename> <string>

Each argument is separated by spaces, and the specified string may not contain any space characters. For example, if the user wished to search all .PRN files in the \123DATA directory for the occurrence of the word "Budget," the command would be entered as:

search \123data *.prn Budget

A confirmation of the arguments entered by the user is displayed at the top of the screen. The above command, for example, would produce the message shown on page 160.

160   HARD DISK MANAGER

```
Searching...   Directory: \hdu\protect    FILE: *.scr    STRING: "example"

----------  INSTRUCT.SCR
[5]             (if any) and the name of the file.  For example, to protect a

----------  PROTECT.SCR

Search is now complete.
The numbers in brackets are line numbers in the file(s).
```

Figure 8.7. Screen Output from Search Utility

```
Searching... DIRECTORY: \123data FILE: *.prn STRING:
"Budget"
```

If the specified directory or filename is not valid or does not exist, an error message is displayed and, after a pause, the Text Search information screen is redisplayed.

If the directory and filename entries are valid, the search process begins. The file is listed on the screen as it is searched. Under the filename is listed each line in the file that contains the specified string. The line number appears in brackets at the beginning of each line. Figure 8.7 shows the screen output generated by search through all .SCR files in the \HDU\PROTECT directory for the string "example." Note that the second file had no occurrences of the "example" string, but the filename is listed anyway.

When the search is finished, the message "Search is now complete" appears. After a pause, the File Management menu is redisplayed.

The Text Search Program Files

The Text Search utility is made up of two batch files and one information screen, all located in the \HDU\FILE directory. The utility is activated by the 4.BAT file, which contains the following commands:

```
   4.BAT
1: echo off
2: cls
3: type search.scr
4: echo ENTER COMMAND:
5: prompt $e[22;16H
```

File Management Utilities

There are no special tricks in the above batch file; its main function is to display the SEARCH.SCR file (shown in Figure 8.6). The program continues when the user enters the SEARCH command and the required arguments. This activates the SEARCH.BAT file.

How SEARCH.BAT Works

Refer to Figure 8.8 to see a listing of the SEARCH.BAT file. Lines 3-5 check for user input of the required arguments; control is passed to the ERROR1 section if all three have not been entered with the command. Line 6 provides a confirmation prompt that displays the arguments, using replaceable parameters.

```
    SEARCH.BAT
 1: echo off
 2: cls
 3: if "%1"=="" goto ERROR1
 4: if "%2"=="" goto ERROR1
 5: if "%3"=="" goto ERROR1
 6: echo Searching...    DIRECTORY: %1    FILE: %2    STRING: "%3"
 7: cd %1
 8: if exist search.bat goto ERROR2
 9: if not exist %2 goto NOFILE
10: for %%x in (%2) do find /n "%3" %%x
11: echo ?
12: echo End of search.
13: echo The numbers in brackets are line numbers in the file(s).
14: pause
15: cd \hdu\file
16: cls
17: type filemenu.scr
18: echo ENTER SELECTION:
19: prompt $e[22;18H
20: setscrn
21: goto DONE
22: :ERROR1
23: echo You must specify all three arguments after command.  Try again.
24: goto END
25: :ERROR2
26: echo     ... your directory does not exist.  Try again.
27: goto END
28: :NOFILE
29: echo Specified file(s) not found.  Try again.
30: :END
31: pause
32: cd \hdu\file
33: cls
34: type search.scr
35: echo ENTER COMMAND:
36: prompt $e[22;16H
37: :DONE
```

Figure 8.8. SEARCH.BAT File Listing

The CD and IF commands in lines 7-9 of SEARCH.BAT are attempts at making the routine somewhat "idiot-proof." If the directory argument is not valid, then the current directory remains \HDU\FILE and the subsequent IF command finds SEARCH.BAT to exist. Control then is passed to the ERROR2 section of the batch file and an error message is displayed. Likewise, the second IF command checks to see if the specified file exists; if not, control is passed to the NOFILE section for the display of an appropriate error message. In both cases, the SEARCH.SCR file and prompt are redisplayed.

If the specified arguments pass these little tests, the search is performed with the FIND command that is embedded in the FOR command (line 10 of SEARCH.BAT). The FOR command is used so that multiple files may be searched when global filename characters appear in the filename parameter. Each filename is displayed on the screen as it is searched. Lines containing the specified string appear under the filename. Nothing is displayed if the string is not found in a file.

When the search is finished, the ECHO commands display some messages, a pause occurs, and the File Management menu is redisplayed (lines 12-19 of SEARCH.BAT). Line 20 resets the screen display attributes with SETSCRN.BAT. Control is shifted to the last line in the file with the GOTO command in line 21 of SEARCH.BAT so that the error conditions are not executed. The ECHO command in line 11 forces a blank line; the "text" of the command is actually an unprintable character, <Alt> 255.

The File Locate Utility

Every hard disk user suffers the frustration of misplacing a file in the hard disk occasionally. (" . . . I know it's here somewhere.") This utility eliminates the necessity of wading through one directory listing after another in search of the elusive file. It works by using two DOS commands: the CHKDSK (Check Disk) command, and the FIND filter. Using the /V switch with the CHKDSK command generates a list of files (and their paths) on the hard disk; this output is redirected to a file that is then searched by the FIND filter.

The program begins when **5** is entered on the File Management menu. This produces the information screen shown in Figure 8.9. The user must enter the command **LOCATE** followed by the filename. The filename *must* be specified in uppercase letters. This is because the CHKDSK commands generates its output in uppercase; the FIND command is case sensitive (i.e., it differentiates between an "A" and an "a").

File Management Utilities 163

LOCATE FILE

```
This routine searches directories on your hard disk for a specified
    file or files.  The filename MUST be entered in upper case.

The command is entered in the following format:
                LOCATE  <filename>

The filename may be with or without extension.  If only the
    extension is entered, all files with that extension will be
    located.  For example, to locate a file called TCRESUME.WK1,
    the command would be entered as
                locate  TCRESUME.WK1

Again, note that upper-case letters must be used for the filename.


            <<<<< Press F1 to Return >>>>>
```

Figure 8.9. File Locate Screen

The command is entered in the following format:

`LOCATE <FILENAME>`

Global filename characters are not permitted. However, by entering only an extension, or other portions of the filename, a list of all files containing those characters is displayed. For example, to locate all files whose first four characters are MEMO, the command is entered as

`locate MEMO`

Or, to find all files with extensions of .DAT, the command is

`locate .DAT`

After the command is entered, a confirmation prompt appears at the top of the screen. If the specified directory or filename is not valid or does not exist, an error message is displayed and, after a pause, the Text Search information screen is redisplayed.

If the directory and filename entries are valid, the program begins the attempt to locate the file(s). The dirve, path, and filename will be listed for every file on the disk that matches the input specified by the user. If no match is found, no file will be listed, only the message "End of search. Press

```
Starting search.  A full disk may take a few minutes; be patient...
Looking for file 3CH8C.

---------- Result
      C:\123DATA\3CH8C.WKS
      C:\123DATA\3CH8C.WK1

End of search.
Strike a key when ready . . .
```

Figure 8.10. Screen Output from Locate Utility

Enter to continue." Figure 8.10 shows the output when a file called 3CH8C is located on the hard disk. Note that two entries are displayed because there are two different extensions on this filename.

When the search is finished, the File Management menu is redisplayed.

Printing the Results

If the output of the Locate File utility exceeds a single screen, the user may send the output to the printer by pressing <Ctrl><PrtSc> before the command is entered. Be sure to press these keys again when finished to turn off this "slaving" of the printer (as it's called); otherwise, it will continue to print everything that appears on the screen.

The Locate File Program Files

The Locate File utility is made up of three batch files and one information screen, all located in the \HDU\FILE directory. The utility is activated by the 5.BAT file, which contains the following commands:

```
   5.BAT
1: echo off
2: cls
3: type locate.scr
4: echo ENTER COMMAND:
5: prompt $e[22;16H
```

The purpose of this file is simply to display the LOCATE.SCR information screen, shown in Figure 8.9. The program continues when the user enters the command LOCATE.

File Management Utilities 165

How LOCATE.BAT Works

When the user enters the command LOCATE, followed by the specified filename, the batch file LOCATE.BAT is activated. This contains the following commands:

```
    LOCATE.BAT
 1: echo off
 2: cls
 3: if "%1"=="" goto BADINPUT
 4: command /c dolocate %1
 5: echo off
 6: goto DONE
 7: :BADINPUT
 8: echo You must specify a filename after the
      command. Try again.
 9: pause
10: cls
11: type locate.scr
12: echo ENTER COMMAND:
13: prompt $e[22;16H
14: goto END
15: :DONE
16: cls
17: type filemenu.scr
18: echo ENTER SELECTION:
19: prompt $e[22;18H
20: setscrn
21: :END
```

Line 3 in the above batch file checks if the user entered an argument with the command. If no argument has been entered, control passes to the BADINPUT section, lines 7-14. Note that in line 4, a batch file subroutine is called. It is DOLOCATE.BAT that contains the heart of the location routine. The program has been structured in this way so that a menu will be redisplayed in the event <Crtl> <Break> is pressed before execution is completed. The DOLOCATE.BAT file contains the following commands:

```
    DOLOCATE.BAT
 1: echo off
 2: cls
```

```
       3: echo Starting search. A full disk may take a few
              minutes; be patient.
       4: chkdsk /v <noinput.txt>result
       5: echo Looking for file %1.
       6: find "%1" Result
       7: echo 
       8: echo End of search.
       9: pause
      10: exit
```

The CHKDSK command in line 4 has its output redirected to the file RESULT. The ECHO in line 5 uses a %1 replaceable parameter to display the user's input in the message. In line 6, the FIND command performs the search on the RESULT file for the user filename, which is %1. Line 7 forces a blank line to be displayed (the "text" is the unprintable character, <Alt> 255). At the end of DOLOCATE.BAT, the EXIT command returns control to LOCATE.BAT, line 5.

The Diskcopy Utility

The Diskcopy utility allows the user to duplicate an entire disk. It uses the DOS command DISKCOPY, and it requires the use of only one disk drive (drive A). It is also one of the simplest routines on the program disk.

It is started by entering **6** at the File Management menu. The screen clears, and the following messages are displayed.

```
      This routine duplicates diskettes using a single
      drive (A). You will be prompted to insert the source
      and target disks...
```

After a pause, the operation begins. Ths user is prompted by DOS to insert the source disk and target disk at various intervals. The target disk is formatted if it is not already. When the diskcopy is finished, DOS displays the message:

```
      Copy another (Y/N)?
```

A response of **Y** repeats the operation; **N** redisplays the File Management menu.

File Management Utilities

The Diskcopy Program Files

There are only two files in this utility: The 6.BAT and DODCOPY.BAT files in the \HDU\FILE directory. The 6.BAT file contains the following commands:

```
      6.BAT
   1: echo off
   2: cls
   3: command /c dodcopy
   4: echo off
   5: cls
   6: type filemenu.scr
   7: echo ENTER SELECTION:
   8: prompt $e[22;18H
   9: setscrn
```

In line 3 of the above file, a subroutine batch file, DODCOPY.BAT, is called, using the COMMAND command. This ensures that a menu is redisplayed if the user does a <Ctrl> <Break> before the program is completed. DODCOPY.BAT contains the following commands:

```
      DODCOPY.BAT
   1: echo off
   2: cls
   3: echo This routine duplicates diskettes using a
            single drive (drive A).
   4: echo You will be prompted to insert the source and
            target disks...
   5: pause
   6: diskcopy a:   a:
   7: exit
```

The DISKCOPY command is performed in line 6 of DODCOPY.BAT. In line 7, control is returned to 6.BAT, line 4. The last five lines redisplay the File Management menu when the diskcopy is complete.

The File Protect/Unprotect Utilities

The File Protect/Unprotect utilities can be used to change the status of a file from Read/Write to Read Only, and vice versa. Note that they can be

```
================ FILE PROTECT/UNPROTECT UTILITY ================
                      (DOS 3.0 or higher)
```

This routine allows you to protect files from inadvertent erasure
   or alteration. Files that have been "protected" are marked as
   Read-Only, and cannot be erased or changed without first
   "unprotecting" them --marking them as Read/Write.

You MUST be using DOS 3.0 or higher. Do not continue if this
   is not the case.

Figure 8.11. File Protect/Unprotect Screen

used only if the system is using DOS 3.0 or higher. This is because these utilities use the DOS command **ATTRIB** (Attribute), which is not available in earlier versions of DOS.

The utilities are accessed by entering **7** from the File Management menu. This displays an information screen that describes the utility and the requirement for DOS 3.0 or higher. The text of this screen is shown in Figure 8.11. If the user responds to the "Continue (Y/N)?" prompt with **N** the File Management menu is redisplayed. If **Y** is entered, an instruction screen is then displayed (Figure 8.12).

To protect a file, the user is required to enter the PROTECT command followed by the pathname/filename of the file. This makes the file Read Only. Similarly, when the UNPROTECT command is entered followed by the pathname/filename specification, the status of the file is changed to Read/Write. In either case, global filename characters may be used to run the utility on multiple files.

```
========================= INSTRUCTIONS =========================
To protect a file, enter the command PROTECT followed by the drive
   and/or path, and the name of the file. For example, to protect a
   file in the \123\DATA directory called RESUME.WKS, the
   command is entered as
             protect \123\data\resume.wks

To unprotect a file, enter the command UNPROTECT followed by the
   drive and/or path, and the name of the file, as in
             unprotect \123\data\resume.wks

              <<<<< Press F1 to Return >>>>>
```

Figure 8.12. File Protect/Unprotect Instructions

File Management Utilities 169

For both utilities, if the directory or filename is not valid, the following error message is displayed:

```
Invalid directory or file does not exist. Try again.
```

The instruction screen then is redisplayed. If there is no problem with the pathname/filename parameter, then a message is displayed indicating that the file has been marked either Read Only or Read/Write. In this case, the user then is returned to the File Management menu.

The Protect/Unprotect Program Files

There are a few more files involved in the Protect/Unprotect utilities than others in the File Management section. This utility includes five batch files and two information screens. The utility is activated by choosing selection 7 on the File Management menu. The contents of this file are as follows:

```
   7.BAT
1: echo off
2: cls
3: cd ..\protect
4: type protect.scr
5: echo Continue (Y/N)?
6: prompt $e[14;18H
```

With the exception of this batch file, all other files associated with these utilites are located in the \HDU\PROTECT directory. The above batch file makes \HDU\PROTECT the current directory (line 3), displays an information screen (PROTECT.SCR in line 4), and positions the cursor at the end of the "Continue (Y/N)?" prompt (line 6). The Y.BAT and N.BAT files that are activated by the user in response to this prompt are shown below.

```
   Y.BAT
1: echo off
2: cls
3: type instruct.scr
4: echo ENTER COMMAND:
5: prompt $e[17;16H

   N.BAT
1: echo off
2: cls
```

```
 3: cd \hdu\file
 4: type filemenu.scr
 5: echo ENTER SELECTION:
 6: prompt $e[22;18H
 7: setscrn
```

The N.BAT file redisplays the File Management menu, whereas the Y.BAT file displays the instructions for entering the PROTECT and UN-PROTECT commands. When the PROTECT command is entered, the PROTECT.BAT file is executed. This file contains the following commands:

```
    PROTECT.BAT
 1: echo off
 2: cls
 3: if not exist %1 goto ERROR
 4: attrib +r %1
 5: echo File(s) now marked Read-Only.
 6: pause
 7: cls
 8: cd \hdu\file
 9: type filemenu.scr
10: echo ENTER SELECTION:
11: prompt $e[22;18H
12: setscrn
13: goto DONE
14: :ERROR
15: echo Invalid directory or filename does not
         exist. Try again.
16: pause
17: cls
18: type instruct.scr
19: echo ENTER COMMAND:
20: prompt $e[17;16H
21: :DONE
```

The IF command in line 3 checks for the existence of the specified file. (A directory path can be used because DOS versions 3.0 and later accept pathnames as part of the EXIST conditions.) If the file is not found, control is shifted to the ERROR section (line 14) of the batch file. There an error message is displayed and, after a pause, the instruction screen is redisplayed. If the filename parameter is valid, then the ATTRIB command

File Management Utilities 171

in line 4 is executed on that file, using the file specified for the %1 replaceable parameter. The confirmation message is displayed and, after the pause, the File Management menu is redisplayed. Line 12 executes SETSCRN.BAT, which resets the screen display attributes (see Chapter 6 for an explanation of this command).

The UNPROTECT command activates the UNPROTEC.BAT file. (The ending "T" in the command is ignored since filenames cannot exceed 8 characters.) The contents of that file are exactly the same as the PROTECT.BAT file except for lines 4 and 5. In line 4, the ATTRIB command is written as

```
attrib -r %1
```

The use of the minus sign in front of the "r" gives the file a Read/Write status. In line 5, the confirmation message indicates that the file is now marked as Read/Write.

8.2
MODIFYING THE FILE MANAGEMENT UTILITES

File management has different requirements for different users. The authors have no expectations that the utilities included in the File Management Utilities will cover the needs of all users. The utilities that were chosen for inclusion generally met one or both of the following criteria:

- the DOS command in its native state is somewhat complicated, easily forgotten, or overlooked
- several DOS operations are required to accomplish the specific task

For this reason, standard DOS file management operations such as COPY, ERASE, and RENAME are not included. These are relatively straightforward operations (for DOS) that are easily executed without the aid of a structured utility. Experienced users will probably find it easier to execute these commands outside of a menu or batch-file environment. (When setting up a main menu, it can be useful to have an "Exit to DOS" menu choice for such situations.)

However, it may be necessary or desirable to totally structure all aspects of file management, particularly if the system is to be used by PC novices. The following section is a "how to" for adding, deleting, or modifying the File Management utilities.

Some Points to Keep in Mind

Here are a few general suggestions and reminders for commands and operations that may be involved in modifying or creating File Management utilities:

1. When using the COPY command, if the drive or path parameters are not specified in either the source or target files, the default drive is assumed. If the target filename is not specified, the file is given the same filename as the source file.
2. The use of global filename characters can be helpful when applying an operation to multiple files in a directory. This is particularly true for commands such as COPY, ATTRIB, etc. Instruction screens should remind users of the availability of these utilities. Standardized filenaming conventions greatly enhance the applicability of global filename characters.
3. The EXIST and NOT EXIST conditions of the IF command are useful for checking the validity of filename parameters entered by the user. It must be remembered that pathnames cannot be used in this command in DOS versions earlier than 3.0. In such cases, it is necessary to change the directory to the current directory containing the file before the IF command is executed.
4. If it is necessary to make sure that the user has supplied the necessary arguments with a command, the IF command can be used for this purpose, as in:

    ```
    if "%1"=="" goto ERROR
    ```

    In other words, IF is checking for a blank (or nonexistent) %1 replaceable parameter; if this is true, the GOTO command is executed.
5. The ATTRIB command in DOS 3.0 and later is useful for protecting files from inadvertent erasure.
6. The COPY command can be used to combine files. Files may be appended to a source file, or they may be combined together into an new summary file. Both binary and ASCII (text) files can be combined, using different switch settings in the command.
7. Execution of the main body of a batch file program through a subroutine batch file is advisable if it is possible that the user may press <Ctrl> <Break> during program execution. This ensures that the utility will return to menu and not leave the user stuck in DOS somewhere. (See Appendix B for using subroutines in batch files.)

Adding and Deleting Menu Selections

Adding and deleting menu choices on the File Management menu does not require a great deal of effort. The sections that describe adding and deleting menu items in Chapter 10 should be consulted for users who wish to follow a step-by-step approach. There are only a few preliminary points that need to be made before the reader proceeds to that chapter.

The File Management menu is named FILEMENU.SCR and is located in the \HDU\FILE directory. All batch and screen files are located in that directory. When adding new menu choices, all batch and screen files should be placed in the \HDU\FILE directory.

There are no Y.BAT and N.BAT files in HDUFILE. This means that the "Continue (Y/N)?" prompt can be used in one new utility that occupies that directory. If more than one utility requires this feature, then it is necessary to create subdirectories for those utilities. This is because only one set of Y.BAT and N.BAT files can occupy the same directory. Likewise, there are no INSTRUCT.SCR files in this directory.

When creating utilities that use the ERASE command, be particularly alert to the possibility of error or misuse by the novice user. Try to anticipate every possible blunder someone might make in using the utility. Then try to build some controls into the batch file to account for these mistakes.

Some Possible Modification and Enhancements

A number of changes can be suggested for the File Management utilities. In addition, depending on the user's needs, more utilities can be developed that build upon the existing ones. The user may modify, delete, or add menu selections to the existing routines. This section describes some suggestions for additional menu choices.

Creating an Audit Trail of File Manipulations

The File Management utilities allow the user to archive files, move files, and combine one or more files. In order to keep track of these modifications, the utilities can be altered to automatically print the changes. This can be done by using DOS's redirection of output facilities.

DOS's redirection facilities allow output to be sent to a number of devices, including the printer. PRN is the reserved device name used by DOS to specify the printer. To direct the output to a printer the symbols

>PRN must follow the command. For example, entering the command at the system prompt:

```
C>DIR>PRN
```

produces a directory listing of the current directory and outputs the contents of the disk to a printer instead of the display. Consider the first 5 lines of the batch file for the File Archive utility described previously:

```
  ARCHIVE.BAT
1: echo off
2: cls
3: if "%1"=="" goto ERROR
4: echo Copying %1 to disk in drive A ...
5: copy %1 a:
```

Functionally speaking, the filename(s) that are entered after the command ARCHIVE are inserted as the %1 replaceable parameter. Thus, by using DOS's redirection features, the names of the files that are archived can be sent to the printer by changing line 5 to read:

```
copy %1 a:>prn
```

This same technique can be used on other utilities included in the File Management programs. For example, the user can obtain a printout of the names of files that have been moved, the names of files that have been combined, etc.

Creating an Archived File Inventory

DOS's redirection facilities also permit the user to output data to a text file. In a process similar to that described above, one can maintain an inventory file of all filenames that have been archived. Using the COPY command, one can continually append newly archived files to an Archived Files Inventory. Consider again the ARCHIVE.BAT file shown above. The output of the archive command can be redirected into a text file (ARCHIVE.TMP):

```
copy %1 a:>archive.txt
```

This temporary file will always hold the most recently archived filename(s).

File Management Utilities

The ">>" symbols could be used instead of of ">" to append output to an existing file:

```
copy %1 a:>>archive.txt
```

If the output is sent to the file ARCHIVE.TXT, the user then may go to this file and view a list of all files that have been archived. This file can be sorted into ascending or descending alphabetic order.

The user can also "time stamp" the last time/date that files were archived by using another feature of the COPY command. This feature allows the user to change the time and date on the file entry (normally, the time and date are NOT changed when the COPY command is used). Another line is added to the batch file after the append operation:

```
copy archive.txt+,,
```

The two commas in the example are used to define the end of the source file (ARCHIVE.TXT). Otherwise, DOS would expect another filename to follow the "+" sign.

Finally, if one wants to be super-organized, the floppy disks that contain the archived files can be numbered. Then, the user can manually edit (with EDLIN or another text editor) the ARCHIVE.TXT file and insert the number of the disk on which the archived file is located.

A Few Other Short Utilities

This section describes some possible additions to the File Management menu. These are utilities that use DOS features not covered in the existing utilities or commands found in the later versions of DOS. The descriptions basically only cover the actual program files.

Copy, Erase, and Rename Utilities

These utilities might be helpful for users who wish to structure all aspects of file management in a menu and batch-file environment. This may be a necessity if the hard disk system is being used by DOS novices. In the case of ERASE, the user may wish to build into it an audit trail such as the one described for the File Archive utility.

The batch file that runs these routines would not have to be very complicated. For example, the following commands would suffice for a rename routine:

```
 1: echo off
 2: cls
 3: if "%2"=="" goto ERROR
 4: echo Renaming %1 to %2 ...
 5: rename %1 %2
 6: goto DONE
 7: :ERROR
 8: echo You must enter two arguments with the
       command. Try again.
 9: :DONE
10: pause
11: cd \hdu\file
12: cls
13: type filemenu.scr
14: echo ENTER SELECTION:
15: prompt $e[22;18H
16: setscrn
```

The use of the replaceable parameters would require the use of a preliminary instruction screen to prompt the user for input. The name of this batch file would be the command that preceded the arguments. The IF command in line 3 checks for the required arguments.

A Copy utility could use the same batch file, substituting a COPY command for the RENAME command. The routine for an Erase utility also could follow the same format. Instead of the RENAME command in the above batch file, the ERASE command would be used, with only one replaceable parameter. For users concerned about inadvertent erasure, the ERASE command could be preceded by a "Y/N" prompt asking users if they wish to copy the file to an archive directory. (Or, for the truly paranoid, the files could be copied automatically.) However, if disk space usage is an issue, this may not be a desirable feature.

A Multiple Directory Copy Utility

For users with DOS 3.2 or later, a utility can be added that uses the DOS command XCOPY. This command was introduced in DOS 3.2. It allows

File Management Utilities

the user to copy all files in a directory plus the files of any subdirectories of that directory. This command can be particularly useful if the user is copying an entire floppy diskette with multiple directories to a hard disk. Or, if a system has two hard disks, one can use this command to copy large chunks of one disk to another. A final use of the XCOPY command might be to create a backup disk on a removable cartridge (when the BACKUP format is not desired).

The XCOPY command has many switches that involve the use of dates, prompting, the archive bit, and the creation of subdirectories. No attempt is made here to use all of these in the suggested utilities. The reader should refer to the Appendix A for a discussion of this command.

A utility that copies a floppy diskette with subdirectories might have the following format:

```
 1: echo off
 2: cls
 3: echo Insert the floppy diskette in Drive A...
 4: xcopy a:\ c:\ /s /w
 5: cd \hdu\file
 6: cls
 7: type filemenu.scr
 8: echo ENTER SELECTION:
 9: prompt $e[22;18H
10: setscrn
```

This utility might be called something like "Copy Entire Floppy To Drive C." The XCOPY command in line 4 copies all files on the floppy diskette to drive C. The /S switch includes files in any subdirectories, creating the necessary directories on the hard disk if they do not already exist. The /W switch makes the XCOPY command wait for the user to insert the floppy diskette in the drive before beginning the search for the source files. Together with the ECHO command preceding it, the following message is displayed:

```
Insert the floppy diskette in Drive A...
Press any key to begin copying file(s)
```

A /P switch could be added that would produce a DOS "Y/N" prompt before each file copied. This would permit copying on a file-by-file basis.

8.3
SOME BACKGROUND INFORMATION ON FILE MANAGEMENT AND HARD DISK MAINTENANCE

When it comes to performing hard disk housekeeping tasks, it is particularly important to be able to quickly locate and identify files. This is because a substantial portion of a user's time must be spent on housekeeping (i.e., moving files from one area of the disk to another, renaming files, combining files, and so on). Since the user is dealing with a fixed-capacity disk, he or she also will periodically want to weed out seldom-used or duplicate files. This can be a tedious, time-consuming task if the user must retrieve every file to determine its contents.

A hard disk system can be organized so that files can be easily identified, located, and manipulated. Using filenaming conventions and a hierarchical directory structure, files can be organized in two fundamental ways:

1. Files may have common identifiers in their filenames so that it is apparent to the user that they have some commonality in content.
2. Files can be logically grouped together in one or more subdirectories, each subdirectory containing files with similar contents.

Using Filenaming Conventions

Filenaming conventions refer to a general agreement on the usage of filenames to identify and describe the contents of files. A carefully designed filenaming scheme is essential to a well-organized hard disk system for three reasons:

1. Well-designed filenaming conventions describe and/or abstract the contents of a file so that it is meaningful to multiple users. Filenaming conventions also provide a framework for naming subsequently created files.
2. Filenaming conventions greatly increase the efficiency of file management and maintenance if they are used in conjunction with DOS commands and global filename characters.
3. Filenaming conventions allow the user to sort his or her directories and obtain an inventory of relevant files. For example, if date information is included in the filenaming scheme, sorting the directory will provide a list by file type in the date order. Although DOS in-

cludes its own date information in the directory listing, the date changes with each update to a file. In contrast, the date information in the filename always reflects the creation or start date of a file.

Filenaming conventions are best established at the time the machine is first installed. This allows one to define a scheme that can be readily understood by multiple users. Users can name new files in accordance with the filenaming conventions, and more importantly, they can quickly locate and identify preexisting files. As the volume of files increases over time, filenaming standards reduce the amount of time required to perform many managerial tasks associated with disk organization and file maintenance.

Using Column Positions in Filenames

Filenaming conventions can be designed in a number of different ways, depending on the needs of the end user and the various types of applications. Perhaps the best way of establishing filenaming conventions is to assign meaning to each of the eight column positions in a filename.

To design a filenaming scheme using column positions, a number of decisions have to be made. Most importantly, the user must decide how to categorize application types (and subtypes, if necessary). Once types and subtypes have been identified, each one must be assigned a unique code (either alpha or numeric).

The user must also decide the detail level that he or she wants to build into the filename. For example, a filename could simply indicate that the file is a memo written on a particular date. Or the filename could contain a reference number to indicate the subject of the memo, the recipient of the memo, and so on.

In designing a filenaming scheme, it is important to construct it with enough flexibility so that more detail may be added at a later time. This could be accomplished by including several "open" positions within the eight-column limitation. When not necessary to the identification of a file, the position(s) could always contain the number "0." If this type of strategy is used, the detail level of the filenaming scheme can be easily modified. Another code number or letter can be added rather than adding or deleting the position itself.

Finally, the user must decide on a logical order of the codes for the various column positions. This order must be consistent for all files on the hard disk. The user then is able to gain maximum benefit from DOS file management features such as directory sorts and global filename characters.

This order also should be meaningful to the user. For example, if the most critical identifier of the data files is application type, then this code should precede all others.

Using Meaningful Syllables in Filenames

An alternative to using column positions to establish a filename convention scheme is to use short, meaningful syllables within the filename. Thus, documentation files may be labelled "DOC," model-related files "MOD," and so on. For example, a file containing expenses accrued for the month of February 1987 might be called "EXP0287." Meaningful syllables can be used very effectively under certain circumstances:

1. When all files to be stored on the hard disk are known at the onset; therefore, a great deal of flexibility for handling new filenames is not required.
2. When they are used in conjunction with a highly organized, many-layered, tree-structured directory. In this case, files can be organized into directories and subdirectories by file type, subtype, date, and so on. If the tree-structured directory contains too many levels, however, DOS search and retrieval time will be quite sluggish.
3. The meaningful syllable always appears in the same column positions for each filename. This permits the use of DOS utilities with global filename characters.

The greatest advantage of using this type of filenaming convention is that the first-time user can readily recognize filenames and identify file contents. Extensive documentation on the meaning of each filename column position is not required.

Using Global Filename Characters with Filenaming Conventions

DOS provides the user with two characters that can be used to perform operations on groups of files rather than individual files. These characters (the symbols ? and *) are called Global Filename Characters or wild cards. Use of the ? character in a filename or extension means that any character can occupy the position. Use of the * character in a filename or extension means that one or more characters can occupy the position.

Used with a hard disk in which filenaming conventions have been established, global filename characters can be extraordinarily useful when performing operations on groups of like files.

Consider a filenaming convention in which monthly expense files are labelled with the prefix EXP followed by a two-digit month and a two-digit year. For example, the file for February 1987 expense data would be called EXP0287. If one wants to archive all expense files for 1986 from a subdirectory called EXPENSE into a subdirectory containing only expense data for 1986 (called EXPENSE6), the following command would be issued:

```
COPY C:\EXPENSE\EXP??86.* C:\EXPENSE6\EXP??86.*
```

Once the 1986 expense files are copied into the archive directory (EXPENSE6), they can be erased in the current EXPENSE directory:

```
ERASE EXP??86.*
```

Using the ? global filename character, the user must include only the prefix code for file type ("EXP") and the year ("86") in the command specification. If, for example, 50 or more files are included in this population, performing this function without using global filename characters could be a highly time-consuming process.

Setting Up a Hierarchical File and Directory Structure

Information stored on the fixed disk of the XT and AT can be organized by function and type. This is one of the most important features of DOS, since thousands of files may be placed on the fixed disk. The storage capacity of a 20-megabyte fixed disk is approximately 56 times greater than that of a single 360-KB floppy disk and 17 times that of a high-capacity disk. With a large amount of information stored on the fixed disk, locating a specific file could be a slow process. However, with DOS, quick access of information on the fixed disk can be achieved through the use of hierarchical directories.

The first task in designing a hierarchical directory system is deciding how the directory system is to be structured. DOS gives the user a great deal of flexibility in setting up a hierarchical directory. When a disk is formatted, DOS starts the basic organization of the directory system by creating one main directory. The structure of the directory system after this point is determined by the user.

Structuring a Hierarchical Directory

The starting point for all hierarchical directories is the root directory. All formatted disks contain a root directory; in DOS versions 2 and 3 the root directory may contain programs, data files, or the names of other directories (subdirectories). However, most individuals prefer to limit the root directory to system or program files. Each directory within the root directory may contain its own set of programs, data files, or directories (sub-subdirectories). This type of organization is referred to as a tree-structured directory. The branching of directories into subdirectories may be extended out as far as necessary.

Hierarchical directories may be structured in any manner that is convenient for the user. To demonstrate how a directory might be organized, consider the following example. The fixed disk on a PC-AT is used to store DOS files, a word processing program, and a spreadsheet program. The root directory contains the DOS files and separate directories for the word processing and spreadsheet programs:

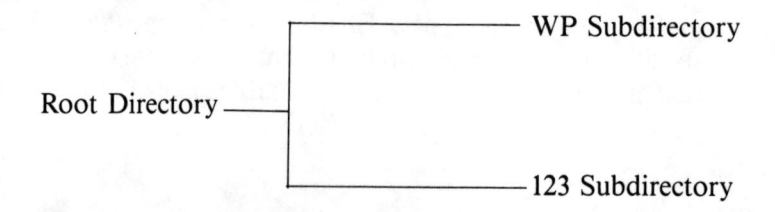

```
                          ┌─────── WP Subdirectory
Root Directory ───────────┤
                          └─────── 123 Subdirectory
```

The word processing directory (WP) might contain all the files necessary to run *DisplayWrite3* as well as three further subdirectories of its own.

```
\WP\DOC (Documentation Subdirectory)
\WP\MEMO (Memo Subdirectory)
\WP\ADMIN (Administrative Reports Subdirectory)
```

Each of the word processing subdirectories might in turn contain further subdirectory divisions. For example, the \WP\MEMO subdirectory might contain separate subdirectories by month. Thus, the subdirectory structure might contain:

```
\WP\MEMO\JAN
\WP\MEMO\FEB
\WP\MEMO\MAR
etc.
```

File Management Utilities

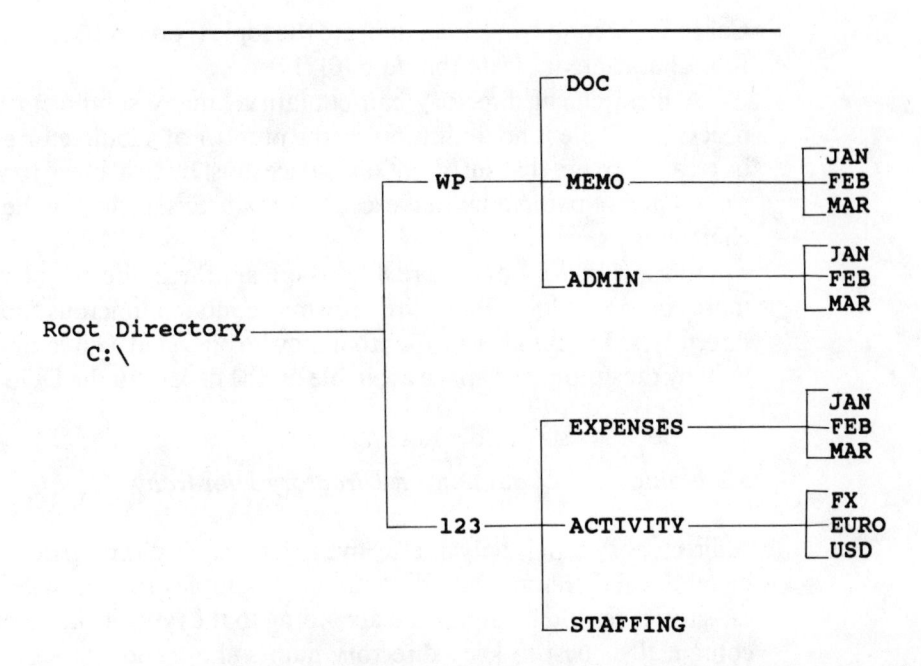

```
                              ┌─ DOC
                              │
                   ┌─ WP ─────┼─ MEMO ──────┬─ JAN
                   │          │             ├─ FEB
                   │          │             └─ MAR
                   │          │
                   │          └─ ADMIN ─────┬─ JAN
                   │                        ├─ FEB
Root Directory ────┤                        └─ MAR
    C:\            │
                   │          ┌─ EXPENSES ──┬─ JAN
                   │          │             ├─ FEB
                   │          │             └─ MAR
                   │          │
                   └─ 123 ────┼─ ACTIVITY ──┬─ FX
                              │             ├─ EURO
                              │             └─ USD
                              │
                              └─ STAFFING
```

Figure 8.13. Sample Hierarchical Directory Structure

A typical hierarchical structure showing these and other subdirectories is displayed in Figure 8.13.

Hierarchical Directory Paths

Hierarchical directories allow DOS to quickly locate a specified file. This is because DOS sees only the files contained in the specified directory when it is searching for a file. The system is able to do this by using a pathname that precedes the filename. A pathname specifies each directory through which DOS must move in order to access the specific file. Each directory in the pathname is separated by the backslash symbol (\). For example, using the hierarchy described above, the path from the Root Directory to a January 19, 1987 memo would be:

```
C:\WP\MEMOS\JAN\NCFX0119.TXT
```

Note that a backslash also separates the directory name from the filename. The filename is NCFX0119. The first two letters indicate the author (Nancy

Cain); the second two letters indicate the topic (Foreign Exchange); the last four characters indicate the date (01/19).

A hierarchical directory can contain as many subdirectory levels as necessary. There is no limitation on the number of subdirectories that may be created, except that sufficient disk space must be available. However, DOS cannot accept pathnames that exceed 63 characters, including the backslash characters.

In the directory of Figure 8.13, there are three directory levels. Many more could be added. Each directory may contain numerous files and subdirectories. The number of files that may be placed in a directory is limited only by the amount of space available on the disk or in the DOS partition.

Managing and Organizing a Directory Hierarchy

A directory system is only as effective as its organization is efficient. A good hierarchical directory should be no more complex than is necessary. Subdirectories should be organized according to the type of files that they will contain. It is best to keep directory names short and simple.

Many applications programs allow the user to store and access data files in multiple subdirectories from within the specific program. If users of such programs are likely to generate hundreds of data files, it is a good idea to create several subdirectories for the program's files. In a program such as *Lotus 1-2-3*, it takes much less time to retrieve a file when the user is not forced to search through a list of all *1-2-3* data files stored on the fixed disk.

chapter 9

HELP Screen Utilities

HELP screens can be very useful tools to have available on a hard disk system. They can eliminate the need to keep a DOS manual, a BASIC reference guide, and a book on DOS next to one's system. However, the disk-space overhead can be very costly for HELP files that are used infrequently. Thus, one must be very careful to choose what information is included on HELP screens and how they are integrated into the system as a whole.

What Are the HELP Screen Utilities?

The HELP Screen utilities contain nine HELP screens. These screens include:

- Documentation that is not easily accessible (e.g., a table of the ASCII Extended Character Set)
- Documentation that is hard to decipher or located in a technical reference manual (e.g., setting the screen attributes, color, and cursor position)
- Documentation that is a condensed version of many pages of text (e.g., the DOS, EDLIN, and batch file commands)

Why Are They Used?

The nine HELP screens were chosen as samples of HELP screens that one may want to incorporate into a hard disk management system. They are useful models for creating HELP screens using the ASCII Extended Character Set.

How to Use the Utilities

The HELP Screen utilities are accessed when selection 6 is chosen from the *Hard Disk Manager* menu. This selection changes the directory to \HDU\HELP and displays the HELP utilities menu. Any of the ten screen selections can be chosen by typing the number of the desired HELP screen.

If at any time, the user chooses not to proceed with the utilities, the <F1> key can be pressed to return to the first menu. After displaying any of the HELP screens, the user also is given the option of returning to the HELP utilities menu or returning to the *Hard Disk Manager* master menu.

Organization of the HELP Screen Utilities

The HELP screens are located in the following subdirectories:

```
\HDU\HELP
\HDU\HELP\DOS
\HDU\HELP\BATCH
\HDU\HELP\EDLIN
```

Seven single-screen HELP files are located in \HDU\HELP. Separate subdirectories exist for the DOS, batch file, and EDLIN HELP files. All HELP files are text files with the extension .HLP. The directory and file structure is presented in Figure 9.1.

The initial menu screen is called HELP.SCR. It gives the users ten HELP screens from which to choose.

Activation of the Utilities

Selection 6 on the main utility menu accesses the HELP Screen utilities by activating the 6.BAT file in the \HDU directory. It contains the following commands:

HELP Screen Utilities 187

```
      6.BAT
1:  echo off
2:  cls
3:  cd help
4:  type help.scr
5:  echo ENTER SELECTION:
6:  prompt $e[22;18H
```

The functions of this file are to change the current directory to \HDU\HELP, display the HELP Screen utility menu (HELP.SCR), and position the cursor at the end of the ENTER SELECTION: prompt.

```
      C:\HDU\HELP        <DIR>

              ASCII.HLP         1.BAT
              ESCAPE.HLP        2.BAT
              CURSOR.HLP        3.BAT
              COLOR.HLP         4.BAT
              SCREEN.HLP        5.BAT
              AUTOEXEC.BAT      6.BAT
              CONFIG.HLP        7.BAT
              HELP.SCR          8.BAT
              Y.BAT             9.BAT
              N.BAT            10.BAT

      C:\HDU\HELP\EDLIN      <DIR>

              EDLIN.HLP
              Y.BAT
              N.BAT

      C:\HDU\HELP\DOS        <DIR>

              DOS.HLP
              Y.BAT
              N.BAT

      C:\HDU\HELP\BATCH      <DIR>

              BATCH.HLP
              Y.BAT
              N.BAT
```

Figure 9.1. Directory and File Structure for the HELP Utilities

9.1
THE HELP SCREEN UTILITIES

Choosing the HELP Screen option on the main utilities menu produces the display shown in Figure 9.2. This screen displays the ten HELP screens available.

This is a very basic utility. When a selection is chosen, the TYPE command is used to display one or more screens. Only the HELP screens for DOS, EDLIN, and Batch Files contain greater than one screen. If the utility contains greater than one screen, the screen passes information through the MORE filter so that only one screen is displayed at a time. At the end of the multiple screen HELP files the user is given the option to redisplay the screens:

```
View Screens Again (Y/N)?
```

At the end of each single screen HELP facility, the user is prompted with:

```
Return to HELP Menu (Y/N)?
```

It is important to note that the HELP screens are accessible only through the HELP menu. This was a design decision to reduce the complexity and

```
========== HELP SCREEN UTILITIES ==========

    1.  ASCII Graphics          6.  EDLIN Commands
    2.  AUTOEXEC.BAT            7.  Escape Characters
    3.  Batch File Commands     8.  Set Cursor Position
    4.  CONFIG.SYS              9.  Set Screen Attributes
    5.  DOS Commands           10.  Set Screen Colors

            <<<<< Press F1 to Return >>>>>
```

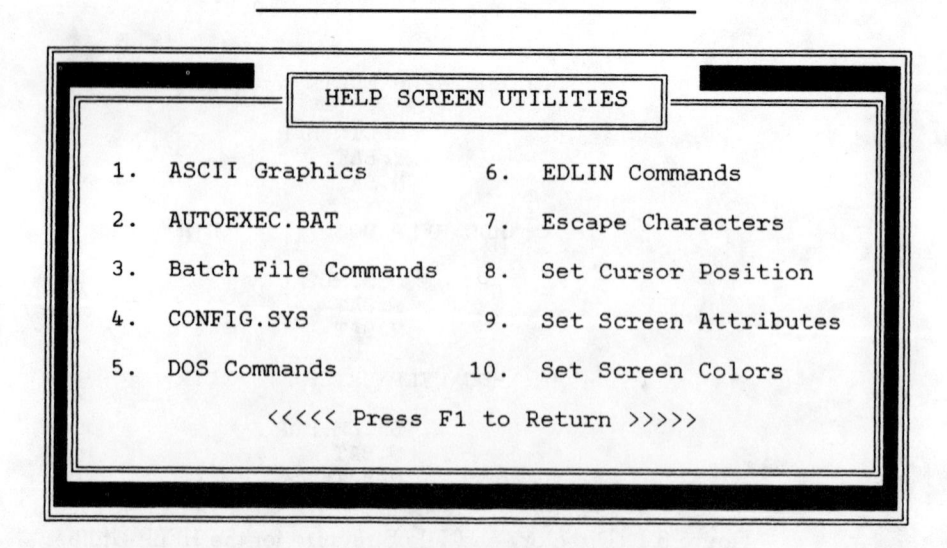

Figure 9.2. HELP Screen Utility Menu

overhead associated with integrating HELP screens as a function key. Of course, it is possible to assign the HELP function to a function key. This option may be attractive to the user and will be discussed in the section on modifying the HELP Screen utility.

An overview of the contents of each HELP screen is described below:

ASCII Graphics HELP

The ASCII Graphics HELP screen is a table of the ASCII Extended Character Set, ASCII codes 176 through 223. These characters are used to produce single-width, double-width, and combination-width borders. Also, the ASCII values for block characters are included. The table of ASCII values can be found in Appendix E.

AUTOEXEC.BAT HELP

The AUTOEXEC.BAT File Creation HELP screen provides a definition of the AUTOEXEC.BAT screen and describes its usage. Two methods for creating an AUTOEXEC.BAT file are given: the COPY CON Method, using the DOS COPY command; and the text editor method, using EDLIN.

Batch File Commands HELP

The Batch File Commands HELP screen is made up of two screens. They contain the command name and the format of all batch file commands.

CONFIG.SYS HELP

The CONFIG.SYS File HELP screen provides a definition of CONFIG.SYS and describes the two most common commands that it contains. These commands are the ANSI.SYS device driver (the Americal National Standards Institute of terminal codes) and the BUFFERS= command.

DOS Commands HELP

The DOS Commands HELP screen is made up of four screens. They contain the DOS command name, the format for using the command, and a description of the optional switch settings. Most of the commonly used commands are included.

EDLIN Commands HELP

The EDLIN Commands HELP screen is made up of three screens. They contain the EDLIN command name, the command notation, the format for using the command, and a key to the notations used.

Escape Characters HELP

The Escape Characters HELP screen describes the definition and usage of escape characters in controlling various aspects of the display screen. Two methods are presented for creating escape characters: A method using the DOS PROMPT command, and a method using the EDLIN text editor.

Setting the Cursor Position HELP

This is a fairly unknown but extraordinarily useful feature of DOS. The Cursor Position HELP screen describes the cursor position functions, the control codes they use, and a key to the notations used.

Setting Screen Attributes HELP

The Screen Attributes HELP screen describes the functions available for altering various aspects of the display screen. The screen also supplies the control codes for each attribute and a key to the notations used.

Setting Screen Colors HELP

The Screen Color HELP screens provide a list of background and foreground color options, the control codes required to activate them, and a key to the notations used.

The HELP Screen Program Files

The HELP Screen utility is made up of a single menu (HELP.SCR), ten batch files (1.BAT through 10.BAT), and ten HELP screen files (.HLP files).

HELP Screen Utilities

In addition, two confirmation prompt files (Y.BAT and N.BAT) are used for the three utilities that contain multiple screens. A second set of Y.BAT and N.BAT files is used with the single-screen HELP facilities to give the user the option of returning to the HELP Screen menu.

All of the HELP screens use the TYPE command to display HELP (.HLP) screens. All HELP screens also allow the user to either return to the HELP menu or to the *Hard Disk Manager* menu. The multiple-screen HELP files contain an option to redisplay the screen contents or to return to the HELP screen main menu. Thus, there are two different categories of batch files for menu selections, depending on the number of screens contained in each HELP option:

1. Batch files for HELP facilities with more than one screen need special commands to break them up into a series of connected display screens. They also need commands that permit redisplay of the screens.
2. There are also batch files for HELP facilities that are contained in a single display screen.

Multiple HELP Screen Batch Files

The batch files used to display multiple screens include the following menu selections:

Selection 3. Batch File Commands
Selection 5. DOS Commands
Selection 6. EDLIN Commands

The batch files used to display and redisplay these selections are described below. Selection 3 (Batch File Commands) is used as an example:

```
    3.BAT
1:  echo off
2:  cd batch
3:  cls
4:  prompt View Screens Again (Y/N)?
5:  type batch.hlp | more
```

The 3.BAT batch file turns off the command display, changes the directory to \HDU\HELP\BATCH, and then clears the screen. Prior to the display of the HELP screen, the PROMPT command is used to set the selection prompt. It precedes the TYPE command so as not to interfere with the MORE filter.

Using the MORE Filter

In the last line of the batch file, the appropriate HELP screen is typed, using the MORE filter. The MORE filter displays a multiple screen HELP file, one screen at a time. At the bottom of each screen display, MORE places the message:

```
--- MORE ---
```

In order to ensure that the display contains only one screen and not parts of another, blank lines must be inserted in the EDLIN file to position the screens properly on the display. Thus, three to four blank lines might precede any of the multiple screens.

It is also important to note that the PROMPT command precedes the display of the HELP screen. This is because the MORE command resets certain attributes of the display screen in order to scroll one display screen at a time. If additional commands must follow the MORE command, ECHO OFF has to be reset; the result is that extraneous command information (e.g., ECHO OFF) appears on the screen display. To avoid this problem, the PROMPT command, which normally ends a selection batch file, in this case precedes the MORE command.

At the bottom of the last screen, the prompt "View Screens Again (Y/N)?" is displayed (see Figure 9.3). This confirmation prompt is included so that the user can opt to redisplay the screen rather than return to the HELP menu and choose the selection again. Thus, a **Y** answer permits the user to rescroll through the previous HELP screens. An **N** answer returns the user to the HELP.SCR menu.

The Redisplay Confirmation Prompt Batch Files

Confirmation prompt batch files Y.BAT and N.BAT are located in each of the subdirectories for the three commands. Selection 3 (Batch File Commands) is used again as an example. The Y.BAT batch file contains the commands shown on page 193.

HELP Screen Utilities

```
          BATCH FILE COMMANDS (CONTINUED)
String1==String2    IF [string1==string2] [command]
Errorlevel          IF ERRORLEVEL [#]
Pause               PAUSE [text of message]
Remark              REM [remark text]
Shift               SHIFT
                                              Screen 2
```

View Screens Again (Y/N)?

Figure 9.3. Example of "View Screen Again" Prompt

```
   Y.BAT
1: echo off
2: cls
3: prompt View Screens Again (Y/N)?
4: type batch.hlp | more
```

This batch file redisplays the three screens that make up Batch File Commands HELP facility. It is identical to 3.BAT except that the directory is not changed since the user is still in \HDU\HELP\BATCH.

The N.BAT file is a bit more complicated since it must return the user to the main HELP menu (HELP.SCR) located in \HDU\HELP. The N.BAT batch file contains the following commands:

```
   N.BAT
1: echo off
2: cd ..
3: cls
4: type help.scr
5: echo ENTER SELECTION:
6: prompt $e[22;18H
7: setscrn
```

This batch file returns the user to the parent directory (\HDU\HELP) with the command:

```
cd ..
```

The HELP Screen menu is displayed along with the ENTER SELECTION: prompt. The cursor position is reset for this screen with the PROMPT command. The last line executes SETSCRN.BAT. This batch file resets the screen display attributes (see Chapter 5 for more information about this command).

Single HELP Screen Batch Files

Batch files used to display HELP screens that are contained on a single screen do not require the use of the MORE command. They also do not require a screen redisplay facility. These batch files have the following format:

```
    #.BAT
1:  echo off
2:  cls
3:  prompt $e[22;30H
4:  type #.HLP
```

Since there is only one screen involved, the prompt at the end of the screen is different. Instead of "View Screens Again (Y/N)?" there is a "Return to HELP Menu (Y/N)?" prompt. A response of **Y** displays HELP.SCR again, whereas an **N** response returns the user to the *Hard Disk Manager* menu. This batch file has the following format:

```
    Y.BAT
1:  echo off
2:  cls
3:  type help.scr
4:  echo ENTER SELECTION:
5:  prompt $e[22;18H
6:  setscrn
```

In this batch file, the HELP.SCR is redisplayed and the cursor is set at the end of the ENTER SELECTION: prompt. The last line executes SETSCRN.BAT.

The N.BAT program file has the following format:

```
    N.BAT
1:  echo off
2:  cls
```

HELP Screen Utilities

```
3: cd ..
4: type hdu.scr
5: echo ENTER SELECTION:
6: prompt $e[22;18H
7: setscrn
```

The N.BAT file changes the directory back to the parent \HDU directory and displays the main *Hard Disk Manager* menu, HDU.SCR. The cursor is then positioned at the end of the ENTER SELECTION: prompt, and the display attributes are reset with SETSCRN.BAT.

HELP selections that are contained on a single display screen include:

1. ASCII Graphics
2. AUTOEXEC.BAT
4. CONFIG.SYS
7. Escape Characters
8. Set Cursor Position
9. Set Screen Attributes
10. Set Screen Colors

9.2
MODIFYING THE HELP SCREEN UTILITIES

Any number of HELP screens can be added to this utility. Similarly, existing HELP screens may be deleted or replaced. In addition, a facility may be set up in which the HELP utilities are activated by a function key rather than a menu screen.

Adding or Modifying HELP Screens

In order to add a HELP Screen, the following steps must be taken:

1. A new HELP screen (.HLP) must be created using EDLIN or a text editor. The user should refer to Chapter 6, "Screen Design Utility," for assistance in creating this screen. This screen should be named for the utility contents.
2. A new selection number batch file (#.BAT) must be created.

3. The HELP menu (HELP.SCR) must be modified to include another selection number. It is advisable to attempt to insert the selection number on the same size screen. Then, the prompt command and cursor setting will not have to be adjusted. Inserting a new selection number can be done using EDLIN. The user should refer to Chapter 10, "Modifying the Hard Disk Utilities," for assistance on altering .SCR files.
4. If the new HELP screen is contained on a single screen, no new directory must be created. However, if the HELP facility contains multiple screens, the MORE command and the Y/N confirmation batch files must be included. This will necessitate setting up a new directory.

HELP screens can be modified using EDLIN. Again, the user might want to refer to Chapter 10.

Deleting HELP Screens

The reverse of the process described above for adding HELP screens must be followed.

1. The HELP screen (.HLP) is deleted using the ERASE or DEL commands.
2. The existing selection number batch file (#.BAT) must be deleted.
3. The HELP menu (HELP.SCR) must be modified. The selection is deleted and the other selections may have to be renumbered.
4. If the HELP screen to be deleted is contained in a subdirectory (i.e., if it contains multiple screens), the subdirectory should be removed. This is done with the Remove Directory (RD) command. In order to remove the directory, it must be empty. Therefore, the corresponding Y.BAT and N. BAT files must be erased using the ERASE or DELETE command.

Creating a HELP Function Key

A HELP function key may be created that allows the user to access the HELP screens from any directory. Perhaps the best way to do this is to reassign a function key (any key but <F1>, since that key is used in the *Hard Disk Manager* utilities for a Return to Menu function).

One point to keep in mind is that function key reassignment can be accomplished not only with the <F1> through <F10> function keys, but

HELP Screen Utilities

also with these keys in combination with the <Alt>, <Ctrl>, and Shift keys. Thus, there are 40 possible combinations of function keys: Unshifted, Shift plus the function key, <Ctrl> plus the function key, and <Alt> plus the function key. Consult Chapter 5 for a discussion of key reassignment.

In assigning HELP to a function key, it is a good idea to use a key assignment that is not likely to be accidently pressed. (For example, if the <F2> key is used, its position next to the <Esc> key makes it vulnerable.) This can be annoying.

The ideal situation for use of function keys for HELP would be to let the user call up HELP screens from any location. When the user finished with the HELP screen, pressing a key would return him or her to that same location. The easy part of this process is displaying the HELP screens; the hard part is getting back to the screen where the HELP was invoked. Unfortunately, there is no quick and easy solution.

The key is to leave the user in the current directory. The main HELP screen could be displayed with a path to the directory containing this screen. Items on the HELP menu could be uniquely labeled, such as H1, H2, etc., instead of the usual 1, 2, 3, or A, B, C. The batch files that ran these topics would have to be placed in all directories. The HELP screens for the individual menu items also would be displayed via a path to the directory containing the batch files. Here is what should happen:

Action	Response	Main Command Executed
1. Press Function Key	Display HELP.SCR	type \hdu\help\help.scr
2. Select HELP Topic	Display TOPIC .SCR	type \hdu\help\topic.scr
3. Press any key	Return	AGAIN.BAT

The trick would be to redisplay the submenu or information screen for whatever directory location happened to be current. This could be accomplished by having a batch file (called AGAIN.BAT, for example) that did just that. It would be found in every directory and it would be different for every directory, since it would be displaying a different menu screen. Here is a summary of the batch files:

1. The user presses a function key that executes a root directory batch file called HELP.BAT, which contains the following commands:

```
HELP.BAT
1: echo off
2: cls
3: type \hdu\help\help.scr
```

```
4:  echo ENTER SELECTION:
5:  prompt $e[22;18H
6:  setscrn
```

The last line is only necessary if the HELP menu resets the display screen attributes, as the *Hard Disk Manager* menus do. This line executes SETSCRN.BAT. (The functions of this command are described in Chapter 5.)

2. The menu selections are numbered H1 through H10. Every directory would contain the execution programs, H1.BAT through H10.BAT files. The individual HELP screens would be located in a single subdirectory, \HDU\HELP. The commands in all of the batch files executed by these menu items would be relatively similar, except for the HELP screen displayed. For example, the first screen might be for ASCII HELP and might be called H1.BAT:

```
    H1.BAT
1:  echo off
2:  cls
3:  type \hdu\help\ascii.hlp
4:  pause
5:  again
```

3. The last command **AGAIN** is a batch file called AGAIN.BAT that also would be found in every directory. However, each batch file would redisplay the menu for its own directory. Suppose that one wanted ASCII HELP while in the process of creating a screen design. In the subdirectory \HDU\DESIGN, the AGAIN.BAT file would have to contain the following commands:

```
    AGAIN.BAT
1:  echo off
2:  cls
3:  type design.scr
4:  echo ENTER SELECTION:
5:  prompt $e[22;18H
```

The elegance of the process might be improved with a little more effort. Instead of using the PAUSE command in H1.BAT to keep the screen from scrolling, confirmation prompts could be used instead. This would be similar to the "View Again (Y/N)?" or "Return to Help Menu (Y/N)?" prompting that was employed in the *Hard Disk Manager* HELP screens. The **N** response would call the AGAIN.BAT file, whereas the **Y** response would execute the H1.BAT file again. However, this would require Y.BAT and N.BAT files in every directory, which would be a problem if other such files already exist.

9.3 SOME BACKGROUND INFORMATION ON HELP SCREENS

HELP screens can be very useful to some individuals and a total annoyance to others. Thus, it is important to determine who will be using a particular system—whether it is one user or multiple users, and the skill levels of each. It is also important to determine what applications the users typically use so that appropriate HELP screens can be developed.

HELP screens are particularly useful if they contain information that is not digested into one source (e.g., using the ASCII Extended Character Set is described in one set of documentation, whereas the ASCII Extended Character Set symbols are listed in the BASIC reference guide). They are also particularly useful if they contain information that is not readily available.

A few rules can be used when developing HELP screens to ensure that they are an effective use of hard disk resources:

1. Plan ahead of time:
   - determine how many users access the system
   - determine the skill levels of users
   - determine which applications are currently in use
   - determine the future plans of users
   - review the documentation currently available to the users
   - determine how much space is available on the system and the maximum percentage of disk storage that should be occupied by HELP screens
2. Ensure that HELP screens are accessible. They might be accessed through a menu system, by depressing a function key, or by including HELP information on informational screens used to perform certain commands. It also might be a good idea to provide a print facility with a HELP screen. This way, the user can refer to a digested HELP screen as other functions are performed.
3. Ensure that HELP screens are readable. Carefully plan how much information can be placed on a screen and how to present that information in a condensed way that the user can follow. Expect to

draft and rewrite the HELP screen information several times before it is right. If necessary, spread HELP information over several screens and link them together with DOS commands.
4. Ensure that HELP screens are useful. Interpret and abstract difficult information rather than simply copying incomprehensible information on a screen. Attempt to tie together information contained in a number of sources. Eliminate the need for users to have multiple manuals stacked around their computer.
5. Use consistent filenaming conventions if there are going to be many HELP screens. This way, DOS global filename characters can be used to delete or move these files when necessary.
6. Use consistent layout formats when developing screens.
7. Be creative—there is no end to the amount of useful HELP facilities that can be developed for novice and intermediate users.

chapter 10

Modifying the Hard Disk Utilities

This book/disk begins with a premise that is quite different from other software packages. The utilities in this package are meant to be customized—modified to suit the needs of the individual user. Indeed, they are designed to be modified by nonprogrammers, by individuals with nothing more than a working knowledge of the operating system. Of course, that is a easy statement to make. What users also need are the tools necessary to make modifications and an understanding of the framework in which the programs were created.

This chapter is designed to prepare the user for modifying the utilities. It describes the analytical process required to determine how utilities might be changed and how screen and batch files are modified and deleted.

It is assumed that one does not have to have any software except DOS. Therefore, all explanations use the EDLIN text editor. For further information on EDLIN, the user should refer to Appendix C.

10.1 ANALYZING UTILITY FILE CHANGES

Once the user has decided what utility he or she wants to modify, two things must be determined: The extent of the desired changes, and the relative benefits to be gained by changing the utility. Then, all users must go through the following process:

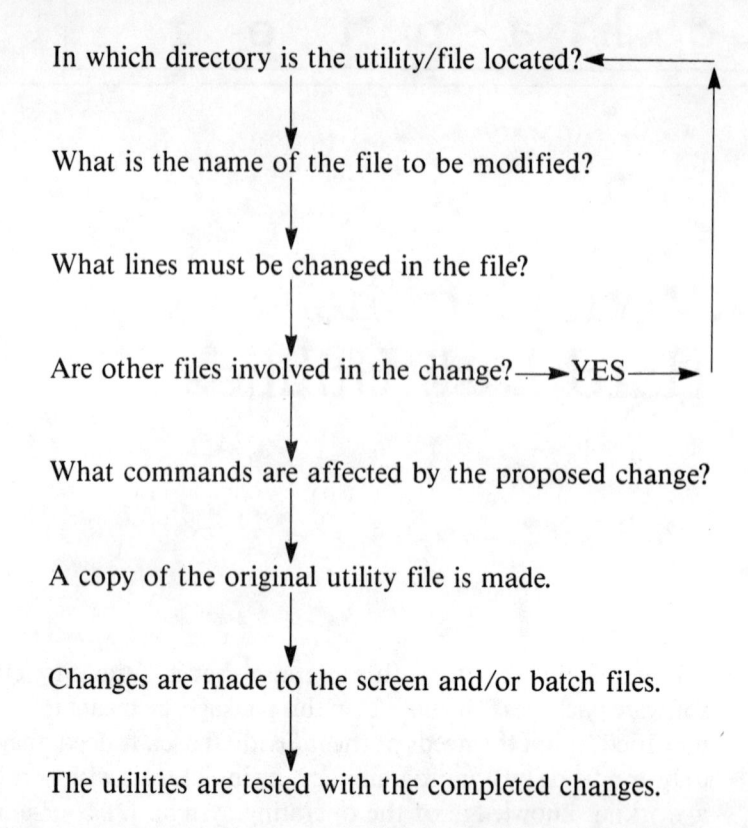

In which directory is the utility/file located? ←┐
        ↓   │
What is the name of the file to be modified?   │
        ↓   │
What lines must be changed in the file?   │
        ↓   │
Are other files involved in the change? ──►YES───┘
        ↓
What commands are affected by the proposed change?
        ↓
A copy of the original utility file is made.
        ↓
Changes are made to the screen and/or batch files.
        ↓
The utilities are tested with the completed changes.

This is a process whereby the user must determine the nature and extent of the change. Then, conceptually the user must trace the change through the entire file and directory structure. The best place to begin this analysis is by examining the diagrams of the directory and file structures at the beginning of each utility chapter.

Some Basic Utility Information

In order to trace through modifications, the user must familiarize himself or herself with the directory, subdirectory and file structures of the *Hard Disk Manager*.

Directory/Subdirectory Structure

All of the utilities are located in the directory \HDU. Each utility is then located in a subdirectory or a number of subdirectories located beneath \HDU. The utility locations are shown on page 203.

Modifying the Hard Disk Utilities 203

Utility	Location
Installation	Root Directory (diskette only)
Disk Utilities	\HDU\DISK
File Utilities	\HDU\FILES
	\HDU\PROTECT
Display Utilities	\HDU\DISPLAY
	\HDU\FOREGRND
	\HDU\BACKGRND
Design Utility	\HDU\DESIGN
Backup Utility	\HDU\BACKUP
Help Utilities	\HDU\HELP

Portions of each utility are further located in lower-level subdirectories.

File Structure

Functionally, five types of files are used in the construction of the *Hard Disk Manager*. In actuality, each of these files are different usages of basic ASCII files. All were created with a text editor. No other programming language other than DOS commands was utilized in their construction. In addition, a DOS-based CONFIG.SYS file was created to take advantage of DOS's Extended Keyboard and Control functions.

Filenaming conventions were used to distinguish between the five different file types; each type has a different filename extension, as discussed in the following text.

Batch Files (.BAT)

These are DOS batch files created for the purpose of the utilities. As with any other batch file, they are activated by their filename. They are used most extensively for:

Menu Selections	1.BAT, 2.BAT, A.BAT, B.BAT, etc.
Commands	ARCHIVE, DESIGN, etc.
Confirmation Prompts	Y/N files

These batch files contain internal and external DOS commands as well as references to other batch files.

HELP Files (.HLP)

These are HELP screens created with a text editor. They provide the user with screen displays of basic DOS reference material. For example, they contain information on EDLIN, creating AUTOEXEC.BAT files, etc.

Screen Files (.SCR)

These are screen files created with EDLIN. They include the menu screens with selection numbers as well as the informational/instructional screens. Menu designs were created with characters included in the ASCII extended character set.

Temporary Files (.TMP)

These are temporary files created by batch files. They seldom appear on the disk because they are created, used, and then renamed. For example, they can be used with the COPY command as a temporary target file. Then this file might be appended to another file through use of the COPY+ command.

Text Files (.TXT)

These files are used two ways: as input to another command or for combining two file fragments with the COPY command. Used as input from a file rather than the keyboard, .TXT files are used to provide input for the EDLIN program when it is activated from within a batch file. (See Chapter 6 for a description of this process.)

10.2 SOME BASIC TOOLS FOR EDITING FILES

Typically, only the batch (.BAT) and screen (.SCR) files must be changed. If one desires to add or change a Help (.HLP) screen, the same process used to modify a screen file is followed. This section describes some fundamental EDLIN commands that may be used to modify files. More specific in-

Modifying the Hard Disk Utilities 205

formation also is discussed in the sections on modifying batch (.BAT) and screen (.SCR) files.

Listing the Contents of a File

Text within a batch file or screen design may be modified by using the EDLIN EDIT LINES command. To determine the line number in which the text is to be changed, the file is typed out on the screen by issuing the LIST LINES command (the * is the EDLIN prompt):

    *L

This command displays up to 23 lines of a batch file: 11 lines before the current line, the current line, and 11 lines after the current line. If the batch file is less than the 23-line maximum, the entire file may be displayed when the current line is line #1.

If the user knows the general range of line numbers in which the potential modification is located, a range of lines may be specified instead. This is done by entering the command in the following format, in which the [line] parameters represent numbered lines in the batch file:

    [line][,line]L

One can also use the Page (P) command to display the contents of a file. The Page command is entered in the same format as the List (L) command:

    [line][,line]P

It permits the user to page through a file; 23 lines are displayed per "page." Unlike the List command, the P command changes the current line.

Editing the Text of a File

Batch files and screen files can be edited on a line-by-line basis using the EDLIN EDIT LINES command. This command is initiated at the EDLIN prompt by typing the desired line number:

    [line#]

EDLIN responds by typing out the existing line number, displaying the text of the line, and prompting the user for new text after the line number:

```
*1
  1:   this is the original text on line #1
  1:*
```

All of the DOS editing keys can be used to edit text within a line displayed with EDLIN. These include the following keys:

<Del>	Deletes characters from within the line
<Ins>	Inserts characters within the line
<Esc>	Cancels the line displayed
<F1>	Copies one character of the line at a time
<F2>	Copies all characters of a line up to a specified character
<F3>	Copies all remaining characters on the line
<F4>	Copies all characters from a specified character to the end of the line

Inserting and Deleting Lines in a File

New lines can be added to an existing line of a file by using the INSERT LINES command. It is entered at the EDLIN prompt in the following format:

```
[line]i
```

EDLIN inserts the new line of text immediately BEFORE the specified line number. If no line number is specified, the new line is placed in the text before the current line (which is the line most recently modified). EDLIN adjusts subsequent line numbers to accommodate the newly added line number.

After the first line is inserted, EDLIN allows the user to continue adding more lines by automatically displaying successive line numbers each time the Enter key is pressed. The Insert mode is terminated by holding down the <Ctrl> key and pressing either the <Break> key or the letter C.

The DELETE LINES command may be use to eliminate one or more lines in a file. It is entered at the EDLIN prompt in the following format:

```
[line][,line]d
```

Modifying the Hard Disk Utilities 207

Either a specific line number or a range of line numbers may be specified with the delete command. When lines are deleted, EDLIN readjusts the remaining line numbers.

Ending the Edit Program

The file editing process in EDLIN can be terminated two ways: with the END EDIT command or the QUIT command.

The END EDIT command ends the current EDLIN session and saves the file under the filename specified at the start of EDLIN. Additionally, when editing an existing .BAT file, the original batch file is renamed with a .BAK filename extension. The End Edit command is processed by entering **E** at the EDLIN system prompt.

The QUIT command allows the user to exit the EDLIN program without saving any changes that have been made during the current edit session. This command is activated by entering **Q** at the EDLIN system prompt. EDLIN responds with a "Abort edit (Y/N)?" confirmation prompt.

10.3
ADDING, MODIFYING, AND DELETING SCREEN FILES

Screen files can be changed in a number of ways: One can modify wording, menu selections, the border type, and width, as well as the screen size and layout. Individual modifications by themselves are not difficult. However, the user must be careful to consider the impact of any change on the entire display screen as well as all files included in the utility.

Adding, Modifying, or Deleting Text and Menu Selections

Adding, modifying, or deleting informational text and/or menu selections can have an impact on some or all of the following aspects of the screen design:

- the screen layout and size
- the parameters of the PROMPT command
- the border design
- the numbering of menu selections

Altering the Screen Layout and Size

When the deletion of informational text requires a decrease in screen size, it is a fairly straightforward process to delete the unnecessary rows using the DELETE LINES command.

However, when additions or modifications require an increase in screen size, it can be a more complicated matter. Two problems may arise: The screen size may exceed that of the display screen, and/or the border must be extended.

When the Screen Size Exceeds the Display Size

Only a limited amount of information can fit on the display screen. Even if one attempts to compact as much information as possible, there is a trade-off between the complexity of the screen and its usefulness. The user has a number of options from which to choose:

1. The screen can be subdivided into a two-part screen: an informational screen and a selection or command screen. These two screens must be linked together to be useful. This can most efficiently be done by using Confirmation prompts (e.g., Continue Y/N?). In this particular case, a **Y** answer would activate a Y.BAT file, which would in turn call the second portion of the screen. An **N** answer would abort the utility. One caution here is that N.BAT and Y.BAT files already exist in certain directories and cannot be duplicated. Therefore, if one is splitting a screen in a directory in which Y.BAT and N.BAT files exist, one would have to devise different confirmation prompt names. For example, C.BAT could be used for "Continue" and E.BAT for "End Process."
2. The PAUSE command also can be used to link two screens, although the process could be somewhat slower. The PAUSE command allows the user to control how much of a batch file is executed at particular time. The PAUSE command would be inserted in the batch file that calls the screen files as follows:

```
1:  echo off
2:  cls
3:  type SCREEN1.SCR
4:  pause
5:  cls
6:  type SCREEN2.SCR
```

Modifying the Hard Disk Utilities 209

```
7: echo ENTER SELECTION:
8: prompt $e[20;18H
```

In this situation, a batch file would type out the first screen file (SCREEN1.SCR) and then pause with the message:

```
Strike a key when ready...
```

Then, when any key is pressed it would resume by clearing the screen and typing out the second screen file (SCREEN2.SCR) with an ENTER SELECTION prompt. Some thought would have to be given as to where to split the file and where a pause would logically make sense.

3. A similar, yet less elegant method would be to use the MORE filter. The MORE filter sends one screenful of data to the display and then pauses with the message:

```
---More---
```

Thus, the MORE filter would be used with a single screen file to divide it into two screens. If for example, the screen file were called SCREEN.SCR, the command would be written as:

```
type SCREEN.SCR | more
```

A full display screen appears with the ---More--- message; after one presses <Enter>, the screen scrolls up to the second portion. It is important to note that the screen display scrolls; that is, portions of the first screen are displayed as it scrolls to part two.

4. One other alternative is to split the screen into two or more menu selections, if possible.

Extending the Border

The addition of text or menu selections may mean that the border size must be extended. This is a process that can be handled readily with EDLIN. The border can be extended vertically by using the COPY LINES command to copy a line of the file containing only border characters. Prior to adding text or menu selections, the following procedure may be followed:

1. In EDLIN, the screen file is first listed out to determine which line should be copied. This is done by entering the LIST LINES command at the * prompt:

```
1 L
```

2. A line or series of contiguous lines is/are chosen that contain(s) ONLY the left- and right-border characters.

3. The COPY LINES command is used to copy that line on to that line (i.e., to duplicate it). For example, if line 8 met the criterion of containing only border characters, the command would be issued as:

   `8,8,8c`

This command tells EDLIN to copy the information in line 8 to line 8. Note that EDLIN expects a range as the "from" parameter, indicated by the numbers 8,8. The third 8 is the "to" parameter. If lines 8 and 9 both met the criterion, the command could be written as:

   `8,9,8c`

4. This procedure is repeated until the border contains the desired number of lines.

NOTE: *The border may not exceed 22 lines if a prompt will be included as the bottom line. Otherwise, the screen will extend beyond a single display screen.*

Extending the width of the border also is a fairly straightforward process, although the need to do so probably will be infrequent. To extend the width of the border, the DOS editing keys can be used:

1. In EDLIN, the screen file is first listed out to determine which line should be extended. This is done with the LIST LINES command:

   `1L`

2. The EDIT LINES command is used to display the border line to be extended. At the * prompt, the line number is entered:

   `*1`
      `1: _____`
      `1:`

3. Then the first two characters on the line are displayed by pressing the right arrow key two times.
4. The <Ins> key is pressed each time for the number of characters to be inserted.
5. The <F3> key is pressed to display the remainder of the line.
6. The <ENTER> key is pressed to enter the new line length.
7. The insert procedure must be repeated for each line of the display screen in which there are border characters and/or text. It can be a *very* tedious process.

Altering the Parameters of the PROMPT Command

If the new screen size exceeds the size of the screen in the current utility; i.e., the new screen has more lines, the PROMPT command must be altered.

In each of the menu screens, the PROMPT command is used to alter the cursor position—to position it after the command **ENTER SELECTION**. The user basically has two choices:

1. The parameters of the PROMPT command can be changed. For example, the command might read:

    ```
    prompt $e[20;18H
    ```

    The two numeric parameters (20 and 18) signify the line (row) and column numbers, respectively. If in this example, the screen is made two lines longer, the first number must be changed to 22. As long as the prompt, ENTER SELECTION:, remains the same, the second numeric parameter remains unchanged.

2. The use of the PROMPT command for setting the cursor position can be eliminated. Instead, the PROMPT command can be used to display the ENTER SELECTION: prompt. For example, in all of the utilities, the text of the prompt is displayed with the batch file lines:

    ```
    echo ENTER SELECTION:
    ```

    This line is followed by the PROMPT command used to set the cursor position. Instead of using the ECHO command, PROMPT could be used:

    ```
    prompt ENTER SELECTION:
    ```

    Then the cursor position setting is not necessary because the cursor will follow the text of the PROMPT command.

    > NOTE: *Although on the surface the second method seems simpler, the first method—changing the PROMPT command parameters—is preferable. This is because the cursor will not move until a valid command is accepted. Thus, if a bad command or invalid selection is entered, the menu will not scroll off the screen. Using the second method, this would be the case.*

Changing the Border Design

The border design may be changed as a result of changes in the text of a screen file. That is, the configuration of the border may be modified to suit the text. For example, changes in the content of the screen may require a rectangular design, a horizontally divided, or a vertically divided border.

In the most basic border configuration, a rectangle or square, six characters from the ASCII Extended Character Set are involved. These include the upper and lower left-side corners; the upper and lower right-side corners; and the horizontal and vertical border characters. Of course, if several different characters make up the width of the border, more characters are involved.

An existing screen design with a border can be divided vertically or horizontally. This can be very desirable when there are two logically distinct types of information on the screen. Such divisions increase readability as well as usability.

To insert a horizontal border, all one has to do is either make sure that there is a space between the text for the border to be placed or insert a space to accommodate the border. The following procedures can be followed to insert a horizontal border, assuming that a space for the divider must first be created.

1. In EDLIN, the screen file is first listed out to determine where the divider must be placed. This is done at the EDLIN * prompt with the LIST LINES command:

    1 L

2. Once the correct space is chosen, a blank line is inserted above that row number with the INSERT LINES command. For example, assume that a blank line will be inserted above line 6:

    6 I

    EDLIN responds with a a prompt for line 6 text as follows:

    6:*

    To make this new line a blank, the <Enter> key is pressed. EDLIN then responds with the next line (line 7) to insert. To end the INSERT LINES command, <Ctrl> <C> is pressed (simultaneously depressing the <Ctrl> and <C> keys produces the characters ^C). This will return the user to the EDLIN command prompt:

    ```
    *6 I
        6: *
        7: *^C
    *
    ```

3. The LIST LINES command is again evoked to ensure that a blank line has been inserted.
4. The most expedient way to place the border divider in the blank row (line 6) is to use the COPY LINES command and copy the top border down. For example, assume that the top border is in line 1. The command would be issued as

    1,1,6 C

    This tells EDLIN to copy from line 1 through line 1 to line 6. However, the user will note that the upper-right and -left corners have been

copied as well. These characters must be changed to characters that are the intersection points between horizontal and vertical borders.
5. The EDIT LINES command is used on the newly copied border characters. Since the first character is the left corner, a new border intersection character is typed by holding down the <Alt> key and typing the numeric ASCII code on the numeric keypad. Then the <F3> key is pressed to display the rest of the line.

   To change the right-corner character to a border intersection character, the user only needs to backspace (to erase the right-corner character) and enter the new ASCII character with the <Alt> key and the numeric keypad. When this is accomplished, the <Enter> key is pressed to record the changes.
6. The EDLIN session is terminated and the changes saved with the END EDIT command. This command (E) is typed at the EDLIN prompt.

A similar procedure is followed to divide the screen with vertical borders. The left or right vertical border is copied to the center of the screen. Different border intersection characters ("T's" and upside-down "T's") are inserted.

Renumbering the Menu Selections

Sometimes the modifications required for a screen file are fairly simple. This might be the case when an entire utility or a utility option has been deleted and it is necessary to delete the menu selection and renumber the remaining selections. This is done using the EDIT LINES command within EDLIN. The procedure to be followed would be very similar to that described above for editing border characters. In brief, the following procedure would be used:

1. The LIST LINES command is used to determine the appropriate line (s).
2. The appropriate line is edited using the EDIT LINES command.
3. The right-arrow key is used to display the line up to the selection number.
4. The new selection number is typed and the <F3> key is pressed to display the remainder of the line. The modification is recorded with the <Enter> key.
5. After each selection is edited, EDLIN is terminated and the modifications are saved with the END EDIT command.

Adding, Modifying, or Deleting Borders

Even though the text of a particular display screen may be appropriate for the user's needs, the user may want to experiment with different borders or remove the border all together. This section describes procedures that may be followed to accomplish these tasks.

Adding New Borders

The design and construction of borders are described in detail in Chapter 6, "Screen Design Utilities." The most important aspects of a successful design are planning out the design and developing a working knowledge of the use of the ASCII Extended Character Set with EDLIN. Both of these elements are emphasized in Chapter 6.

Modifying Borders

Using EDLIN's REPLACE TEXT command, the user can change an existing border with ease. As mentioned above, a basic menu design contains six characters: the four corner characters and the horizontal and vertical border characters. Thus, the most expedient method of altering a border design is to use the REPLACE TEXT command twice: once to replace the the horizontal characters and once to replace the vertical characters. Then the EDIT LINES command must be used to change the corner characters. The following procedures might be used:

1. In EDLIN, the LIST LINES command is used to determine which lines are to be replaced.
2. The REPLACE TEXT command is issued, replacing the existing character(s) with the new character(s). This command is entered at the EDLIN prompt. The replacement operation in this example begins with the first row of the screen file (line 1):

    `1,R[old characters]<F6>[new characters]`

    This command tells EDLIN to start with line 1 and replace all of the old characters with new characters. The <F6> specification means that the <F6> function key must be pressed; this will generate the characters ^Z. It is important to note several things:

    a. The ASCII Extended Character Set can be used in this command. When the ASCII character is entered as either an old or new

character, the <Alt> key and the numeric keypad are used for the appropriate ASCII code.
  b. More than one character can be included in either the old or new character designations. This might be the case, for example, if the border were made up of several contiguous characters (e.g., a double border, a solid border, and a single inner border). If the border is more than one character wide, several lines will have to be edited when changing the corner characters.
3. The LIST LINES command is again issued to ensure that what was supposed to happen did indeed happen. Also, this shows the lines containing corner characters; these lines must be changed.
4. To change a corner character, the appropriate line is edited using the EDIT LINES command.
5. The new corner character is typed by holding down the <Alt> key and typing the numeric ASCII code on the numeric keypad.
6. The <F3> key is pressed to display the rest of the line. To change the old right-corner character to the new corner character, the backspace is pressed (to erase the right-corner character) and the new ASCII character is typed with the <Alt> key and the numeric keypad. When this is accomplished, the <ENTER> key is pressed to record the changes.
7. The LIST LINES command is again issued to ensure that what was supposed to happen did indeed happen.
8. At the prompt, the EDLIN session is terminated in one of two ways:
  a. If the new design is not aesthetically pleasing or the user wants to try another modification, the QUIT command can be issued. This command *does not save* the previous modifications.
  b. If the new change is acceptable, EDLIN is terminated and the *file is saved* with the END EDIT command.

10.4
ADDING, MODIFYING, AND DELETING BATCH FILES

The mechanics for adding, modifying, or deleting batch files are very similar to those for screen files. The tricky part about modifying batch files is that one must be able to determine how such modifications affect every other part of the utility or utilities.

Adding, modifying, or deleting batch files can have an impact on some or all of the following aspects of batch and screen files:

- batch file changes may require the addition or deletion of lines in other batch files
- batch files may need to be deleted
- entire menus and/or screens may have to be deleted
- menu selections may need to be deleted
- batch files may need to be renamed

Adding and Deleting Batch File Lines

In cases where batch file lines must be added or deleted, the EDLIN INSERT LINES and DELETE LINES commands are used. Brief procedures for performing each operation are described below.

1. In EDLIN, the LIST LINES command is used to determine the appropriate line(s) to delete or the location in which to add more lines.
2. To insert a line, the line number location is chosen and the INSERT LINES comand is issued; the new line will appear just *before* the specified line number. When EDLIN responds with a new line prompt, the text is entered. As many lines as necessary can be added. To end the INSERT LINES command, the <Ctrl><C> keys are simultaneously depressed.
3. To delete a line, the line number is chosen and the DELETE LINES command is issued. If greater than one line must be deleted, they must be sequential lines (e.g., lines 2, 3, and 4). If they are not sequential lines, the DELETE LINES command must be issued as many times as necessary. This is because each time EDLIN deletes a line, subsequent lines are renumbered.
4. After the necessary insertions and deletions, EDLIN is terminated and the modifications are saved with the END EDIT command.

Deleting Batch Files

Batch file deletions are accomplished by using the DOS ERASE (or DEL) command. In order to delete a batch file, the file must be in the current directory. Otherwise, a path to the file's directory location must be specified. Global filename characters (the * and ? symbols) may be used to delete more than one batch file at a time. However, deleting more than one file at a time can be a risky endeavor. The following procedures may be used to delete a batch file. In this example the ERASE command is used.

Modifying the Hard Disk Utilities

1. If the file to be erased is in the current directory, the directory does not have to be changed. Otherwise, the directory must be changed. This is done with the Change Directory (CD) command:

    `CD\ Directory name`

2. The Directory command (DIR) is issued to ensure that the file to be deleted is located in the current directory. The /W parameter can be specified so that the files will be listed across the screen.

    `DIR /W`

3. The batch file to be deleted is typed out using the TYPE command:

    `TYPE filename.BAT`

    The contents of the file are scanned for any references to other batch files; since these no longer may be necessary, they also can be deleted.

4. The file is erased using the ERASE command:

    `ERASE filename.BAT`

5. The DIR command can again be issued to ensure that the file was deleted as specified.

Deleting Menus, Screens, and Menu Selections

The same procedure described above is used to delete menus, instructional screens, and specific menu selections. Care must be given to any linkages between menus, screen files, and batch files. Before any file is deleted, the user should be 100% confident that the deletion will not affect other program and screen files.

Renaming Batch Files

A number of instances will require that a particular batch (or screen) file be renamed. This might result from the renumbering of menu selections, the substitution of a new batch file for an existing batch file or menu selection, or the need to use a backup (.BAK) batch file.

The names of batch files are changed using the DOS RENAME command. The RENAME command uses the following format:

`RENAME [old filename.ext] [new filename.ext]`

If a file by the new filename already exists, DOS will display an error message and abort the procedure.

Using Backup Batch Files (.BAK Files)

Once a batch file has been modified, DOS saves a backup of the file. DOS stores the last version of the file under the same filename as the .BAT file with the extension .BAK. This automatic backup facility can be most useful. Should a batch file be lost or overwritten, the latest version of the file can be reconstructed using the .BAK file. In order to use the .BAK file, it must be renamed. This is done using the RENAME command described above. It should be noted that the .BAK file *cannot* be named the same name as the original batch file if that filename is still valid.

If the user knows that he or she has a valid batch file, it saves disk space to periodically erase the .BAK files. This can be done using the ERASE command with Global Filename Characters:

```
ERASE *.BAK
```

Every time the batch files are modified thereafter, DOS creates another .BAK backup batch file.

c·h·a·p·t·e·r   11

Creating Your Own Utilities: Tips and Techniques for Programming with DOS

By this time you have mastered the *Hard Disk Manager* utilities and have decided to try your hand at writing your own. Where do you start? This chapter discusses the components of a DOS-based utility program and the creation of utility menu screens and program files. It also provides a number of tips and techniques for creating screen designs and progam files. Each tip and technique is cross-referenced with an example from the *Hard Disk Manager*.

How to Begin

Behind each of the *Hard Disk Manager* utilities is a DOS batch file program. This is a program file created with a text editor (such as EDLIN) that executes, line-by-line, a series of DOS commands. DOS contains its own special set of batch file commands; these are described in Appendix B. A quick review of DOS's basic commands (Appendix A) and DOS's batch file commands (Appendix B) is a good place to begin. Then, just like any other application program, a utility must be planned, designed, and coded.

Planning a Utility Program

To create a useful and effective utility, a number of questions must be asked during the planning and design phase:

1. For whom is the utility designed? What is his or her skill level, how often will the utility be used, and for what will the utility be used?
2. What does the utility need to do?
3. What DOS commands are required to perform these functions?
4. What is the simplest and most efficient way for the user to interact with the utility?
5. Does the utility require user input?
6. What risks are you taking and should any controls be built into the utility?
7. Does the utility or portions of the utility need to reside in separate directories? What directories need to be created?
8. What kind of informational screens will the utility require? Can an existing menu screen be utilized or does a new menu screen need to be developed?

Once you have the answers to the relevant questions, it is necessary to determine how they impact the two components of DOS-based utilities: program files and screen design.

Components of a Utility

A DOS-based hard disk utility is basically made up of two components: program (or batch) files and informational screens. In actuality, a utility can be made up of any number of interconnected program files. Informational screens can be either menu screens that drive the utilities or explanatory screens that prompt users for input.

Creating Program (Batch) Files

DOS program files can be created with any text editor or program that produces an ASCII file. If you do not own a text editing package, DOS's text editor, EDLIN, will suffice. Procedures for creating a batch file are described in Appendix B on Batch files.

Some Fundamental Batch File Rules

1. Batch files are executed whenever the system encounters a command with the extension **.BAT**. Thus, all program files must have the extension .BAT.

Creating Your Own Utilities 221

2. Batch files execute DOS and/or batch file commands. DOS commands perform specified actions on files and directories; they include such operations as COPY, ERASE, BACKUP, etc. Batch file commands are the programming commands that link together these DOS operations into executable programs.

3. As each command in a program file is executed by DOS, the command appears on the display screen, unless it is suppressed.

4. The batch file command **ECHO OFF** is necessary to suppress the screen display of each command. Thus, ECHO OFF should be the first line of any program file unless it is desirable to have the commands displayed on the screen as they are executed.

5. Thereafter, the command **ECHO** can be used to display necessary information on the screen. ECHO must precede the comments on a program line. It is most often used to display remarks or instructions on the screen. ECHO can also be used to place control codes in a file to change various attributes of the display screen.

6. The command Clear Screen (CLS) is useful to "clean up" the display before an informational or menu screen is displayed. Typically the command CLS would always appear on the program line preceding the use of the TYPE command to display a screen (.SCR) file.

7. User input can be provided by DOS replaceable parameters. They take the form of %1, %2, %3, etc. The %0 replaceable parameter can be used to reference the name of the batch file itself.

8. The PROMPT command can be used to place an escape character in a batch file and execute control codes. Escape characters are necessary whenever screen attributes need to be altered. For example, the PROMPT command can be used to set the cursor position and to change the color the display foreground and background.

9. If a batch file command calls a second batch file, control is passed to the second file. Unless the call to the second batch file is made as a subroutine batch file, the remainder of the first batch file will not be executed. A subroutine batch file is executed by using the commands **COMMAND /C** and **EXIT**.

10. A quick and dirty way to create short batch files is to use the **COPY CON:** command. In effect, this command accepts or copies input from the console into a text file. Files created using the COPY CON: command, however, can only be corrected by using a text editor.

Creating Screen Files

Screen files can be created with any text editor or program that produces an ASCII file. If you do not own a text editing package, DOS's text editor, EDLIN, will suffice. Throughout the different utilities, procedures are described for creating informational screens and menu designs.

Some Fundamental Rules for EDLIN-Based Screen Files

1. Screen files that fill the display screen are a maximum of 80 characters wide and 25 lines long.
2. The spacing between rows is greater than column widths are across. Hence, a block character that shades an entire cell (row#/column# location) is a rectangular shape rather than a square. The ASCII character <Alt> 219 shades a cell completely.
3. When creating a screen file with the EDLIN text editor, the cursor will wrap around when it reaches column position 72; however, 80 characters can be typed for a full screen width.
4. Since lines typed with EDLIN wrap around at column 72, and the screen width is 80 characters, centering a design on a screen can be difficult. Remember that column 40 is the center, even though the screen may appear off-center in EDLIN. When it is displayed as a screen file with the TYPE command, it will be centered.
5. Screen designs can include any character typed from the keyboard as well as ASCII characters 128 through 254.
6. In addition to ASCII characters, a screen design can include control codes that set the foreground and background colors of the display as well as various attributes of the screen display (e.g., blinking characters, reverse video, etc.).

11.1 SCREEN AND BATCH FILE TECHNIQUES

This section summarizes many useful and frequently unknown tips and techniques that can be employed in the development of imaginative screen and batch file designs. All of these tricks have been used throughout the *Hard Disk Manager* programs.

Using the *Hard Disk Manager* Techniques

Ten screen design techniques and ten batch file design techniques are described in this section. They describe what the technique does and then cross-reference its usage in an example from the *Hard Disk Manager*. Each technique supplies the following information:

- the utility name where it is used
- the directory name where the example is found
- the filename of the example
- a page reference in the book for the example

To look at the batch or screen files referred to in the examples, the user can use the TYPE command:

```
TYPE <directory>\<filename>
```

To obtain a printout of the batch file as it is displayed on the screen, the user can press <Ctrl><P> prior to issuing the TYPE command. The <Ctrl><P> instructs the printer to act as a "slave"; i.e., as information is typed on the screen it is also sent out to the printer (<Ctrl><P> turns it off). DOS's redirection capabilities could be used to produce a hard copy as well. In this case, a greater-than-sign > and the device name (PRN) follow the directory and filename:

```
TYPE <directory>\<filename>>prn
```

11.2
TEN TECHNIQUES FOR CREATIVE SCREEN DESIGN

Using the ASCII Extended Character Set

In screen and menu design, the user is not restricted to the characters displayed on the computer's keyboard. The ASCII Extended Character Set includes a number of additional symbols and characters. Interesting screen designs can be created using these characters and a text editor. The ASCII Extended Characters include ASCII values 128 to 255, which go beyond the upper- and lowercase alphabetic and numeric characters. They are typed by:

- holding down the <Alt> key
- typing the ASCII value on the *numeric keypad*
- releasing the <Alt> key

Included in the extended character set are some fifty graphic characters that allow the user to create various types of border and screen designs. The ASCII HELP screen in *Hard Disk Manager* shows some of the more popular and useful graphics characters and their code numbers.

Section 6.2 in Chapter 6 describes the use of these special characters in screen design in more detail.

Example Cross-Reference

UTILITY:	*Hard Disk Manager* Main Menu
DIRECTORY:	\HDU
FILENAME:	HDU.SCR
PAGE REFERENCE:	102

Control Codes: Changing Full-Screen Attributes

DOS uses special character sequences, known as control codes or character control sequences, to manipulate various aspects of the video screen (i.e., the screen attributes). These control character sequences can be used to alter or enhance many attributes of the display. Control codes are generated by a command that includes the escape character, the specific numeric value for the desired attribute, and the letter "M," as in:

```
^V[31m
```

Control codes can be activated in two ways: using the PROMPT command containing the control codes, or through the TYPE command that displays a file containing the control codes. In the PROMPT command, the escape character are the symbols $e, as in:

```
prompt $e[31m
```

The author's preferred method is the TYPE command in a text file. The trick is generating the escape character in a text file. This is done by:

- pressing the keys <Ctrl> <V>
- then typing one left-hand bracket character ([)

Control codes may be used in screen design to make characters typed on the screen invisible, to make portions of the display screen blink, to increase the intensity of display characters, to reverse the video screen image, to underscore display characters, to set the cursor position, and to change the color of the screen foreground and/or background. For example, one may activate control codes that display screen foreground characters in white against a blue background.

A general discussion of these control codes is found in Chapter 2 under the heading "Programming with DOS's Advanced Features."

Example Cross-Reference

           UTILITY: Foreground Color Selector, accessed from Customized Display Utilities
       DIRECTORY: \HDU\FOREGRND
        FILENAME: 1.BAT through 8.BAT
PAGE REFERENCE: 73

Control Codes: Used in Screen Design

In addition to controlling an entire screen display, the DOS character control sequences or control codes can also be used to control selective aspects of screen design. Additionally, the ASCII Extended Character Set can be used in combination with control codes to create multicolored screen designs or to otherwise selectively control specific aspects of the screen data.

A single screen may make use of multiple colors or other screen attributes by selectively activating different codes on a line-by-line or character-by-character basis. For example, screen designs may be developed in which an inside border is one color, the outside border is another color, and the text is yet another color.

Note also that control codes can be used in any text or information screen file for the purposes of calling attention to specific instructions with attributes such as reverse video, high-intensity characters, underlining, and so on.

The section entitled "Using Color in Screen Design" in Chapter 6 discusses the procedures for this technique.

Example Cross-Reference

           UTILITY: *Hard Disk Manager* Main Menu
       DIRECTORY: \HDU
        FILENAME: HDU.SCR
PAGE REFERENCE: 113

Controlling the Cursor and System Prompt

The DOS PROMPT command can be used for a variety of screen design purposes. One common usage of PROMPT is to replace the standard "C>" system prompt. In this capacity, it can be used to invoke date/time prompts, directory location prompts, or prompts with text of one's own choosing.

Better still, the PROMPT command can be used to control cursor positioning. This is particularly useful in menu design. After a menu screen or information screen is displayed with the TYPE command, the cursor can be positioned at a specific point on the screen. This point could be at the end of the line that said "ENTER COMMAND." This ENTER COMMAND line could be a part of the menu screen or could be displayed with an ECHO command. Then, the PROMPT command is used to "freeze" the cursor at the end of the ENTER COMMAND line.

The great advantage of this technique is that the menu screen does not scroll up when the <Enter> key is pressed, or when the user types invalid command input. In effect, the menu itself is "frozen" on the screen until a valid command is entered.

A general discussion of how the PROMPT command can be used for cursor and screen control is found in Chapter 2 under the heading "Programming with DOS's Advanced Features."

Example Cross-Reference

UTILITY:	Backup/Restore Menu, accessed from *Hard Disk Manager* Main Menu
DIRECTORY:	\HDU, and \HDU\BACKUP
FILENAMES:	\HDU\4.BAT, which displays \HDU\BACKMENU.SCR
PAGE REFERENCE:	124

Using "What If" in Screen Design

In the process of developing screens, there is a fun and effective way to quickly judge the effects of different graphics characters, colors, or display attributes on the overall design. This is done by manipulating the screen characters with a text editor's Search and Replace function while the screen is being edited. In EDLIN, this is done using the REPLACE TEXT command.

The idea is to build the screen using easily typed characters for different sections of the screen. For example, the top border and bottom borders of

Creating Your Own Utilities 227

a screen could be built using plus signs, while the side borders could be entered as periods. Then, using the REPLACE TEXT command, each of these characters is replaced with a more elaborate graphics character. Perhaps the character could be preceded and followed by a control code that activated and then deactivated a specific color for that character.

Example Cross-Reference

         UTILITY: Screen Design utility. Using it as described in Chapter 6 illustrates the technique in detail.
PAGE REFERENCE: 110

Forced Line Spacing in Information Screens

In batch files using the ECHO command to display messages, the screen layout of the messages can often be improved by the use of blank lines between statements or paragraphs. There are two easy ways to generate these blank lines.

    In one method, a blank line can be forced with a wrap-around effect of a preceding line. In other words, the preceding line is made "longer" by adding space characters to the end text so that it wraps around to the next line. The additional length must go up to approximately 20 positions into the next line.

    Another convenient method of creating a blank line is to make the text of an ECHO command an unprintable character, such as <Alt> 255. The ECHO command must have some text, otherwise it generates the message "ECHO is ON/OFF" when the batch file is executed. The use of an unprintable character will suffice as "text," even though nothing will appear on the screen.

Example Cross-Reference

         UTILITY: Locate File utility, File Archive utility
      DIRECTORY: \HDU\FILE
       FILENAME: DOLOCATE. BAT and ARCHIVE.BAT
PAGE REFERENCE: 165

Displaying Information Screens

When a utility must have some instructions or some type of information screen, it is generally better to set up the information screen in a separate text file if more than 3 to 4 lines of text are involved. Information screen files can be created using EDLIN or any other text editor. This file is then displayed at the appropriate time during the execution of the utility through the use of the TYPE command.

The advantage of this approach is speed. DOS displays these screen files faster than the line-by-line display that occurs using multiple ECHO commands in a batch file.

Example Cross-Reference

UTILITY:	Full Backup utility
DIRECTORY:	\HDU\BACKUP
FILENAME:	1.BAT, which calls FULLBACK.SCR
PAGE REFERENCE:	126

Multiple Information Screens

In situations where one screen cannot accommodate all of the necessary information, multiple screens can be displayed sequentially, using the DOS MORE filter. In this scenario, the display of the screen file is executed through the TYPE command, with its output passed through the MORE filter. If the file contains more than one screen of information, the result is the message "---More---." This message is displayed for each 23 lines of information until the last screen is reached; pressing any key scrolls the screen to the next 23 lines.

This facility is very handy in displaying instructional screens or HELP screens that exceed 21 to 22 lines. Screens longer than this will scroll past the top line after the prompt is displayed. The MORE command allows the user to control the segments of the text file that scroll.

Example Cross-Reference

UTILITY:	HELP Screen for DOS Commands, accessed from Help Screen utilities
DIRECTORY:	\HDU\HELP
FILENAME:	3.BAT
PAGE REFERENCE:	191

Creating Your Own Utilities. 229

Executing Menu Selections

One of the easiest and most effective ways to have menu items executed is through the use of batch files with letter or number filenames. It provides a high level of simplicity and consistency in menu screens with multiple selections. It must be remembered that the whole idea behind menus is that they are supposed to make an operation easy to perform. Program execution using batch files such as 1.BAT or A.BAT requires only two keystrokes: the number or letter, and <Enter>. For multiple menus, different directories can be used for each menu.

Example Cross-Reference

UTILITY: *Hard Disk Manager* Disk Directory Menu
DIRECTORY: \HDU\DISK
FILENAME: 1.BAT and following; A.BAT and following
PAGE REFERENCE: 30

Screen and Menu Layout: Organization and Brevity

The objective in screen design for menus and information screens is to make it easy for the user to know what he or she is supposed to do. This means that menus should be short, easy to read, and organized by functionality. In the best-designed menu environments *(Lotus 1-2-3,* for example), one can find this principle in effect. A menu with much more than seven or eight choices is apt to appear confusing and busy. Try to keep menus organized by function.

    The best approach in developing information and instruction screens is to strive for conciseness and brevity. If an operation requires a number of complicated steps, consider breaking up the operation into separate stages so that the user is not required to read and understand all the steps at one time. Several different screens presented at different stages of the program are more likely to be read by the user than in an all-at-once approach.

Example Cross-Reference

UTILITY: Backup/Restore menu, and the Partial Restore screens
DIRECTORY: \HDU\BACKUP

HARD DISK MANAGER

FILENAME: BACKMENU.SCR and screens beginning with 6.BAT
PAGE REFERENCE: 126; 129

11.3

TEN TECHNIQUES FOR CREATIVE BATCH FILE DESIGN

User-Interactive Batch Files

The DOS COPY command can be used in the COPY CON format in a batch file to develop routines that get input from the user after program execution has begun. When the batch file encounters this command, it pauses and waits for user input. Pressing <F6> followed by <Enter> causes the batch file to resume. The user's input is stored in the file specified in the COPY CON command.

This technique can be used for routines in which the input data are combined with other text files; the combined files could be another batch file that is executed later in the program. It is a way of developing self-modifying batch files. This procedure was used extensively in the menu-building programs found in the menu creation utilities, and in the installation routines in *Hard Disk Manager*.

Example Cross-Reference

UTILITY: Main Menu and Directory Setup utility
DIRECTORY: \HDU\DISK
FILENAME: Program files that begin with 1.BAT.
PAGE REFERENCE: 35

Redirecting Input from a File

This technique allows the user to develop routines in which commands or programs executed in batch files get their input from a text file rather than the keyboard. The sophistication of this technique can range from supplying a Yes/No response to a DOS command, to the complete execution of programs such as EDLIN or DEBUG.

In the simplest case, redirected input can be used for DOS commands that stop for a Yes/No response, such as "Are you sure (Y/N)?" in the ERASE command used with global filename characters. The input for such a

Creating Your Own Utilities.

response could come from a text file containing the **Y** or **N** response. On the other hand, an entire EDLIN sequence can be developed with the same technique. For example, an EDLIN operation that involves transferring a file into an existing file might be completely automated, using a redirected input file with the execution of EDLIN.

Example Cross-Reference

        UTILITY: Locate File utility; Screen Design utility
    DIRECTORY: \HDU\FILE (File Locate);
                         \HDU\DESIGN (Screen Design)
     FILENAME: DOLOCATE.BAT; DESIGN.BAT
PAGE REFERENCE: 165; 100

Redirecting Output to Files and Devices

This technique allows the user to send the output of a command or program to a file or a device instead of the display screen. The device is typically a printer, although the specification of a "Null" device suppresses the output display (i.e., the output is simply thrown away). Suppressing program output can be useful when the display of normal DOS messages and command output may be confusing or distracting.

Equally useful is redirecting screen output into a text file. One may design batch files in which a command's output is sent to a file, and then the output file is subjected to processing, such as a text search or a file combine.

Example Cross-Reference

        UTILITY: Locate File utility
    DIRECTORY: \HDU\FILE
     FILENAME: DOLOCATE.BAT
PAGE REFERENCE: 165

Key Reassignment

One interesting use of the PROMPT command is to reassign the keys on the keyboard. This is particularly useful for assigning specific tasks to the function keys. Using the ten function keys plus the <Shift>, <Alt>, and <Ctrl> keys gives the user forty available keys.

These function keys can be assigned to execute batch file functions. A key can be assigned to type the name of the batch file followed by a carriage return <Enter)>. If the batch file resides in a directory that is part of the search path, such as the DOS directory, the function key can be pressed anywhere in DOS.

This technique is used in *Hard Disk Manager* to make <F1> return the user to the *Hard Disk Manager* Menu (or the Main Menu, if one is installed). Key reassignment is discussed in detail at the end of Chapter 5.

Example Cross-Reference

UTILITY:	<F1> key
DIRECTORY:	Root directory
FILENAME:	HDU.BAT
PAGE REFERENCE:	92

Validation of User Input

It is generally a good idea to build as many control mechanisms into batch files as possible, particularly when user input is involved. Batch file programs using replaceable parameters must have the arguments included when the batch file is executed. There are various methods of checking for user input at the beginning of the program. The IF command can be used to determine whether or not the user has actually entered the required number of parameters. Execution can be halted if there are problems.

When the required input has been entered, one might also build routines that pass the input through validity checks. For example, if a directory path is one of the required arguments, one might use the CD command on the input. The validity of the input could be determined by using the IF command to test for the existence of a file that is present in the directory prior to the CD command.

Example Cross-Reference

UTILITY:	Text Search utility, accessed from File Management utilities
DIRECTORY:	\HDU\FILE
FILENAME:	SEARCH.BAT
PAGE REFERENCE:	161

Creating Your Own Utilities 233

Using Batch File Subroutines

One of the lesser-known capabilities of DOS is the trick of calling batch files as subroutine functions from within a batch file. This means that a batch file can execute another batch file and, when the second batch file ends, control returns to the original batch file at the point where it left off. This is done using the DOS command processor COMMAND.COM and the EXIT command (see Appendix B for details).

There are some useful applications for this technique. For example, batch files with a number of iterations of the same commands could execute these commands via a subroutine batch file. This technique can also be used to maintain a controlled environment in the event the user presses <Ctrl><Break> during the execution of the batch file. This application is used frequently in the programs of *Hard Disk Manager*.

Example Cross-Reference

UTILITY:	Diskcopy utility
DIRECTORY:	\HDU\FILE
FILENAME:	6.BAT and DODCOPY.BAT
PAGE REFERENCE:	167

Confirmation Prompts

DOS uses confirmation prompts in a number of situations where thoughtless program execution may generate unwanted results. It is generally a good idea to emulate this practice. The technique is not difficult. The batch file simply displays the required information and ends in a directory where these two batch files reside: a Y.BAT file and an N.BAT file. The prompt line is a yes/no question, such as "Continue (Y/N)?". The user then enters a **Y** or **N**, executing the appropriate batch file. The desired routine continues in the Y.BAT file, whereas the N.BAT file returns the user to the point of origin.

Example Cross-Reference

UTILITY:	File Protect/Unprotect utility
DIRECTORY:	\HDU\FILE
FILENAME:	7.BAT
PAGE REFERENCE:	169

Different Uses of Replaceable Parameters

Replaceable parameters allow batch files to contain program variables that are specified each time the batch file is run. There are several overlooked uses of replaceable parameters. One technique that is purely cosmetic in function is to use replaceable parameters in ECHO messages. For example, a batch file using a filename as a replaceable parameter for a COPY command could use the same parameter to display a message such as "Moving _____ file to Archive directory." The filename specified in the replaceable parameter would appear as the specified file.

There are other, more functional techniques. For example, replaceable parameters used in one batch file can be passed to other batch files. Still another technique is to use a replaceable parameter as the name of a batch file. The batch file would treat the replaceable parameter as any other batch file name. (In Chapter 6, the description of modifications to the Design utility outlines such a routine.)

Example Cross-Reference

UTILITY:	Locate File utility
DIRECTORY:	\HDU\FILE
FILENAME:	LOCATE.BAT and DOLOCATE.BAT
PAGE REFERENCE:	165

Chaining Together Batch Files

This is an interesting technique for developing self-modifying batch file programs. Processing that is begun in one batch file can be continued in another. The second batch file (or third, fourth, etc.) may use the results of the previous batch file. It can be useful to string together batch files in this way when each is segregated by function. For example, two different starting batch files may both pass control to a third batch file. This might be a more efficient solution than incorporating the third batch file into both of the starting batch files, particularly if many lines of code are involved.

Example Cross-Reference

UTILITY:	Main Menu and Directory Setup utility
DIRECTORY:	\HDU\DISK
FILENAME:	A.BAT
PAGE REFERENCE:	36

Self-Modifying Batch Files

A batch file can be made to modify itself as it goes along by having the batch file create its own new text files. It can combine user input with other text file fragments into a new batch file. Control is then passed to the newly combined file.

In several programs in *Hard Disk Manager*, this technique is used in conjunction with the COPY CON command. Components of the self-modifying batch file may be input by the user with the COPY CON command. For example, consider the following situation in which user input is required to identify the appropriate directory for an operation:

1. A COPY CON command obtains from the user the name of a specific directory in which an operation is to take place.
2. Then the results of the user's input are combined with a text file that places a CD command in front of the user's input; this forms a single line file. This ensures that the current directory is changed to the directory name input by the user.
3. To the two just-combined text files is added another text file, to form a complete batch file.
4. Control is then passed to this new batch file.

In step 2 above, the COPY CON command is used to make sure that the end-of-file marker (^Z) for the first text file is on the same line as the text itself, as in:

    CD ^Z

Otherwise, when the user input file is appended to this, the directory name will be placed on the line *below* the CD command, rather than on the same line. Thus, this would cause the batch file commands to execute incorrectly. To create this kind of text file in COPY CON, you must type the <F6> key (generating the end-of-file marker, ^Z) at the end of the line of text; then press <Enter>.

> NOTE: *The forced placement of this kind of end-of-file marker in this way cannot be done in EDLIN.*

Example Cross-Reference

UTILITY:	Main Menu and Directory Setup utility
DIRECTORY:	\HDU\DISK
FILENAME:	A.BAT
PAGE REFERENCE:	36

appendix a

An Overview of Selected DOS Commands

Command	Page
The ASSIGN Command	238
The ATTRIB Command (DOS 3.X)	239
The BACKUP Command	240
The CHDIR (CD) Command	242
The CHKDSK Command	243
The CLS (CLEAR SCREEN) Command	244
The COPY Command	244
Copying Files from Directory to Directory	244
Combining Files	246
Combining Files into a Summary File	247
Combining Files into the Original Source File	247
The COPY CON: Command for Creating Batch Files	247
The DIR Command	249
The DISKCOPY Command	250
The ERASE and DELETE Commands	251
The FIND Filter	252
The FORMAT Command	253
The MKDIR (MD) Command	255

Command	*Page*
The MORE Filter	255
The PATH Command	256
The PROMPT Command	257
The RENAME Command	258
The RESTORE Command	258
The RMDIR Command	260
The SORT Filter	261
The SYS Command	262
The TREE Command	263
The TYPE Command	264
The XCOPY Command (DOS 3.2 and Later)	264

The ASSIGN Command

The ASSIGN command is used to temporarily reassign a currently specified drive to another drive. This is most often done when an applications software package is configured for one drive (e.g., C drive) and the user wants the package to run off a different drive (e.g., B drive). The ASSIGN command has the following format:

```
ASSIGN [X=Y]
```

In this command, the "X" refers to the currently specified drive and the "Y" refers to the new drive; thus, X is assigned to Y. For example, suppose that *MultiMate* is configured to read its data files from the B drive; the user wishes to temporarily use the program on data files on the C drive without reconfiguring the program. This can be done by changing the current directory on the C drive to the one containing the *MultiMate* data files, and then issuing the following command:

```
assign b=c
```

NOTE: *Drive assignments are restored to the default by issuing the ASSIGN command without arguments.*

Appendix A

The ATTRIB Command (DOS 3.X)

The DOS command ATTRIB (Attribute) can be used to protect sensitive files from inadvertent erasure. It is available only in DOS 3.X (DOS 3.0 or later). This command allows a file to be marked as read-only. *Read-only* means that the file can be read, but any attempts to alter or erase it will fail. The ATTRIB command has the following format:

```
[d:][path]ATTRIB [+/-R] [+/-A] [d:][path]filename[.ext]
```

These parameters have the following meaning:

d:	This specifies the disk drive. Placed before the ATTRIB command, it designates the disk drive containing the ATTRIB command. Placed after the ATTRIB command, it designates the drive of the file whose read/write status is to be changed. With no drive specification, the default drive is used.
path	A path parameter placed before the ATTRIB command designates a specific directory in the hierarchy where the ATTRIB command is located. Placed after the command, it specifies the directory location of the file whose attribute is to be changed. The current directory is used if no path is specified.
filename	A single file may be designated. More than one file may be specified through the use of global filename characters.
.ext	This specifies the filename extension. Global filename characters may be used.
+/−R	This switch sets the attribute of the file(s). When +R is specified, the file is marked as read-only. When −R is specified, the file is marked as read/write. If this parameter is omitted, the status of the file is displayed; the output for read-only files will show an "R" in front of the filename.
+/−A	This switch setting is available only in DOS 3.2 and later. A +A setting turns on the archive bit; a −A setting resets it (turns it off). Normally, DOS sets the

archive bit only when the BACKUP or XCOPY commands are used. This allows the user to control the backup status of a file.

Once the attribute has been set to read-only, any attempt to alter or erase the file will result in the DOS error message "Access denied." The error message may be different when erasure or alteration is attempted from within an application program.

The BACKUP Command

BACKUP copies fixed disk files to floppy or fixed disks in a special format that allows a single file to occupy more than one disk. Files copied with the BACKUP command may be used only after they have been processed through the RESTORE command. Floppy diskettes must be formatted prior to being used for backup. The BACKUP command has the following format:

```
BACKUP [d:][path][filename][.ext] d:[/S][/M][/A][/D:mm-dd-yy]
```

The first group of parameters refers to the source file(s), whereas the second set of parameters specifies the target file(s). These parameters have the following meaning:

    d: This specifies the disk drive. Drive specifications differ for DOS 2.X and 3.X:

        DOS 2.X Unless the user's system has a second hard disk, the first drive specification is C. If the system has a single floppy drive, the second drive specification is A. Note that the second drive specification (the target drive) *must* be included in this command.

        DOS 3.X The source and target drives can be of any type. That is, files can be backed up from a fixed disk to a fixed disk, from a diskette to a diskette, from a fixed disk to a diskette, and from a diskette to a fixed disk.

Appendix A

path
: This designates a specific directory in the hierarchy where the file or files to be copied are located. If no path is specified, then the current directory is used.

filename
: A single file may be designated. More than one file may be specified through the use of global filename characters. All files in the designated directory are copied when this parameter and the **.ext** parameter (the filename extension) are omitted.

.ext
: This specifies the filename extension. Global filename characters are permitted.

/S
: When this parameter is included in the command, BACKUP copies the files in all subdirectories below the directory level specified in the path parameter. Thus, if the path parameter specifies the root directory, this parameter causes all files in the directory system to be copied. This is called a full backup.

/M
: This parameter is used only after a full backup has been performed. This parameter backs up only those files that have been modified since the last backup was performed. For example, to back up only those files that have been modified since the last time the directory C:\LOTUS was backed up, the command would be:

```
backup C:\lotus /m
```

/A
: DOS normally erases all the existing files on a diskette before it starts copying files under the BACKUP command. This does not happen when the /A parameter is included in the command; backed up files are added to a diskette's existing files.

/D:mm-dd-yy
: This parameter backs up only those files that have been created or modified on or after a specified date. For example, if backups are needed only for files modified or created on or after June 30, 1984, this parameter is written as /d:6-30-84.

NOTE: *With DOS 3.X, the parameter [d:][path] may be placed in front of the command. Since BACKUP is an external command, this allows the user to specify the particular drive and directory in which the command file is located. The pathname is separated from the command by a backslash (\ ).*

Before a complete backup is made of all files on the fixed disk, the user should have enough formatted diskettes available to accommodate the files on the fixed disk. To determine roughly how many diskettes will be needed, the CHKDSK (Check Disk) command can be used to find out how many bytes contain files. Then divide this number by 360,000 (the number of bytes in a floppy disk) to determine the number of floppy disks required. A fixed disk filled to capacity will require 28 diskettes for a complete system backup.

After entering the BACKUP command, DOS prompts the user to insert a diskette. If the number of files on the fixed disk exceeds the capacity of a floppy diskette, the user is prompted to insert another one. The first one is removed and labelled "1." This process continues until all files have been copied. Diskettes must be numbered in the order in which they are used. As the backup process for each file is completed, the filename is displayed on the screen.

It is good practice to have two separate sets of backup diskettes. Should a power or system failure occur before BACKUP completes, all existing backup files on the disk will be lost. This is because BACKUP first erases the contents of the floppy diskette. Thus, the user should alternate between two sets of diskettes whenever a complete or partial backup is performed.

The CHDIR (CD) Command

Many times it is easier to change the current directory rather than use pathnames in DOS commands. This is most logical when the same directory is frequently accessed for data files or commands. The current directory is changed with the CHDIR (Change Directory) command, also abbreviated as CD. The CHDIR command has the following format:

```
CHDIR [d:][path]
```

These parameters have the following meaning:

    d: This specifies the disk drive intended to be the current drive.

Appendix A

    path   This is a series of directory names that leads DOS from the current or root directory through the hierarchy to a newly designated current directory. A backslash separates each directory name in a path.

Entering the CD command with no parameters will display the current directory. The drive specification is optional. If no drive is specified, the default drive is assumed.

The CHKDSK Command

The CHKDSK command displays a disk status report, providing data on total disk space, files, directories, free disk space, disk capacity, and total memory. It also displays any error messages. The CHKDSK command provides these data through analysis of the directory and File Allocation Table (FAT). The CHKDSK command has the following format:

```
CHKDSK [d:][filename][/F][V]
```

These parameters have the following meaning:

    d: This specifies the disk drive.
    filename If a filename is included, DOS displays all sector locations for that particular file.
    /F   This switch instructs DOS to correct any errors it finds on the disk.
    /V   With this switch, CHKDSK displays informational messages as it proceeds and provides more detailed error reporting.

NOTE: *With DOS 3.X, the parameter [d:][path] may be placed in front of the command. Since CHKDSK is an external command, this allows the user to specify the particular drive and directory in which the command file is located. The pathname is separated from the command by a backslash (\).*

The CHKDSK command can be most useful for determining how badly a disk is fragmented. Fragmentation refers to files that are spread over too many noncontiguous areas of the disk. It is caused by extensive file creation and deletion and results in poor system performance. When global filename characters (e.g., *.*) are included as the filename parameter, DOS searches the current directory only. By checking each file, the user can determine the degree of fragmentation on his or her disk. To eliminate fragmentation, each file must be copied off the hard disk and replaced with the COPY command. DISKCOPY cannot be used because it will simply transfer the files as well as the fragmentation.

It should be noted that the CHKDSK command cannot be used with the /F parameter when redirecting the output to a file. Errors will be reported on that file.

The CLS (CLEAR SCREEN) Command

This command clears the display screen upon execution. If foreground and background colors have been set using the Customized Display utilities or through any other method that utilizes the Extended Screen and Keyboard functions, the screen colors remain unchanged. The CLS command has the following format:

```
CLS
```

This command is particularly useful for controlling the contents of the screen display during batch file execution. The second line of almost every batch file in the *Hard Disk Manager* is CLS; CLS follows the ECHO OFF command.

The COPY Command

The DOS COPY command has a multitude of uses. It can be used to copy files from one disk to another and from one directory to another. It also can be used to append one file to another or to combine two files into a third file. Finally, it can be used to create files, in effect by copying information typed from the keyboard (the console) into a file.

Copying Files from Directory to Directory

Sometimes it is necessary to move a file to another directory. This can be accomplished with the COPY command. When copying files from one directory to another, the command's parameters first must describe the source

Appendix A

file, and then the target file. The source file is the file being copied; the target file is the duplicate. The COPY command has the following format:

```
COPY [/A][/B][d:][path][filename][/A][/B]
[d:][path][filename][/A][/B][/V]
```

The source file parameters in the above command are defined up to and including the first filename parameter; the parameters for the target file are all those thereafter. A space separates the source and target parameters. Although there are many parameters, only a few of these are required when a file is being copied to another directory. These parameters have the following meaning:

/A   Used with the source file, /A specifies that the file is copied as an ASCII (text) file. Used with the target file, it adds an end-of-file character to the end of the file.

\B   If used with the source file, the entire file is copied, based on its directory file size. If used with the target file, no end-of-file character is added to the file.

d: This specifies the drive location for both the source and target files.

path   The path parameter guides DOS to the appropriate level in the directory system for the source and target files.

filename   As the source file, this is the file to be copied; as the target file it is the duplicate filename.

/V   This parameter verifies that the copy has been recorded correctly.

If no drives are specified when copying files, then the default drive is assumed. Although errors in recording data are rare, the /V parameter can be used to ensure that critical data have been duplicated correctly.

The only parameters required to copy files from one directory to another are the path and filename parameters. DOS will not copy a file with the same filename into a different directory without these parameters.

A few points should be remembered when copying files from one directory to another:

1. A file cannot be copied into the same directory under the same filename.

246   HARD DISK MANAGER

  2. When the drive or path parameters are omitted in either the source or target files, the default drive and current directory are assumed.
  3. If the filename is not specified for the target drive, the copied file will be given the same filename.
  4. The use of global filename characters (wild cards) is permitted in both the source and target file specifications.
  5. The /V parameter causes the COPY command to run slightly more slowly. This parameter has the same effect as the VERIFY ON command.

Combining Files

A lesser-known function of the COPY command is its file combination or concatenation facility. Using conventional file specifications, several of the COPY command switches, and "+" signs, any number of files may be linked together. Combining files using the COPY command uses the following format:

```
COPY [/A][/B][d:][path][source filename 1
     [.ext]][/A][/B]+
     [/A][/B][d:][path][source filename
     n[.ext]][/A][/B]
     [/A][/B][d:][path][target filename[.ext]][/A]
     [/B][/V]
```

The parameters in this command have the following meanings:

d:	The drive specification for each file.
path	The path parameter guides DOS to the appropriate level in the directory system for the specified files.
filename	The "source" files are the files to be combined (1...n). The "target" file is the file containing the linked files.
+	The filename specification that follows the "+" is added to the previously specified filename.
/A	This signifies an ASCII file.
/B	This signifies a binary file.
/V	This switch verifies that sectors written to in the target file are recorded intact.

  The placement and use of the /A and /B switches are crucial to the command's outcome:

Appendix A 247

1. A switch following the COPY command, thus preceding all file specifications, sets the switch globally for all files in the command. The /A switch setting is the default setting.
2. A switch following a filename refers to that filename and all other filenames until the next switch is encountered.
3. The /A and the /B switches have different meanings when they refer to source and target files. Basically, the switches can be used to control how the COPY command uses and reads the end-of-file marker (the symbol ^Z).

Combining Files into a Summary File

The conventional format of the COPY command combines the source files into a new or existing summary file:

```
COPY C:SOURCE1.EXT+C:SOURCE2.EXT C:TARGET.EXT
```

Combining Files into the Original Source File

When no target file is specified, the COPY command combines all of the source files into the first source file specified. The DOS COPY command, in effect, sequentially chains subsequent source files to the first source file. The following command combines three files in the first source file specified (SOURCE1.EXT).

```
COPY C:SOURCE1.EXT+C:SOURCE2.EXT+C:SOURCE3.EXT
```

The COPY CON: Command for Creating Batch Files

DOS allows the user to treat input from the keyboard as if it were input from a file; i.e., DOS reads the contents of a disk file as a series of characters. DOS can be fooled into believing that a series of characters coming from the keyboard is actually coming from a disk file. This is the basis for creating batch files with the COPY command. Data are copied from one "file" (the keyboard) to a new file, the batch file. The COPY CON: command has the following format:

```
COPY CON: filename
```

The elements of this command have the following meaning:

CON: This portion of the command specifies a reserved device name in DOS. CON stands for console. It actually has two meanings: When it designates an input device in a command, it represents the keyboard; when it designates an output device in a command, it represents the video screen. CON represents the keyboard in the above command.

filename This is the name of the batch file being created. Any filename may be chosen that conforms to the normal rules of naming files. However, to be a batch file, the filename *must* have .BAT as the filename extension.

When the COPY CON: command is issued, each text line entered at the keyboard is incorporated into the batch file. When the batch file is complete, an end-of-file marker (^Z) must be entered as the last line of the batch file. This is done by pressing the <F6> key and then the <Enter> key. The end-of-file marker also can be specified by holding down the <Ctrl> key and pressing the "Z" key; this also is followed by an <Enter>.

An example follows in which a batch file is created that automatically formats a floppy disk, copies some files onto the disk, and then displays the contents of the floppy disk. The batch file is named ARCHIVE.BAT. At the prompt, the procedure begins with issuing the command, followed by the filename. The batch file contents are then entered on each line:

```
C>copy con: ARCHIVE.BAT
format a:
copy c:\123\*.wks a:
dir a:
^Z
```

The last line is the end-of-file marker; it is generated by pressing the <F6> function key. This ^Z ends the COPY CON: routine, completing the batch file.

Before a newly created batch file is activated, it is advisable to review the contents of the batch file. This is done to make sure that it contains all the desired commands, and that they have been typed correctly. The contents of batch files can be viewed with the TYPE command, which has the following format:

```
TYPE [d:][path][filename][.ext]
```

Appendix A 249

If the file contains errors, the user has two choices: the entire batch file can be rewritten, starting over with the COPY CON: command; or the line or lines with the errors can be edited with the DOS text editing program, EDLIN (an overview of EDLIN commands can be found in the EDLIN Help section of the disk and in Appendix C).

The DIR Command

The DOS command DIR (Directory) displays the contents of a directory. This includes the filename or directory name, the number of bytes in each file, and the date and time the file was last modified. The DIR command has the following format:

```
DIR [d:][path][filename][/P][/S]
```

These parameters have the following meaning:

- d: This specifies the disk drive containing the directory that is to be displayed.
- path   This is a series of directory names that leads DOS from the current or root directory through the hierarchy to the directory to be displayed. A backslash separates each directory name in a path.
- filename   A specific filename or a category of files (if global filename characters are used) is displayed when this parameter is used.
- /P   This causes the display to pause after the screen is full.
- /W   Filenames are shown in a horizontal (wide) display, with five filenames on each line. Only the filename or directory name is displayed.

All of the above parameters are optional. If no drive is specified, then the default drive is assumed. If no path or filename is given, then DOS displays the contents of the current directory.

DOS displays some slightly different information if the DIR command is issued outside the root directory. The entry for the first file shows a period in place of a filename. The second entry shows two periods in place of a filename. Both are listed as directories. The single-period entry denotes the directory being listed. The double-period entry denotes the parent directory of the directory being listed. The parent directory is the higher-level directory that contains the subdirectory.

The double-period notation can be used to display the contents of a subdirectory's parent directory. This can be accomplished by writing the DIR command as:

```
DIR ..
```

Any DIR command parameters may be used with this notation.

The DISKCOPY Command

The entire contents of one floppy diskette can be duplicated on another floppy diskette with this command. The source and target diskettes may be in the same drive or they may be in different drives. If the operation is done on the same drive, DOS prompts the user alternately to insert the source and target diskettes at the appropriate times. The user may find this command more convenient than the COPY command as a way of copying files from one diskette to another. The DISKCOPY command has the following format:

```
DISKCOPY [d:] [d:][/1]
```

These parameters have the following meaning:

- d: The source and target drives are specified with this parameter. If this parameter is omitted for either drive, a single-drive copy operation is performed on the default drive.
- /1   When this parameter is included, only the first side of the diskette is copied.

This command is handy for hard disk systems with only one floppy disk drive. To duplicate a floppy diskette, this command can be entered as

```
diskcopy a: a:
```

DOS will prompt the user to first insert the source disk, and then the target disk. Depending on the amount of system memory and the amount of data on the source disk, DOS may request several swaps of source and target disks. DOS will automatically format an unformatted target disk.

Appendix A

The ERASE and DELETE Commands

Although the fixed disk can store a great deal of information, it has a finite capacity. Eventually, it will become necessary to eliminate unnecessary files. The ERASE and DEL (Delete) commands are used for ongoing maintenance of this type. These two commands have identical functions and format:

```
ERASE [d:][path][filename]
DEL [d:][path][filename]
```

These parameters have the following meaning:

- d: This specifies the disk drive containing the file that is to be erased.
- path This leads DOS through the hierarchy to the directory containing the file that is to be erased.
- filename The file to be eliminated is specified by this parameter. If a path is specified, a backslash separates the pathname from the filename.

If no drive or path is specified, the file is deleted from the current directory of the default drive. Files that have been marked read-only cannot be erased. (Files are marked read-only with the ATTRIB command.)

More than one file may be erased at a time when global filename characters (wild cards) are used. These characters are the * and ? symbols. They are used to designate files in a more generalized, less exacting manner. The * symbol permits substitution of up to eight characters for the stmbol. The ? symbol allows substitution of a single character for the symbol in a filename.

The ERASE and DELETE commands are very powerful and must be used with caution. The following points should be noted:

1. The *.* filename designation should be used with caution. Because the *.* filename specification designates all files in a directory, DOS displays the following warning prompt when *.* is used with ERASE or DEL:

    ```
    Are you sure (Y/N)?
    ```

    Entering **N** cancels the command. A **Y** answer must be followed by an ENTER.

2. The DIR command should always be issued before using ERASE or DEL commands that contain global filename characters. The same

global filename can be used to display the files that will be affected by the erasure. Thus, the user will be certain that only the intended files are deleted.
3. The current directory and default drive are assumed. It is recommended that the commands ERASE and DEL be used only within the current directory. However, just in case, one should always specify a path when using the *.* designation in the ERASE and DEL commands. This helps prevent the inadvertent erasure of data.
4. It is possible to recover erased files if no new information is placed on the disk after the ERASE or DEL commands have been issued. This is because these commands do not actually wipe out areas of the disk, but rather specify that the space occupied by the "erased" files is now available for data storage; if no new information is added to the disk, the files remain intact. To recover these files, a special utility program must be used. The DOS command RECOVER cannot be used for this purpose.

The FIND Filter

FIND searches for all occurrences of a particular string in each of the filenames specified. It also includes three switches that can be activated to provide the user with basic data on the number, placement, and contents of matching and mismatching lines. The FIND filter is used with the following format:

```
FIND [/C][/N][/V]"string"[d:][path][filename][.ext]...
```

The switches /C, /N, and /V *must* precede the string. The string also must be enclosed in double quotes. Single switches may be specified or combinations of switches may be used. The switches have the following meaning:

/C	Displays a count of the number of matched lines.
/N	Displays the line number and contents of each matching line.
/V	Displays all mismatched line contents.
/C/V	Displays a count of the number of mismatched lines.
/N/V	Displays the line number and contents of each non-matching line.

Appendix A

NOTE: *With DOS 3.X, the parameter [d:][path] may be placed in front of the command. Since FIND is an external command, this allows the user to specify the particular drive and directory in which the command file is located. The pathname is separated from the command by a backslash (\).*

Although the FIND filter is a powerful tool, it has several limitations:

1. Global filename characters are not permitted in filenames and extensions. Thus, if one wants to search through the text of a number of files, each filename and extension must be specified.
2. The FIND filter is ASCII-based and searches only for exact matches. This means that upper- and lowercase letters, for example, have different ASCII representations and are treated differently. Using "The" as the string to be matched would produce different results from using the string "the."

The FORMAT Command

The FORMAT command initializes a disk in the specified drive so that it can be used by DOS. It causes the disk to be analyzed for any defective areas on the disk. It also prepares the disk for file storage by setting up a directory and the File Allocation Table. As an option, FORMAT also will copy onto the target disk the DOS files necessary for a system startup. All fixed disk partitions and floppy diskettes must be formatted before they can be used.

When a disk is formatted, DOS installs markings that divide the disk's areas into smaller parts. The disk is divided into a series of concentric circles called *tracks*. Each track is divided into smaller sections called *sectors*. A sector can store 512 bytes of information. Thus, the difference between the storage capacities of a fixed disk, a high-capacity disk, and a floppy diskette is a function of the number of tracks and sectors. The FORMAT command is written as follows:

```
FORMAT [d:][/S][/1][/8][/V][/B][/4]
```

NOTE: *The "/4" option is not available in DOS 2.0 or 2.1 and is a feature unique to DOS 3.0 and 3.1 for formatting 360-KB diskettes with a high-capacity drive. With DOS 3.X, the parameter [d:][path]*

may be placed in front of the command. Since FORMAT is an external command, this allows the user to specify the particular drive and directory in which the command is located. The pathname is separated from the command name by a backslash (\ ).

These parameters have the following meaning:

- d: This specifies the drive containing the disk to be formatted.
- /S When this parameter is included in the command, the following operating system files are copied to the disk or being formatted:

    IBMBIO.COM
    IBMDOS.COM
    COMMAND.COM

    When these files are contained on a disk, a system startup can be performed using that diskette or disk partition. This makes the partition or diskette "bootable." That is, one is able to "boot" or start the system from the disk.
- /1 This switch is included only when formatting floppy diskettes. It formats the diskette as a single-sided diskette, for use in single-sided disk drives. If it is not included, DOS formats diskettes as dual-sided. Dual-sided diskettes cannot be used in single-sided disk drives.
- /8 This formats a floppy diskette with eight (8) sectors per track instead of the usual nine. It cannot be used when formatting the fixed disk.
- /V When this parameter is included in the command, DOS prompts the user for a volume label. It is written on the disk; its function is to identify the disk or diskette. It cannot be used with the /8 switch.
- /B This formats a diskette with eight sectors per track, leaving space for the operating-system files. It is used to create a diskette onto which any version of DOS (1.0, 1.1, or 2.0) can be placed. It cannot be used in formatting the fixed disk or with the /S and /V parameters.
- /4 This formats a 360-KB double-sided diskette from the high-capacity drive.

Any data stored on a disk partition or a floppy diskette are destroyed when the disk or diskette is formatted. If the /S parameter is used, various messages and statistics are displayed when the formatting is complete.

Appendix A   255

The MKDIR (MD) Command

The MKDIR (Make Directory) command is used to create directories and subdirectories. It is abbreviated as MD. The MKDIR command has the following format:

```
MKDIR [d:][path][dirname]
```

These parameters have the following meaning:

- d: This specifies the disk drive that is to contain the new directory.
- path This is a series of directory names that leads DOS from the current or root directory through the directory hierarchy to the level at which the new directory is to be placed. A backslash separates each directory name in a path.
- dirname This is the name of the new directory. The directory name is separated from the path by a backslash.

The drive and path specifications are optional. When they are not specified in the command, the new directory is placed in the current directory of the default drive. It should be noted that the current, or active, directory is the location in the hierarchy from which DOS is reading files at any particular point in time. A new directory created with the MKDIR command is always placed as a subdirectory of the current directory unless a path is specified.

The MORE Filter

This filter reads data from an input device and then sends data to the display screen one screenful at a time. After each screenful of information, a pause occurs and displayed in the lower left corner of the screen is the message:

```
---More---
```

Pressing any character key causes the display to resume, with another pause if the remaining information exceeds one screen's worth. This process is repeated until all data have been displayed.

The MORE filter has the following format:

```
MORE
```

It has no value when used by itself. A typical application of the command might be as follows:

```
TYPE SAMPLE.TXT | MORE
```

In this case, the output of the TYPE command is passed through the MORE filter via piping. If the contents of the text file SAMPLE.TXT exceed the size of one display screen, a pause will occur after the first screen of information is displayed. The HELP screens for items with more than one screen in the *Hard Disk Manager* make use of this technique.

The PATH Command

The PATH command instructs DOS to search through a specified directory or directories for commands and/or batch files not found in the current directory. More than one path may be specified, and the drive may be specified as well. The PATH command is particularly useful with hierarchical directories because DOS does not permit the execution of a program or batch file that is not in the current directory. The PATH command has the following format:

```
PATH [d:]path1;[d:]path2;[d:]path3;...
```

d: This specifies the disk drive of the directory that is to be searched for commands or batch files.

path1; path2; ...   These are pathnames that direct DOS to the directories in the hierarchy where commands or batch files may be found. When more than one is specified, each is separated by a semicolon.

A few rules can assist the user when the PATH command is used:

1. If no disk drive is specified for a path, the current drive is used.
2. More than one directory path may be specified; each must be separated by a semicolon.

Appendix A

3. Paths should always start with the root directory. If the root directory is not the starting point, DOS assumes that the path begins with the current directory. This may result in an invalid path.
4. Any path that contains invalid information will be ignored.
5. Only program command files and batch files are affected by the PATH command (i.e., files with filename extensions of .EXE, .COM, or .BAT).
6. The PATH command can be most useful when it is included in an AUTOEXEC.BAT file. This file type is automatically executed when a system or program is booted. If included in the AUTOEXEC.BAT file, DOS will automatically search the specified directories for any subsequent command not found in the current directory.
7. Without parameters, the PATH command displays the current path.

The PROMPT Command

The PROMPT command allows the user to modify the appearance of the DOS system prompt. The standard DOS prompt (a letter followed by the > symbol) can be converted into an informational prompt that tells the user the date, the time of day, or the current directory. Or, the prompt may simply display a directive, such as ENTER COMMAND >. The prompt command has the following format:

```
PROMPT [prompt-text]
```

Special characters (called metastrings) also can be included after the PROMPT command. All of these special characters are preceded by the $ (carriage return plus line feed) character. These metastrings can be used with each other and with other character strings to produce customized system prompts. The following is a list of symbols used in metastrings.

- b   The | character.
- d   The date.
- e   The ESCAPE (ASCII 027) character.
- g   The > character.
- h   Backspace
- l   The < character.
- n   The default drive.
- p   The current directory of the default drive.
- q   The = character.

- t   The time.
- v   The version number.
- $ The $ character.
- _   A carriage return/linefeed sequence (go to the beginning of the next line on the display screen).

The system prompt is returned to normal by entering the PROMPT command with no arguments.

The RENAME Command

This command may be abbreviated to REN. It allows a user to change the filename and/or extension of a specified file. An error message is generated if there is another file with the same name in the same directory. RENAME has the following format:

```
RENAME [d:][path]filename[.ext] filename[.ext]
```

The parameters in this command have the following meaning:

- d: This specifies the drive containing the file that is to be renamed.
- path This specifies the directory location of the file that is being renamed.
- .ext This designates the filename extension.

Global filename characters are permitted.

Note that no drive or path is permitted in the second filename parameter: The drive and path of the first parameter are assumed.

The RESTORE Command

The RESTORE command is used to place one or more files copied by the BACKUP command back onto the fixed disk. In addition, if a file is accidently destroyed but has been copied onto a floppy diskette with the BACKUP command, it may be recreated with this command. If a fixed disk has failed, this command restores the BACKUP copies after the repair. Note

Appendix A

that files copied with the BACKUP command can be used only after they have been placed back onto the fixed disk with RESTORE.

BACKUP and RESTORE do not have to be reserved for solving or preventing data-loss problems. The commands also can be used to transfer data from one fixed disk system to another. When many files are involved, or when some of the files might be too large to fit onto floppy diskettes, the BACKUP command can be used to make the duplicates. The RESTORE command is then issued to place the floppy backup files onto the other system's fixed disk. The RESTORE command has the following format:

```
RESTORE d: [d:][path][filename][.ext][/S][/P]
```

NOTE: *With DOS 3.X, the parameter [d:][path] may be placed in front of the command. Since RESTORE is an external command, this allows the user to specify the particular drive and directory in which the command file is located. The pathname is separated from the command by a backslash (\).*

These parameters have the following meaning:

- **d:** This specifies first the source drive and then the target drive. In an XT or AT with a single fixed-disk drive and a single floppy-disk drive, these parameters are specified as A and C, respectively. Note that the source drive *must* be included in the command.
- **path** The directory to which the file or files are to be restored is specified by this parameter. Files are restored to the current directory if no path is specified.
- **filename** This parameter allows specific files to be restored to the fixed disk. Global filename characters may be used to designate more than one file. If no filename or filename extension is specified, then all files in the directory are restored.
- **.ext** This designates the filename extension. Global filename characters are permitted.
- **/S** All subdirectories below the directory level specified in the path parameter are restored when this parameter is included in the command.
- **/P** When this parameter is included in the command, DOS displays a prompt before restoring files that have been changed since the last backup, or before restoring files that are marked read-only.

If a complete system backup has been performed, all backup copies on floppy diskettes can be restored to the fixed disk with the command:

```
restore a: c:\/s
```

The user is instructed to place the first backup diskette into the floppy drive. After this is done, pressing any key initiates the process. If the system backup uses more than one diskette, DOS pauses and prompts the user to insert each numbered diskette in turn. The diskettes must be restored in the correct sequence; if not, DOS will pause and display an error message. The operation will resume when the correctly numbered diskette is placed in the disk drive.

If partial backups have been made since the last full backup, the full backup should be restored first. Only then should the partial backups be done, beginning with the oldest data. This process adds to the fixed disk all those backup files that have been created or modified since the last full backup. If the fixed disk contains new files that are not on the backup diskettes, they are not erased. Unlike the BACKUP command, RESTORE does not erase files on the disk before copying the backup files from the floppy diskettes.

The RMDIR Command

Occasionally, it is necessary to eliminate an entire directory from a directory system. The DOS command RMDIR (Remove Directory) is used for this purpose. It is abbreviated as RD. This Remove Directory command has the following format:

```
RMDIR [d:][path]
```

These parameters have the following meaning:

- d: This is the drive specification.
- path This specifies a directory path, with each directory separated by a backslash. The last name in the path is the directory to be deleted.

A few rules that must be followed when the RD command is used:

1. The root directory and the current directory cannot be deleted.

Appendix A 261

2. The directory to be deleted must be empty, except for the "." and ".." listings. Thus, command **ERASE *.*** must be issued first. When a DIR command is used to display the contents of an empty directory, only two files will be listed: the parent directory (..) and the current directory (.).
3. The name of the directory to be deleted must be specified in the command. If a path is specified, the directory to be deleted must be the last name in the path.
4. If the drive is not specified, the current drive is assumed.

The SORT Filter

The SORT command reads information from an input device, sorts it in ascending (A to Z) alphabetical order, and sends it to an output device. The SORT command also includes two switches that sort information in descending (Z to A) alphabetical order and perform a sort using a specified column as the primary sort key. The SORT command has the following format:

```
SORT [/R][/+n]
```

The two switches, /R and /+n, are used either as single switches or in combination; they must precede the input source. These parameters have the following meaning:

/R   Sorts the information in descending (Z to A) alphabetical order.

/+n   The primary sort key is set to start at column "n"; the default is column 1. For example, setting this switch as /+14 when sorting a directory listing produces a list of directory entries in file size order.

NOTE: *With DOS 3.X, the parameter [d:][path] may be placed in front of the command. Since SORT is an external command, this allows the user to specify the particular drive and directory in which the command file is located. The pathname is separated from the command by a backslash (\).*

The SORT command can accept keyboard input as its source and typically outputs information to the video display. The output of the SORT command also can be redirected to another device (such as the printer). The greater-than symbol (>) indicates the redirection of the output to a specified device.

Other DOS commands also can be filtered through the SORT command. For example, the DIR and SORT commands can be chained together by the ¦ symbol:

```
DIR ¦ SORT
```

This command tells DOS to display the directory entries (DIR) and pass them through the SORT filter to alphabetize them. Note that the SORT command in the previous example does not permanently alter the order of the directory listing. Subsequent issuance of the DIR command alone would produce an unalphabetized directory listing.

Just as was the case with the FIND filter, the SORT filter has its limitations:

1. The maximum file size that can be sorted is 63,000 characters.
2. File contents are sorted in ASCII sequence. Thus, capital letters will always precede lowercase letters.
3. Numeric sequences other than 0 through 9 cannot be sorted because numbers in ASCII files are treated as characters.
4. The end-of-file marker, Control-Z, appears before alphanumeric characters in a listing of ASCII characters. When SORT is used with a file containing the ^Z character, and the result is output to a file, the resulting file cannot be edited or typed out. This is because DOS reads the end-of-file marker and fails to recognize that additional lines in the file come after the ^Z.

The SYS Command

The SYS (System) command is used to transfer the operating system files from the default drive to the specified drive. The directory entry of the target disk must be empty or the disk must have been formatted with the /S or /B options of the FORMAT command. This is because specific disk space must be available for the IBMBIO.COM and IBMDOS.COM files. The SYS command has the following format:

```
SYS d:
```

Appendix A

The parameter d: is a specified disk drive. If the required space is not available on the target disk, an error message is displayed.

This command is generally used in two specific circumstances. If the user wishes to install a different version of DOS on his or her hard disk, this command can be used instead of reformatting the hard disk. Also, many applications programs are designed to be used with DOS but are not sold with DOS installed. If the program already has space allocated for the necessary DOS files, the SYS command can be used to make the program disk a boot (or system) disk.

The TREE Command

The TREE command (Display Directory) allows the user to view the structure of the disk's entire directory system, including all directories, subdirectories, and their contents. The difference between this command and the DIR command is that the latter permits the display of only one directory at a time. The TREE command has the following format:

```
TREE [d:][/F]
```

These parameters have the following meaning:

- d: This specifies the disk drive containing the directories to be displayed.
- /F   When this parameter is included, the TREE command displays the names of files contained in each directory.

NOTE: *With DOS 3.X, the parameter [d:][path] may be placed in front of the command. Since TREE is an external command, this allows the user to specify the particular drive and directory in which the command file is located. The pathname is separated from the command by a backslash (\).*

Both the drive and the /F parameters are optional. If the drive parameter is not specified, the TREE command displays the directories on the default drive. TREE displays only directory names and directory paths unless the /F parameter is used. The TREE command can be a particularly effective method of keeping track of what is contained in an extensive directory system.

The TYPE Command

This simple command is used to display the contents of a file on the screen. It is useful only for the display of text (ASCII) files. It has the following format:

```
TYPE [d:][path]filename[.ext]
```

The parameters have the following meaning:

- d: This is the drive containing the file whose contents are to be displayed.
- path The directory location on the specified or default drive is designated with this parameter.
- .ext This specifies the filename extension of the file that is to be displayed. Global filename characters are not permitted.

The XCOPY Command (DOS 3.2 and Later)

This command is useful for copying selective groups of files, which may include lower-level subdirectories. For example, suppose a user wishes to copy an entire directory plus its subdirectories to another disk. This command could be used in this case. It has one of three formats:

```
[d:][path]XCOPY [d:][path]filename[.ext]
[d:][path][filename[.ext]][/A][/D][/E][/M][/P]
[/S][/V][/W]
```

or

```
[d:][path]XCOPY [d:]path[filename[.ext]]
[d:][path][filename[.ext]][/A][/D][/E][/M][/P]
[/S][/V][/W]
```

or

```
[d:][path]XCOPY d:[path][filename[.ext]]
[d:][path][filename[.ext]][/A][/D][/E][/M][/P][/S]
[/V][/W]
```

The source and target destinations are separated by a space.

Appendix A 265

The user should not be intimidated by the excessive number of parameters in this command. The various permutations of the command simply add to its flexibility. The parameters have the following meaning:

[d:][path] Before the filename, this specifies the drive and/or the directory location of XCOPY command file.

[d:][path][filename[.ext]] As the source specification, this designates the starting drive, path, and/or file.

[d:][path][filename[.ext]] As the target specification, this designates the destination drive, directory, and/or filename.

/A This causes only files with the archive bit set to one to be copied.

/D This will designate only files with a date equal or later than a specified date to be copied. The format is /D:dd-mm-yy, /D:mm-dd-yy, or /D:yy-mm-dd, depending on the setting of the SELECT or COUNTRY commands.

/E This causes subdirectories to be created on the target, even if they are empty. If not specified, empty ones will not be created.

/M Files whose archive bit is set will be copied when this parameter is included.

/P A prompt is displayed before each file is copied when this parameter is used.

/S This parameter will copy the contents of subdirectories of the source as well as the source directory contents. Empty directories are not copied unless /E is included.

/V This causes DOS to verify that the target data are recorded properly.

/W When this parameter is used, DOS will wait until a key is pressed to begin the search for the source, displaying the message "Press any key to begin copying file(s)."

The authors found this command useful in copying portions of the *Hard Disk Manager* to their hard disk. For example, this command copied all of the Backup/Restore Utilities to drive C:

```
xcopy a:\hdu\backup c:\hdu /s
```

appendix b

A Batch File Reference Guide

Behind the *Hard Disk Manager* utilities are a number of programs written using the operating system's command language. These programs are known as batch files. They contain one or more commands that can be executed by DOS. When a batch file is activated, each command in the file is automatically executed in a batch mode. The beauty of batch files is their simplicity. They can be written or modified by nonprogrammers; all that is needed is a working knowledge of DOS's commands.

Batch files vary in complexity and type. They may contain the usual DOS commands, or they may use a special set of commands found only in batch files. Some of these special batch file commands have decision-making capabilities. These capabilities permit the user to develop routines that use sophisticated, higher-level programming techniques.

This appendix provides an overview of batch file commands, their usage, and some tips for using batch files to their fullest advantage.

Creating Batch Files

Batch files can be created several ways. They can be created using a standard text editor or the DOS EDLIN program. In addition, short routines can be created most expediently by utilizing advanced features of the COPY command.

Appendix B

Creating Batch Files with the COPY Command

The COPY CON: command can be used to create batch files. In effect, the COPY CON: command treats the input from the keyboard as input from a file. Data are copied from the keyboard (the console) to a new file (the batch file). The major advantage of this method is that it is very expedient. The major disadvantage is that errors cannot be corrected using the COPY CON: method.

The Format of COPY CON:

The following format is used to tell DOS to copy input from the keyboard to a batch file:

```
COPY CON: filename.bat
```

These parameters have the following meaning:

- CON: This portion of the command specifies a reserved device name in DOS. CON stands for console or the keyboard.

- filename This is the name of the batch file being created. The filename must conform to the normal rules of naming files. The filename *must* have .BAT as the filename extension.

Each text line entered at the keyboard is incorporated into the batch file. At the end of the batch file, an end-of-file marker (^Z) must be entered as the last line. This is done by either pressing the <F6> key or by holding down the <Ctrl> key and pressing **Z**. The end-of-file marker must be followed by <Enter>.

For example, to create a batch file that copies all *Lotus 1-2-3* files from a hard disk to a floppy disk in drive A, the following batch file might be written.

```
copy con: 123copy.bat
copy c:\123\*.wks a:
dir a:
^Z
```

Making Changes and Correcting Mistakes

If the file contains errors, the user has two choices: (1) The entire batch file can be rewritten, starting over with the COPY CON: command from the beginning, or (2) the line or lines with the errors can be edited with the DOS text-editing program, EDLIN, as is discussed in the next section.

Creating Batch Files with EDLIN

Batch files may be created with any text editor or DOS's text editor, EDLIN. EDLIN can be used to create, change, or display text files. Since EDLIN is a line editor, the text of files created or edited in EDLIN is displayed in numbered lines. Each line may be up to 253 characters wide.

The Edlin Format

The EDLIN program is started by entering the EDLIN command and the batch filename with a .BAT extension. The EDLIN command is entered in the following format:

```
EDLIN [d:][path]filename.bat
```

These parameters have the following meaning:

- d: (Optional) This specifies the drive of the disk where the batch file will be located.
- path   (Optional) The location of the file in the directory hierarchy is specified by this parameter.
- filename   This specifies the name of the batch file. Batch files must have the .BAT extension.

NOTE: *With DOS 3.X, the parameter [d:][path] may be placed in front of the command. Since EDLIN is an external command, this allows the user to specify the particular drive and directory in which the command file is located. The pathname is separated from the command by a backslash (\).*

Appendix B

Creating or Editing a Batch File in EDLIN

To create a new batch file with EDLIN or to edit an existing one, the EDLIN command is entered followed by the filename of the batch file. Thereafter, lines can be inserted, deleted, altered, copied, etc. using EDLIN's commands. A guide to EDLIN and the EDLIN commands can be found in Appendix C.

Batch File Subroutines

A batch file can be executed from within another batch file as a subroutine. This means that when the subroutine batch file ends, control will return to the original batch file and resume executing commands where it left off. For example, suppose batch file A in line 5 executes batch file B. Control is then passed to batch file B. When batch file B ends, control can be returned to line 6 of batch file A.

Two special commands are used to make batch files run as subroutines. The call to the subroutine batch file is made in the following format:

```
COMMAND /C <batch file name>
```

COMMAND is the DOS command processor, COMMAND.COM. The name of the subroutine batch file follows the /C switch. To return to the originating file, the subroutine batch file must end with the following command:

```
EXIT
```

The COMMAND /C command, followed by the batch file name, causes a secondary copy of COMMAND.COM to be loaded into memory. Execution of the batch file is processed by this secondary version of COMMAND.COM. The EXIT command instructs DOS to eliminate the secondary command processor from memory; control then returns to the first batch file.

An interesting application of this technique is as a control mechanism for use of <Ctrl><Break>. If these keys are pressed while the second batch file is in execution, control returns to the first batch file. If users are apt to press these keys during batch file execution, this technique will permit a controlled environment (e.g., a menu) to be maintained.

> NOTE: *Echoing of batch file commands resumes when control moves from one batch file to another. If this is not desirable, the command ECHO OFF should be the first line of the subroutine batch file, and should also follow the COMMAND /C command.*

Batch File Commands

DOS has a number of commands that are used exclusively in batch files. These commands allow the user to construct batch routines of even greater versatility and sophistication. The commands are REM, ECHO, PAUSE, IF, GOTO, FOR, and SHIFT. These commands may be used *only* in batch files. The CLS command is not restricted to batch files, but is particularly useful in batch routines. All of these commands are discussed below.

REM (Remark)

REM is used to place remarks or descriptive comments within batch files. Each remark (REM) can contain up to 123 characters. As the batch file is executed, the remarks appear on the screen. Thus, they can be used to describe the various components of a batch file as it is being executed. The command has the following format:

```
REM [remark]
```

It should be noted that DOS 2.X also allows the period (.) to be substituted for the REM command (DOS 3.X, however, does not). In a batch file, a command line that begins with a period is interpreted to mean REM. This can be useful when the word REM may be otherwise confusing to the user.

ECHO

ECHO has two main functions: It is used to display or suppress batch file commands as they appear on the screen during the execution of a batch file; and it can be used to place remarks or commentary on the screen during batch file execution.

The ECHO command is one of the most useful batch file commands. It can be used to give as much description as necessary to the user. Full

Appendix B   271

paragraphs of instructions or help screens can be built into batch files. At the same time, ECHO can be used to prevent the user from seeing confusing or distracting command syntax as it appears on the screen. To produce these two states, ECHO has an on/off switch; ECHO OFF suppresses the display of commands during batch-file execution; and ECHO ON turns the display back on. ECHO used alone displays only the comments it precedes. Used alone, it has the following format:

```
ECHO [message]
```

If the user does not wish to have the batch commands displayed as they are executed, the first command in the batch file should be ECHO OFF. The ECHO OFF command itself is displayed, but no other batch command after it will appear on the screen until an ECHO ON command is encountered. There is no need to end the batch file with ECHO ON, as DOS automatically returns to the ECHO ON mode when the batch routine ends.

It is important to note that the ECHO OFF prevents only the batch file commands from being displayed on the screen; it has no effect on the display of information generated by the commands themselves. For example, a DIR command in a batch file will still show a listing of filenames on the screen, even if ECHO OFF is in effect.

When ECHO commands are used to display messages, blank lines can be displayed by specifying the "text" of the message as an unprintable character, such as <Alt> 255.

PAUSE

PAUSE halts the execution of a batch file and displays an optional command of up to 121 characters. Then it displays the message:

```
Strike a key when ready...
```

When any key is pressed, the batch file resumes from where it was halted. The PAUSE command is particularly helpful when it is necessary for the user to pause and perform another task before the batch file continues. For example, if a batch file is created that archives old files and sends a list of the files to the printer, the PAUSE command might be used to instruct the user to check to see that his or her printer is on and ready. PAUSE has the following format:

```
PAUSE [message]
```

The [message] parameter is optional. This command is useful for situations when the user must perform some task before the batch routine can proceed.

CLS (Clear Screen)

CLS is not a command that is restricted to batch files. CLS can be used anywhere in DOS. However, it is particularly useful in batch routines as a way of controlling the screen display. When this command is entered, all information on the screen is cleared. The prompt or cursor then moves to the upper left-hand corner of the screen. For example, a batch file might display a message or call up a user-designed menu. The CLS command can be used to blank the screen just before the message or menu is displayed. The screen then contains only the desired information.

IF

IF is a batch file command that allows the user to make the execution of certain commands conditional. If a specified condition is true, the command is executed; if the condition is false, the command is ignored. Without the IF command, one could not have branching logic within a batch file. Writing command sequences would be far more complicated and the code far less efficient. IF has the following format:

```
IF [NOT] [condition] [command]
```

The condition parameter may be expressed in one of three ways. Each is described below. Also included in the discussion is the [NOT] parameter.

The Exist Condition

This condition tests for the existence of a specified file. When used with the IF command, it has the following format:

```
IF EXIST [filespec] [command]
```

or

```
IF NOT EXIST [filespec] [command]
```

The filespec parameter is a filename and an optional filename extension. An optional drive specification may be included as well. Pathnames are not

Appendix B

allowed in versions of DOS prior to 3.0. This condition performs a specified command only if a particular file exists when the batch file is executed. Conversely, when the NOT parameter is used, a specified command is performed only if a particular file does not exist.

The String1==String2 Condition

This condition in the IF command tests whether one character string is equal to another character string. It has the following format when used with the IF command:

```
IF [string1==string2] [command]
```

Translated, this means "If the string entered by the user (string1) is equal to this specific string (string2), then do this command." Notice that two equal signs are used in the command. If the two strings match, character for character, then the condition is true and the command is performed. If the two strings do not match, then the command is ignored and the next line of the batch file is executed. The two strings also must be identical in their use of upper- and lowercase letters.

The Errorlevel Condition

This condition in the IF command can be used to test if specific DOS commands or programs have been completed successfully. The error code scheme currently is used by only two DOS commands, BACKUP and RESTORE.

Applications programs that use error code schemes typically set the error level at 0 if the program has been completed successfully. When such programs do not successfully complete their operations, the error level usually is set at different positive values, depending on the nature of the error. Typically, the seriousness of the error increases as the value of the error code increases. The user's manual accompanying the program should be consulted for the error-level code scheme used by that program, if any.

GOTO

GOTO is used to alter the sequential order of a batch file's execution. This command permits the batch file to jump from one series of commands to another. It is most often used in conjunction with the IF command; i.e., if a certain condition exists, the batch file goes to another location to continue.

Descriptive labels in the batch file are used as location points for the GOTO command. A batch file LABEL begins with a colon (:) followed by any character string from one to eight characters long. Command execution can be shifted to any of these points with the GOTO command. The command has the following format:

```
GOTO [label]
```

Labels may be longer than eight characters, but DOS recognizes only the first eight. In a batch file, these labels are never displayed when the file is executed. This means that they can be used throughout a batch file for descriptive purposes as an alternative to the REM command. (REM statements are displayed unless ECHO OFF is in effect.) If a GOTO command directs command execution to a label that does not exist in the batch file, the batch routine is ended and the following error message is displayed:

```
Label not found
```

FOR

FOR is used to perform a command or a series of commands on a list of files. As such it enhances the efficiency of batch files because it eliminates the need to enter the same command(s) for a series of files. This command has the following format:

```
FOR %%variable IN (set) DO [command]
```

These parameters have the following meaning:

- variable   This is a single upper- or lowercase letter, and it represents a dummy filename. During the execution of the FOR command, the files specified in set (which is a list of filenames) are substituted sequentially for variable (the dummy filename).
- set   This is the list of filenames that are the subject of the command. Each item in the list is separated by a space. File specifications may include the filename, the filename extension, and the drive specification.

Appendix B

                    Pathnames are not allowed. Wild-card characters (the * and ? symbols) may be used in filenames.

command   This is the action that is to be taken on each of the items in the set. It is any internal DOS command such as DIR, COPY, or DEL.

NOTE: *Although pathnames are not allowed in the set parameter in DOS 2.X, they are permitted in DOS 3.X.*

Notice in particular the syntax used in the FOR command. The variable parameter must be preceded by two percent signs (%%) and the filenames in the set parameter are enclosed in parentheses.

SHIFT

SHIFT allows the user to increase the number of replaceable parameters used in a batch file. As indicated below, up to ten variables or replaceable parameters can typically be used in a batch file. Each time this command is encountered in a batch file, the numbering of the variables supplied with the batch filename moves one position to the left. That is, the %1 variable is treated as %2, the 2% variable becomes %3, and so on. This command can be useful when a batch file is receiving input from a text file.

Using Replaceable Parameters with Batch Files

Batch files can be written so that they can accept variable input, i.e., filenames, drive specifications, paths, etc. Batch-file input variables are indicated by the symbol %, and are called *replaceable parameters*. The % notation indicates that the parameter is specified by the user each time the batch file is executed. As a result, the user may input different parameters for those commands every time the batch file is run, without having to change the contents of the file.

    Up to ten different replaceable parameters may be specified in a batch file. All replaceable parameters begin with the percent sign (%), followed by a number from 0 to 9. The replaceable parameter %0 is reserved for designating the name of the batch file itself in the batch file, if this is necessary. It may not be used for any other purpose. The numbering for all other valid command parameters begins with %1. The SHIFT command can be used when more than ten replaceable parameters are required (see above).

In a batch file with replaceable parameters, the user does not necessarily have to specify all the parameters when the batch routine is executed. Although replaceable parameters %1 to %3 are specified in a batch file, the user does not necessarily have to enter all three variables. Consider the following example in which the COPY and DIR commands accept variable input:

```
copy c:%1 %2%3
dir %2%3
```

The first replaceable parameter (%1) can be used to specify the source file for the COPY command. The second replaceable parameter (%2) may specify either another drive or a directory path for the target file of the COPY command. The third replaceable parameter may specify the new filename for the target file. The third replaceable parameter need not be specified; for example, if the drive is omitted, DOS simply ignores the %3 parameter in the batch file.

A Special Batch File: AUTOEXEC.BAT

AUTOEXEC.BAT is DOS's special facility for automatic execution of batch files. Whenever the computer is turned on or a system restart is performed (i.e., <Ctrl><Alt><Del>), DOS searches for a file with this name. If such a file exists, DOS automatically executes this file before other system activities begin.

The AUTOEXEC.BAT file must reside in the root directory of the disk that is used for the system startup. The XT and AT will read from a floppy disk drive (drive A) if there is a diskette in this drive and the drive door is closed. If this is not the case, the system will read from the fixed disk. Thus, the user has the option of placing AUTOEXEC.BAT files on floppy diskettes, high-capacity floppy diskettes, or the root directory of the fixed disk. The AUTOEXEC.BAT file on the fixed disk is ignored when a floppy drive is used for the startup.

AUTOEXEC.BAT files are created like any other batch file. Either the COPY CON: command or the EDLIN program may be used to create them. The only difference between this type of batch file and normal batch files is in the use of the AUTOEXEC.BAT filename.

appendix c

An EDLIN Reference Guide

Command	Page
The APPEND LINES Command (A)	277
The COPY LINES Command (C)	278
The DELETE LINES Command (D)	278
The EDIT LINES Command	278
The END EDIT Command (E)	278
The INSERT LINES Command (I)	278
The LIST LINES Command (L)	279
The MOVE LINES Command (M)	279
The PAGE Command (P)	279
The QUIT EDIT Command (Q)	279
The REPLACE TEXT Command (R)	280
The SEARCH TEXT Command (S)	280
The TRANSFER LINES Command (T)	280
The WRITE LINES Command (W)	280

The APPEND LINES Command (A)

This command (A) is used when the file to be edited is too large to fit into memory. The number of lines [n] is specified. These lines are added from disk to the end of the current line in the file being edited. If *no* lines are specified, lines are appended until memory is 75% full. Use the following format:

    [n]A

The COPY LINES Command (C)

Lines in a specified range (line numbers in the first two parameters) are copied to a line number (the third parameter). The number of times this operation is to be performed [, count] also may be specified. Use the following format:

```
[line],[line],line[,count]C
```

The DELETE LINES Command (D)

Line numbers in a specified range (first parameter to second parameter) are deleted. All line numbers are renumbered accordingly. Single lines (first parameter only) or the current line (no parameters) may be specified for deletion. Use the following format:

```
[line][,line]D
```

The EDIT LINES Command

This command displays the line number and the text to be edited. Control and editing keys can then be used to alter the text. Use the following format:

```
[line]
```

Entering a period (.) instead of a line number displays the current line for editing.

The END EDIT Command (E)

The EDLIN session is terminated and the edited file is saved under the initially specified filename using the following format:

```
E
```

The INSERT LINES Command (I)

The I command permits the user to insert line(s) immediately preceding the specified line [line] or the current line (.). Creation of *new* files requires that the I command be entered prior to inserting text. Use the following format:

    [line]I

The LIST LINES Command (L)

The L command types out the line numbers and the text in a specified range (first two parameters). Twenty-three lines, beginning with the specified line, are displayed if only the first parameter is entered; eleven lines plus the current line are displayed if only the second parameter is entered. Eleven lines before and after the current line are displayed if *no* parameter is entered. Use the following format:

    [line][,line]L

The MOVE LINES Command (M)

Lines in a specified range (line numbers in the first two parameters) are moved ahead of the specified line # (third parameter). All line numbers are renumbered accordingly. Use the following format:

    [line],[line],lineM

The PAGE Command (P)

The P command types out the line numbers and text in a specified range (first two parameters). Twenty-three lines are displayed if only the first parameter is entered; the current line plus one are displayed if only the second parameter is entered. The user can then "page" through a file, 23 lines at a time. Use the following format:

    [line][,line]P

The QUIT EDIT Command (Q)

The EDLIN session is terminated and the edited file *is not saved* using the following format:

    Q

The REPLACE TEXT Command (R)

Lines in a specified range (line numbers in the first two parameters) are scanned for the occurrence of a text string (first [string] parameter) and replaced with the text in the second [string] parameter. A confirmation prompt can be inserted before the replacement by including the [?] parameter. The search ends with the last line in memory if only the first parameter [line] is entered; the search begins following the current line if only the second parameter [, line] is entered; if both line parameters are omitted, lines following the current line to the last line in memory are searched. (Note that <F6> refers to the DOS function key setup or to <Ctrl> Z.) Use the following format:

```
[line][,line][?]R[string][<F6>string]
```

The SEARCH TEXT Command (S)

Lines in a specified range (line numbers in the first two parameters) are scanned for the occurrence of a text string [string] and the first line is displayed. A confirmation prompt to continue or discontinue searching can be displayed if the [?] parameter is included. (Omissions either of one or both [line] parameters produce the same results as those described for the Replace Text command.) Use the following format:

```
[line][,line][?]S[string]
```

The TRANSFER LINES Command (T)

Contents of a specified file ([d:]filename) are brought into the file currently being edited. These contents are placed ahead of the line number specified in the first parameter [line] or ahead of the current line (if no [line] parameter is specified). Use the following format:

```
[line]T[d:]filename
```

The WRITE LINES Command (W)

A specified number of lines [n], starting with line number 1, are written to disk. This command is used when the file being edited is too large to

Appendix C

fit into memory. This command is the opposite of the APPEND LINES command; it must be used to write edited lines to disk *before* loading additional unedited lines into memory. Use the following format:

    [n]W

NOTATIONS USED FOR EDLIN PARAMETERS

[line]	=	a line number is specified *or*
		a # sign is entered to indicate the next available line in memory *or*
		a period (.) is entered to indicate the current line
[n]	=	number of lines
[string]	=	series of characters/text is entered
<F6>	=	DOS function key, F6, is pressed to signal end of string; <Ctrl> Z keys can be used as well
[?]	=	? is entered to insert a confirmation prompt (a yes/no decision alternative) in the Search/Replace operations

appendix d

Control Character Sequences

FUNCTION	TEXT File Format	PROMPT Format
Change Display Attributes:		
Restore display to normal	^[[0m	prompt $e[0m
Make characters invisible	^[[8m	prompt $e[8m
Create blinking characters	^[[5m	prompt $e[5m
Increase character brightness	^[[1m	prompt $e[1m
Reverse video screen	^[[7m	prompt $e[7m
Underscore characters	^[[4m	prompt $e[4m
Change Foreground/Background Colors:		
Foreground Colors		
Black	^[[30m	prompt $e[30m
Blue	^[[34m	prompt $e[34m.
Cyan	^[[36m	prompt $e[36m
Green	^[[32m	prompt $e[32m
Magenta	^[[35m	prompt $e[35m
Red	^[[31m	prompt $e[31m
White	^[[37m	prompt $e[37m
Yellow	^[[33m	prompt $e[33m
Background Colors		
Black	^[[40m	prompt $e[40m
Blue	^[[44m	prompt $e[44m
Cyan	^[[46m	prompt $e[46m
Green	^[[42m	prompt $e[42m

Appendix D

FUNCTION	TEXT File Format	PROMPT Format

Change Foreground/Background Colors:

Background Colors

Magenta	^[[45m	prompt $e[45m
Red	^[[41m	prompt $e[41m
White	^[[47m	prompt $e[47m
Yellow	^[[43m	prompt $e[43m

Change Cursor Position:

Move cursor to row #/column #	^[[#;#H	prompt $e[#;#H
Move cursor up row #'s	^[[#A	prompt $e[#A
Move cursor down row #'s	^[[#B	prompt $e[#B
Move cursor forward column #'s	^[[#C	prompt $e[#C
Move cursor backward column #'s	^[[#D	prompt $e[#D
Save current cursor position	^[[s	prompt $e[s
Restore cursor to normal	^[[u	prompt $e[u
Erase display, move to home	^[[2J	prompt $e[2J
Erase from cursor position to end of line	^[[K	prompt $e[K

NOTES FOR CHANGING THE CURSOR POSITION:

The # symbols represent row and/or column numbers. Note that these commands must use the upper- and lowercase designation shown above. The first command shown above is used extensively in the batch files of the *Hard Disk Manager*.

appendix e

ASCII Extended Character Set: Selected Values

| ┌ 218 191 ┐ | ┌ 195   180 ┐ | ┌ 194 ┐ | ┌   │   ┐ |
| └ 192 217 ┘ | └   ┘ | └ 193 ┘ | │ 197 │ |

| ╔ 201 187 ╗ | ╔ 204   185 ╗ | ╔ 203 ╗ | ╔   ║   ╗ |
| ╚ 200 188 ╝ | ╚   ╝ | ╚ 202 ╝ | ║ 206 ║ |

| ╒ 214 183 ╕ | ╒ 199   182 ╕ | ╒ 210 ╕ | ╒   │   ╕ |
| ╘ 211 189 ╛ | ╘   ╛ | ╘ 208 ╛ | │ 215 │ |

| ╓ 213 184 ╖ | ╓ 198   181 ╖ | ╓ 209 ╖ | ╓   ║   ╖ |
| ╙ 212 190 ╜ | ╙   ╜ | ╙ 207 ╜ | ║ 216 ║ |

─	196	■	223	Ω	234	⌡	245
═	205	α	224	δ	235	+	246
│	179	β	225	∞	236	≈	247
║	186	Γ	226	φ	237	°	248
░	176	π	227	ε	238	•	249
▒	177	Σ	228	∩	239	·	250
▓	178	σ	229	≡	240	√	251
█	219	μ	230	±	241	ⁿ	252
▄	220	τ	231	≥	242	²	253
▌	221	Φ	232	≤	243	■	254
▐	222	Θ	233	⌠	244	blank 'FF'	255

appendix f

Extended ASCII Codes for Key Reassignment

These tables list the extended ASCII codes for the 40 possible keystroke combinations using the function keys. These keystrokes are:

- the ten function keys, <F1> through <F10>
- the <Shift> key plus the function keys
- the <Ctrl> key plus the function keys
- the <Alt> key plus the function keys

Also listed are standard and extended ASCII codes for some other non-alpha/numeric keys. These codes can be used in key reassignment routines. This is done using control code sequences in either a text (EDLIN) file or via the PROMPT command. The syntax of each format is as follows:

For Text Files: ^[[#,#;"string";p   or   ^[[#,#;...p
In PROMPT: PROMPT $e[#,#;"string";p   or
           PROMPT $e[#,#;...p

The above notations have the following meaning:

#;#   These # signs are the two values representing the ASCII value for the function keys; for the function-key reassignment, the first value is always 0.

"string"   A character string may be assigned to a function key, such as batch filenames or commands; the string is enclosed in quotation marks.

285

p   This signifies to ANSI.SYS that this is a key reassignment command. The lowercase letter must be used at the end of the command.

...   One or more keystrokes and strings may be reassigned to the function keys; each is represented by its ASCII value and is separated by a semicolon. For example, <F10> could be assigned to type the string "lotus" followed by a carriage return. This would be written as follows:

```
^[[0,68;"lotus";13p
```

The ASCII value of the carriage return <Enter> is 13.

Appendix F

EXTENDED ASCII CODE FOR FUNCTION KEYS

FUNCTION KEYSTROKES	ASCII VALUE
\<F1\>	0,59
\<F2\>	0,60
\<F3\>	0,61
\<F4\>	0,62
\<F5\>	0,63
\<F6\>	0,64
\<F7\>	0,65
\<F8\>	0,66
\<F9\>	0,67
\<F10\>	0,68
\<Shift\>\<F1\>	0,84
\<Shift\>\<F2\>	0,85
\<Shift\>\<F3\>	0,86
\<Shift\>\<F4\>	0,87
\<Shift\>\<F5\>	0,88
\<Shift\>\<F6\>	0,89
\<Shift\>\<F7\>	0,90
\<Shift\>\<F8\>	0,91
\<Shift\>\<F9\>	0,92
\<Shift\>\<F10\>	0,93
\<Ctrl\>\<F1\>	0,94
\<Ctrl\>\<F2\>	0,95
\<Ctrl\>\<F3\>	0,96
\<Ctrl\>\<F4\>	0,97
\<Ctrl\>\<F5\>	0,98
\<Ctrl\>\<F6\>	0,99
\<Ctrl\>\<F7\>	0,100
\<Ctrl\>\<F8\>	0,101
\<Ctrl\>\<F9\>	0,102
\<Ctrl\>\<F10\>	0,103
\<Alt\>\<F1\>	0,104
\<Alt\>\<F2\>	0,105
\<Alt\>\<F3\>	0,106
\<Alt\>\<F4\>	0,107
\<Alt\>\<F5\>	0,108
\<Alt\>\<F6\>	0,109
\<Alt\>\<F7\>	0,110
\<Alt\>\<F8\>	0,111
\<Alt\>\<F9\>	0,112
\<Alt\>\<F10\>	0,113

STANDARD AND EXTENDED ASCII CODES FOR OTHER KEYS

KEY	ASCII VALUE
\<Tab\>	9
\<Enter\>	13
\<Space\>	32
\<Home\>	0,71
\<Cursor Up\>	0,72
\<PgUp\>	0,73
\<Cursor Left\>	0,75
\<Cursor Right\>	0,77
\<End\>	0,79
\<Cursor Down\>	0,80
\<PgDn\>	0,81
\<Ins\>	0,82
\<Del\>	0,83
\<ShiftTab\>	0,15
\<Ctrl\>\<Home\>	0,119
\<Ctrl\>\<PgUp\>	0,132
\<Ctrl\>\<PrtSc\>	0,114
\<Ctrl\>\<Cursor Left\>	0,115
\<Ctrl\>\<Cursor Right\>	0,116
\<Ctrl\>\<End\>	0,117
\<Ctrl\>\<PgDn\>	0,118

Index

A.BAT, 36-37, 39, 41, 65
Access control, security, 147
AGAIN.BAT, 198
AGAIN command, 198
ANSI.SYS, 82
   cursor control, 92-93
   DOS, 12
      display attributes, altering, 87-88
      keyboard reassignment, 87-88
/A parameter, adding, 144-145
APPEND LINES command, EDLIN
      command, use of, 277
ARCHIVE.BAT, 152-153
ARCHIVE command, 151
ARCHIVE.TXT, 175
ASCII characters
   display, Help utilities, 102
   extended set, 14
      block letters, 105
      border designs, 102-103, 106
      colored screen designs, 111-113
      creating screen with, 102-103, 105, 223-224
      for function keys, 287
      generation of, 105-106
      input shortcut with EDLIN
         REPLACE TEXT, 106-107, 117
      for key reassignment, 285-286
      listing of, 284
ASCII Graphics HELP, 189
ASSIGN command, general information/
      use of, 238
ATTRIB command, 168, 170, 171
   general information/use of, 239-240

Audit trails, security, 147
AUTO.BAT, 43-44, 45
AUTO command, 35
AUTOEXEC.BAT, 44-45
   general information/use of, 276
   purpose of, 83-84
   screen attributes, setting, 83-84
AUTOEXEC.BAT HELP, 189

BACKUP command, 122, 125, 142-143, 146
   /A parameter, 129
   general information/use of, 240-242
Backup files, batch, use of, 218
Backup Files by Date, 132-134
   program files, 133-134
   running of, 132
Backup/Restore utilities, 121-147
   activation of, 124-125
   Backup Files by Date, 132-134
      program files, 133-134
      running of, 132
   floppy disk needed, 125-126
   Full Backup, 125-128
      and copy-protected software, 127
      program files, 127-128
      running of, 126-127
   Full Restore, 137-139
      program files, 138-139
      running of, 137-138
   menu, 124
   modification of, 142-145
      /A parameter, adding to, 144-145
      guidelines/tips, 143

menu items, adding/deleting, modifying, 144
New File/Modified File Backup, 135-137
    program files, 136
organization of, 122-123
    HD BACKUP, 122
    HDU BACKUP DATEBACK, 123
    HDU BACKUP FULLREST, 123
    HDU BACKUP MODIFY, 123
    HDU BACKUP PARTIAL, 123, 145
    HDU BACKUP PARTREST, 123
Partial Backup, 129-132
    program files, 130-132
Partial Restore, 139-142
    program files, 141-142
    running of, 140
usefulness of, 121-122
.BAK files, 218
Batch file design, 230-235
    chaining batch files, 234
    confirmation prompts, 233
    key reassignment, 231-232
    redirecting input, 230-231
    redirecting output, 231
    replaceable parameters, uses of, 6, 234, 275-276
    self-modifying batch files, 235
    subroutines, use of, 233
    user-interactive files, 230
    validity of input, 232
Batch files, 8-10
    AUTOEXEC.BAT, 276
    Backup Files by Date, 133-134
        BYDATE.BAT, 134
        3.BAT, 133
        Y.BAT, 133, 134
    Change Background Color, 78-79
        2.BAT, 79
    Change Foreground Color, 75-76
        codes for color display, 75-76
        9.BAT, 76
        1.BAT, 75
        SETSCRN.BAT, 76, 77
    Change Screen Attributes, 81-82
        3.BAT, 81
    characteristics of, 8-9
    commands
        CLS (Clear Screen) command, 272
        ECHO command, 270-271
        FOR command, 274-275
        GOTO command, 273-274
        IF command, 272-273
        PAUSE command, 271

Batch files, continued
        REM command, 270
        SHIFT command, 275-276
    contents of, 9
    creation of, 267-270
        with COPY CON command, 267
        with EDLIN, 268-269
        subroutines, 269-270
    Diskcopy
        DODCOPY.BAT, 167
        6.BAT, 167
    File Archive, 152-153
        ARCHIVE.BAT, 152-153
        1.BAT, 152
    File Combine, 157-158
        COMBINE.BAT, 158
        3.BAT, 157
    File Protect/Unprotect, 169-171
        PROTECT.BAT, 170
        7.BAT, 169
        UNPROTECT.BAT, 171
        Y.BAT, 169-170
    format utilities
        DOFORM3.BAT, 55
        DOFORM4.BAT, 56
        DOFORM5.BAT, 57
        5.BAT, 57
        4.BAT, 56
        3.BAT, 55
    Full Backup
        1.BAT, 127-128
        Y.BAT, 128
    Full Restore, 138-139
        5.BAT, 138
        Y.BAT, 138
    Help Screen, 190-195
        confirmation prompt batch files, 192-193
        MORE filter, use of, 192
        multiple screen display, 191-192
        N.BAT, 192, 193, 194-195
        #.BAT, 194, 195, 196
        single HELP screen, 194-195
        3.BAT, 191, 193
        Y.BAT, 192-193, 194
    Locate File, 164-166
        DOLOCATE.BAT, 165-166
        5.BAT, 164
        LOCATE.BAT, 165
    and Menu/Directory Setup utility, 36-45
        A.BAT, 36-37, 39, 41
        AUTO.BAT, 43-44, 45
        and AUTOEXEC.BAT file, 44-45

Index

Batch files, continued
   and COPY CON command, 37, 38–39
   DOCOPYC1.BAT, 37–38, 41
   DOCOPYC2.BAT, 37, 41
   G.BAT, 42
   MENU.BAT, 43
   N.BAT, 44
   1.BAT, 35–36, 40–41
   RETURN.BAT, 45
   WPMORE.BAT, 37, 39–40
   WPSTART.BAT, 37, 39–40
   Y.BAT, 44
  modifying, 215–218
   deleting batch files, 216–217
   lines, adding/deleting, 216
   menus/screens/menu selections, deleting, 217
   renaming batch files, 217
  Move File, 154–158
   MOVE.BAT, 155–156
   2.BAT, 154–155
  New File/Modified File Backup, 135–136
   4.BAT, 136
   MODIFY.BAT, 136
  Partial Backup
   PARTIAL.BAT, 130, 132
   2.BAT, 130
   Y.BAT, 130, 132
  Partial Restore
   PARTIAL.BAT, 142
   6.BAT, 141
   Y.BAT, 141, 142
  programming commands, 10
  RD utility, 60–61
   ERASEDIR.BAT, 61
  Screen Design utility, DESIGN.BAT, 100–101, 119
  Text Search
   4.BAT, 160–161
   SEARCH.BAT, 161–162
  uses of, 9–10
  using (.BAK) backup batch files, 218
  View/Print utilities
   DOPRINT.BAT, 51–52
   DOTREE.BAT, 52–54
   DOVIEW.BAT, 50–51, 59–60
   PRINT.BAT, 51–52
   VIEW.BAT, 50–51, 59–60
Blank line, creation of, screen design, 227
Borders
  adding/deleting/modifying, 214
  adding new, 214
  changing design of, 211–213
  in color, 112
  with EDLIN REPLACE TEXT, 106–107
  with extended ASCII characters, 102–103, 106
  extending, 209–210
  modifying, 215
  planning of, 108–110
  prefabricated, 119–120
BUFFERS, DOS, 11
BYDATE.BAT, 134

CD command. *See* CHDIR command
Chaining batch files, batch file design, 234
Change Background Color, 78–79
  color options, 78
  program files, 78–79
Change Foreground Color, 73–78
  color options, 74
  menu, 74
  program files, 75–76
  SETSCRN command, 76–78
Change Screen Attributes, 79–82
  blinking characters, setting, 80
  character intensity, increasing, 80
  display restored to normal, 81
  invisible characters, setting, 81
  menu, 80
  program files, 81–82
  reverse video, 81
  SCREEN.SCR. 82
Character attributes. *See* Change Screen Attributes
CHDIR (Change Directory) command, general information/use of, 217, 242–243
CHKDSK (Check Disk) command, 126, 162, 166
  general information/use of, 243–244
CLS (CLEAR SCREEN) command, 83, 89, 221
  batch file command, use of, 272
  general information/use of, 244
Colors
  with ASCII extended character set, 111–113
  Change Background Color, 78–79
  Change Foreground Color, 73–78
  and EDLIN REPLACE TEXT command, 113–114
  multicolor menu screen, 86–87

COMBINE.BAT, 158
COMBINE command, 156
Command /C, 6, 38, 51, 54, 58, 221, 233, 269-270
Command files, DOS, 6
Compatibility, of storage media, 62-63
CONFIG.SYS HELP, 189
Configuration files (CONFIG.SYS), 11
  BUFFERS, 11
  DEVICE, 12
  FILES, 12
  format of, 11
Confirmation prompts, batch file design, 233
Control characters
  DOS, 13-14
  sequences for, 282-283
Control codes, use of, screen design, 224-225
COPY command, 172, 174, 175, 176, 204
  general information/use of, 244-247
COPY CON command, 37, 38-39, 41, 221, 230, 235
  general information/use of, 247-249
  suggestions for use, 57-58
COPY LINES command, 115, 116, 209-210, 212
  EDLIN command, use of, 278
Copy-protected software, backup of, 127
Copy protection, security, 147
Cursor control, ANSI.SYS, 92-93
Cursor Position HELP, 190
Customized Display utilities, 70-94
  activation of, 73
  categories of, 70
  Change Background Color, 78-79
    color options, 78
    program files, 78-79
  Change Foreground Color, 73-78
    color options, 74
    menu, 74
    program files, 75-76
    SETSCRN command, 76-78
  Change Screen Attributes, 79-82
    functions performed, 80-81
    menu, 80
    program files, 81-82
  modifications of, 82-87
    display attributes, setting, 83-84
    guidelines/tips for, 82-83
    menu, creating in multicolor, 86-87
    menu items, adding/deleting, 83
    utility attributes, combining, 84-85

  organization of, 71-73
    HDU BACKGRND, 72, 79, 83
    HDU DISPLAY, 71, 73, 75, 81, 82
    HDU DISPLAY SCREEN, 72, 82, 83
    HDU FOREGRND, 71, 75, 83
  usefulness of, 71

Data disk, formatting, 55-56
Data storage, 6-7
  logical, 7
  physical, 6-7
DELETE command, 155, 156
  general information/use of 251-252
DELETE LINES command, 111, 114, 206, 208, 216
  EDLIN command, use of, 278
DESIGN.BAT, 100-101, 119
DESIGN.SCR, 99, 118
DEVICE, DOS, 12
DIR command, 217
  general information/use of, 249-250
Directory paths, hierarchical directory system, 183-184
Directory sort utility, 59-60
Directory utility, removing, 60-61
Diskcopy, 166-167
  DISKCOPY command, 166
  program files, 167
DISKCOPY command, 166
  general information/use of, 250
Disk/Directory utilities, 28-69
  accessing of, 29
  activation of, 31-32
  format utilities, 54-57
    data disk, formatting, 55-56
    data disk utility, formatting, 55
    program files, 56, 57
    system disk, formatting, 56
    360-KB/High-Capacity disk utility, formatting, 56-57
  menu, 31
  Menu/Directory Setup utility, 32-35
    batch files, 36-45
    installing new menu, 34-35
    menu choices, 32-33
    menu construction, 34
    Miscellaneous Programs option, 45-48
    program files, 35-45
    resetting menu, 48-49
  modification, 57-61
    directory sort utility, 59-60

Index

directory utility, removing, 60-61
menu items, adding/deleting, 58
tricks/suggestions, 57-58
operations not included, 57
organization of, 29-31
  file types used (.BAT, .SCR, .TXT), 31
  HDU DISK AUTO directory, 29, 30
  HDU DISK directory, 29, 30, 32
  HDU DISK MP directory, 29, 30
  HDU VIEW directory, 30, 31
usefulness of, 28-29
View/Print utilities, 49-54
  Print Contents of All Directories, 53-54
  program files, 50-54
  View Contents of All Directories, 52-53
  View/Print Contents of Directory, 49-50
Display attributes, changing, DOS, 14
DOCOPYC1.BAT, 37-38, 41, 65
DOCOPYC2.BAT, 37, 41
DODCOPY.BAT, 167
DOFORM3.BAT, 55
DOFORM4.BAT, 56
DOFORM5.BAT, 57
DOLOCATE.BAT, 165-166
DOPRINT.BAT, 51-52
DOS
  ASCII extended character set, 14
  AUTOEXEC.BAT, purpose of, 83-84
  batch files
    characteristics of, 8-9
    contents of, 9
    programming commands, 10
    uses of, 9-10
  command files, 6
  commands
    ASSIGN command, 238
    ATTRIB command, 239-240
    BACKUP command, 240-242
    CHDIR command, 242-243
    CHKDSK command, 243-244
    CLS (CLEAR SCREEN) command, 244
    COPY command, 244-247
    COPY CON command, 247-249
    DELETE command, 251-252
    DIR command, 249-250
    DISKCOPY command, 250
    ERASE command, 251
    FIND filter, 252-253
    FORMAT command, 253-254
    MKDIR command, 255
    MORE filter, 255-256
    PATH command, 256-257
    PROMPT command, 257-258
    RENAME command, 258
    RESTORE command, 258-260
    RMDIR command, 260-261
    SORT filter, 261-262
    SYS command, 262-263
    TREE command, 263
    TYPE command, 264
    XCOPY command, 264-265
  configuration files (CONFIG.SYS)
    BUFFERS, 11
    DEVICE, 12
    FILES, 12
    format of, 11
  control character sequences, 13-14
  cursor control, ANSI.SYS, 92-93
  data storage, 6-7
    logical, 7
    physical, 6-7
  display attributes
    altering, ANSI.SYS, 87-88
    changing, 14
  editing keys, 206
  file management, 6
  /4 option, 62-63
  hierarchical directory system, 63-64
    setting up, 181-184
  keyboard reassignment, 13
    ANSI.SYS, 87-88
  redirection, 12-13, 93-94
  screen/keyboard control
    EDLIN, 88-89
    PROMPT command, 89-91
  utilities, 7-8
    batch files, 8-10
    configuration files (CONFIG.SYS), 11
DOTREE.BAT, 52-54
DOVIEW.BAT, 50-51, 59-60

ECHO command, 77, 79, 221, 228
  batch file command, use of, 270-271
ECHO OFF command, 221
  effect of, 76, 90
Editing tools
  editing text of file, 205-206
  ending edit program, 207
  inserting/deleting lines, 206-207
  listing contents of file, 205

EDIT LINES command, 205, 210, 213, 214, 278
EDLIN, 84
  attribute screens, modifying, 85
  commands
    APPEND LINES command, 277
    COPY LINES command, 278
    DELETE LINES command, 278
    EDIT LINES command, 278
    END EDIT command, 278
    INSERT LINES command, 278-279
    LIST LINES command, 279
    MOVE LINES command, 279
    PAGE command, 279
    QUIT EDIT command, 279
    REPLACE TEXT command, 280
    SEARCH TEXT command, 280
    TRANSFER LINES command, 280
    WRITE LINES command, 280-281
  editing tools, 205-207
  HELP screens, 196
  key reassignment, 91
  notations used, 281
  screen files, basic facts about, 222
  screen/keyboard control, 88-89
  suggestions for use, 58
  See also Screen Design utility
END EDIT command, 111, 207, 213, 215
  EDLIN command, use of, 278
END.TXT, 41
ENTER SELECTION command, 211
ERASE command, 173, 216, 217
  general information/use of, 251
ERASEDIR.BAT, 61
Erasing
  erasing files, 176
  Hard Disk Manager, 24-25
Escape character, generating, 85, 87-89, 111, 224
Escape Characters HELP, 190
EXIT command, 39, 55, 221, 233

File Archive, 151-153
  ARCHIVE command, 151
  program files, 152-153
File Combine, 156-158
  COMBINE command, 156
  program files, 157-158
File management
  DOS, 6
  filenaming schemes, 178-179
    column positions, use of, 179-180

global filename characters, use of, 180-181
meaningful syllables, use of, 180
hierarchical directory system, 181-184
  directory paths, 183-184
  management of, 184
  structure of, 182
organization, methods of, 178
File Management utilities, 148-184
activation of, 150-151
Diskcopy, 166-167
  DISKCOPY command, 166
  program files, 167
File Archive, 151-153
  ARCHIVE command, 151
  program files, 152-153
File Combine, 156-158
  COMBINE command, 156
  program files, 157-158
File Protect/Unprotect, 167-171
  ATTRIB command, 168, 170, 171
  program files, 169-171
  PROTECT command, 170
  UNPROTECT command, 170, 171
Locate File, 162-166
  LOCATE command, 162, 164-165
  printing output, 164
  program files, 164-166
modification of, 171-177
  archived file inventory, creating, 174-175
  copy, multiple directory copy, 176-177
  copy/erase/rename utilities, 175-176
  guidelines/tips for, 172
  menu selections, adding/deleting, 173
  print changes automatically, 173-174
Move File, 153-156
  MOVE command, 153-154, 155
  program files, 154-158
organization of, 149-150
  HDU FILE, 149, 173
Text Search, 158-162
  program files, 160-162
  SEARCH command, 159
usefulness of, 148-149
FILEMENU.SCR, 173
Filenaming schemes. *See* File management, filenaming schemes
File Protect/Unprotect, 167-171
  ATTRIB command, 168, 170, 171
  program files, 169-171
  PROTECT command, 170

Index

UNPROTECT command, 170, 171
FILES, DOS, 12
Filter, defined, 158
   general information/use of, 252-253
FIND filter, 158, 162, 166
   general information/use of, 252-253
5.BAT, 57, 138, 164
Floppies
   backups, multiple-sets, 146
   formatting
      data disk, 55-56
      high-capacity disk, 56-57
      system disk, 56
   multiple directory copy, 176-177
FOR command, batch file command, use of, 274-275
FORMAT command, 54, 56, 62, 63
   general information/use of, 253-254
Format utilities, 54-57
   data disk, formatting, 55-56
   data disk utility, formatting, 55
   program files, 56, 57
   system disk, formatting, 56
   360-KB/High-Capacity disk utility, formatting, 56-57
4.BAT, 56, 136
/4 switch, 57, 62-63
Full Backup, 125-128
   and copy-protected software, 127
   program files, 127-128
   running of, 126-127
Full Restore, 137-139
   program files, 138-139
   running of, 137-138
Function key, HELP, creating, 196-199

G.BAT, 42
Global filename characters, use of, 129, 140, 180-181
GOTO command, batch file command, use of, 273-274
Greek characters, as design element, 114-115

Hard Disk Manager
   Backup/Restore utilities, 121-147
   Customized Display utilities, 70-94
   Disk/Directory utilities, 28-69
   File Management utilities, 148-184
   HDU root directory, 17
   HELP screen utilities, 185-200
   installation, 16-24
      of entire program, 17-19

   part of program, 19-21
   problems of, 21-24
   requirements of, 16-17
   modifying utilities, 201-218
   quick start, 3
   removing from hard disk, 24-25
   Screen Design utility, 95-120
   starting program, hdu commands, 18
   users of, 3
   uses of, 2
HDU BACKGRND, 71, 79, 83
HDU BACKUP, 122
HDU BACKUP DATEBACK, 123
HDU BACKUP FULLREST, 123
HDU BACKUP MODIFY, 123
HDU BACKUP PARTIAL, 123, 145
HDU BACKUP PARTREST, 123
HDU.BAT, 92
Hdu command, starting program, 18
HDU DESIGN, 98
HDU DISK, 29, 30, 32, 36, 55, 56
HDU DISK AUTO, 29, 30, 36
HDU DISK MP, 29, 30, 36
HDU DISPLAY, 71, 73, 75, 81, 82
HDU DISPLAY SCREEN, 72, 82, 83
HDU FOREGRND, 71, 75, 83
HDU HELP, 186, 187, 193
HDU HELP BATCH, 186, 191, 193
HDU HELP DOS, 186
HDU HELP EDLIN, 186
HDU VIEW, 30, 31
Help files (.HLP), 204
HELP.SCR, 190, 192, 193
HELP screens, 199-200
   planning stage, HELP screens, 199-200
   usefulness of, 199
HELP screen utilities, 185-200
   activation of, 186-187
   ASCII Graphics HELP, 189
   AUTOEXEC.BAT HELP, 189
   CONFIG.SYS HELP, 189
   Cursor Position HELP, 190
   DOS commands HELP, 189
   EDLIN commands HELP, 190
   Escape Characters HELP, 190
   menu, 188
   modification of, 195-199
      adding/modifying HELP screens, 195-196
      deleting HELP screens, 196
      HELP function key, creating, 196-199
   organization of, 186

HDU HELP, 186, 187, 193
HDU HELP BATCH, 186, 191, 193
HDU HELP DOS, 186
HDU HELP EDLIN, 186
program files, 190–195
Screen Attributes HELP, 190
Screen Color HELP, 190
usefulness of, 185–186
Hierarchical directory system, 63–64, 181–184
advantages of, 64
directory paths, 183–184
management of, 184
and menu access, 64
structure of, 182
High-capacity drives, compatibility of, 62–63

IBMBIO.COM, 6
IBMDOS.COM, 6
IC command, 221
IF command, 155, 156, 158, 162, 172
batch file command, use of, 272–273
suggestions for use, 58
Information screens, displaying, screen design, 227–228
INSERT LINES command, 115, 206, 212, 216
EDLIN command, use of, 278–279
Installation, 16–24
of entire program, 17–19
part of program, 19–21
problems of, 21–24
invalid directory specification, 21–22
odd characters after prompt, 22–23
PATH commands, conflicts with, 23–24
requirements of, 16–17
INSTRUCT.SCR, 99, 118

Key reassignment
ANSI.SYS, 87–88, 91–92
batch file design, 231–232
DOS, 13
in *Hard Disk Manager*, 13, 92, 231–232
for HELP Screens, 196–197
with extended ASCII characters, 285–286

LIST LINES command, 109, 111, 116, 205, 209, 212, 213, 215 216
EDLIN command, use of, 279
LOCATE.BAT, 165
LOCATE command, 162, 164–165
Locate File, 162–166
LOCATE command, 162, 164–165
printing output, 164
program files, 164–166
LOGOAID, 99

MAINMENU.SCR, 43, 44
MANUAL command, 35, 42
MENU.BAT, 43
MENU command, 33, 34, 35
Menu/Directory Setup utility, 32–35
batch files, 36–45
installing new menu, 34–35
menu choices, 32–33
menu construction, 34
menu selections, 33–34
Miscellaneous Programs option, 45–48
program files, 46–48
submenu display, 45–46
program files, 35–45
adding menu selection, 36–37
installing menu, 42–45
operation of, 37–42
resetting menu, 48–49
See also Batch files, Menu/Directory Setup utility
Menu items, adding/deleting, 58
Menu selections, executing, screen design, 229
Metastring activation, PROMPT command, 90
Miscellaneous Programs option, 45–48
MKDIR command, 137
general information/use of, 255
MODIFY.BAT, 136
MODIFY command, 135–136
Modifying utilities, 201–218
batch files, 215–218
considerations, pre-modification, 202
editing tools
editing text of file, 205–206
ending edit program, 207
inserting/deleting lines, 206–207
listing contents of file, 205
foreknowledge needed
batch files (.BAT), 203–204
directory/subdirectory structure, 202–203
file structure, 203
screen files, 207–215
See also specific types of files
MORE filter, 53, 58, 192, 209, 228

Index

general information/use of, 255-256
use of, HELP Screen, 192
MOVE.BAT, 155-156
MOVE command, 153-154, 155
Move File, 153-156
   MOVE command, 153-154, 155
   program files, 154-158
MOVE LINES command, EDLIN
      command, use of, 279
MOVE.SCR, 155
Multiple screens, displaying, screen
      design, 228

N.BAT, 44, 192, 193, 194-195, 233
New File/Modified File Backup, 135-137
   program files, 136
9.BAT, 76
NUL, 12, 101

1.BAT, 35-36, 40-41, 75, 127-128, 152

PAGE command, EDLIN command, use
      of, 279
Partial Backup, 129-132
   program files, 130-132
PARTIAL.BAT, 130, 132, 142, 145
Partial Restore, 139-142
   program files, 141-142
   running of, 140
PATH command, general information/use
      of, 256-257
Pathname, defined, 183
PAUSE command, 208
   batch file command, use of, 271
Piping, defined, 94
#.BAT, 194, 195, 196
Prefabricated designs, creating, 119-120
PRINT.BAT, 49, 51-52
PRINT command, 49
Printing
   Locate File, 164
   print changes automatically, 173-174
PRN, 12, 52, 54, 93, 173-174, 223
Program files
   Menu/Directory Setup utility, 35-45
      adding menu selections, 36-37
      installing menu, 42-45
      operation of, 37-42
Programming. *See* Utility (creation of)
PROMPT command, 82-83, 191, 221, 231
   altering parameters, 210-211
   and cursor position, 92-93, 143
   general information/use of, 257-258

key reassignment, 91
metastring activation, 90
screen/keyboard control, 89-91
use of, screen design, 226
PROTECT.BAT, 170
PROTECT command, 170

QUIT command, 207, 215
QUIT EDIT command, EDLIN
      command, use of, 279

RD command. *See* RMDIR command
   adding of, 60-61
Redirection, 41, 93-94, 101
   capabilities, 12-13
   of input, batch file design, 93-94, 101,
      230-231
   of output, 52, 54, 173-174
      batch file design, 230-231
   output data to text file, 75-76, 93,
      174-175
REM command, batch file command, use
      of, 270
Removing *Hard Disk Manager*, 24-25
RENAME command, 176, 217
   general information/use of, 258
Rename files, 176
Renumbering, menu selections, 213
Replaceable parameters, uses of, batch
      file design, 6, 234, 275-276
REPLACE TEXT command, 214
   ASCII input shortcut with, 106-107,
      111
   border designs, 106-107
   with color designs, 113-114
   EDLIN command, use of, 280
   filling in ASCII characters, 110-111
   screen design, 107, 226-227
   use of, 107
Resetting menu, Menu/Directory Setup
      utility, 48-49
RESTORE command, 122, 125, 142-143,
      146
   general information/use of, 258-260
RETURN.BAT, 45
RMDIR command, 57, 60-61, 196
   general information/use of, 260-261
Root Directory
   explanation of, 63-64, 182
   hierarchical nature of, 64

Screen Attributes HELP, 190
Screen Color HELP, 190

Screen design, 223-230
  ASCII extended character set, use of, 223-224
  blank line, creation of, 227
  control codes, use of, 224-225
  information screens, displaying, 227-228
  menu selections, executing, 229
  multiple screens, displaying, 228
  PROMPT command, use of, 226
  screen/menu layout, 229-230
  "what if" approach to, 226-227
Screen Design utility, 95-120
  creating screen, 101-116
    with ASCII extended character set, 102-103, 105
    color in, 111-114
    creating design, 105-106
    and EDLIN REPLACE TEXT command, 106, 107, 110-111, 113-114
    setting up screen, 108-110
    sketching design, 104-105
    template borders, removing, 114-116
  DESIGN command, 96-97, 99
  information/instruction screens, 96-97
  modifications of, 116-120
    guidelines/tips for, 117
    menu selections, adding/deleting, 117-118
    prefabricated designs, creating, 119-120
    template spacing, changing, 118-119
  organization of, 98-99
    HDU DESIGN, 98
  program files, 99-101
    DESIGN.BAT, 100-101
  screen files
    DESIGN.SCR, 99
    INSTRUCT.SCR, 99
    LOGOAID, 99
  usefulness of, 95-96
Screen display. See Customized Display utilities
Screen files (modifying)
  borders
    adding/deleting/modifying, 214
    adding new, 214
    changing design of, 211-213
    extending, 209-210
    modifying, 215
  layout/size alteration, 208-209
  menu selections, renumbering, 213

PROMPT command, altering parameters, 210-211
  text, adding/deleting/modifying, 207
Screen files (.SCR), 204
Screen/keyboard control
  EDLIN, 88-89
  PROMPT command, 89-91
Screen markings, changing with EDLIN, 118-119
Screen/menu layout, screen design, 229-230
SCREEN.SCR, 82
SEARCH command, 159
SEARCH TEXT command, EDLIN command, use of, 280
Security, 145-147
  areas of, 147
    access control, 147
    audit trails, 147
    copy protection, 147
  DOS-based security systems, 146
Self-modifying batch files, batch file design, 235
SETSCRN.BAT, 76, 77, 79, 128, 139, 194
SETSCRN command, 76-78
7.BAT, 169
SHIFT command, batch file command, use of, 275-276
6.BAT, 141, 167
SORT filter, general information/use of, 59-60, 93, 261-262
Sort utility, adding, 59
/S switch, 56
Starting program, hdu command, 18
Storage, 61-69
  compatibility of storage media, 62-63
  formatting disks, 61-62
  hierarchical directories, 63-64
    advantages of, 64
    and menu access, 64
  logical data storage, 7
  physical data storage, 7-8
Subroutines, use of, batch file design, 233
SYS command, general information/use of, 262-263

Temporary files (.TMP), 204
Text files (.TXT), 204
Text Search, 158-162
  program files, 160-162
  SEARCH command, 159
3.BAT, 55, 81, 133, 157, 191, 193

Index

360-KB/High-Capacity disk utility, formatting, 56–57
Time-stamping, archived files, 175
TRANSFER LINES command, 119
   EDLIN command, use of 280
TREE command, general information/use of, 53, 263
2.BAT, 79, 130, 154–155
TYPE command, 155, 191, 224, 228
   general information/use of, 264

UNPROTECT.BAT, 171
UNPROTECT command, 170, 171
User-interactive files, batch file design, 230
Utilities, DOS, 7–8
Utility (creation of)
   batch file design, 230–235
      chaining batch files, 234
      confirmation prompts, 233
      key reassignment, 231–232
      redirecting input, 230–231
      redirecting output, 231
      replaceable parameters, uses of, 234
      self-modifying batch files, 235
      subroutines, use of, 233
      user-interactive files, 230
      validity of input, 232
   batch files, basic facts about, 220
   planning program for, 219
   screen design, 223–230
      ASCII extended character set, use of, 223–224
      blank line, creation of, 227
      control codes, use of, 224–225
      information screens, displaying, 227–228
      menu selections, executing, 229
      multiple screens, displaying, 228
      PROMPT command, use of, 226
      screen/menu layout, 229–230
      "what if" approach to, 226–227
   screen files, basic facts about, 222

Validity of input, batch file design, 232
VIEW.BAT, 50–51, 59–60
VIEW command, 49
View/Print utilities, 49–54
   Print Contents of All Directories, 53–54
   View Contents of All Directories, 52–53
   View/Print Contents of Directory, 49–50
/V switch, 55

WDESIGN.BAT, 119
Wildcards. *See* Global Filename Characters
WPBEGIN2.TXT, 41
WP command, 34, 41
WPDIR.TMP, 39, 41
WPMORE.BAT, 37, 39–40, 65
WPSTART.BAT, 37, 39–40, 65–67
WRITE LINES command, EDLIN command, use of, 280–281

XCOPY command, general information/use of, 176–177, 264–265

Y.BAT, 44, 67–69, 128, 130, 132, 133, 134, 138, 141, 142, 169–170, 192–193, 194, 233

Fasten your seat belt!

For the serious computer user who wants to soup up his PC—make it faster, more powerful, more fun—the experts at PC WORLD have a fascinating new book and software program that can make your personal computer truly personal.

Called *The Fully Powered PC* with *PC World Utilities Disk*, it takes you under the hood of your PC. It shows you how to construct your own system, how to combine many single-purpose systems, and how to call up a dozen or more applications with little more than a keystroke.

It puts you on the fast track by showing you how to put applications programs into active memory so they run faster, design menus to guide you through systems you've created, even customize your computer to find and dial telephone numbers. It even includes public-domain software that add still more powerful features to your PC.

In other words, *The Fully Powered PC* helps you create a system that performs exactly the way *you* want it to. And isn't that why you bought a PC in the first place?

For the IBM PC, XT, AT or compatible. $39.95 at all computer stores. To order direct, call TOLL FREE: 1-800-624-0023, (in N.J. 1-800-624-0024), or use the coupon below.

Please send me a copy of *The Fully Powered PC*. Enclosed is a check, money order or credit card information for $39.95 plus sales tax (if applicable) and $2.00 for postage and handling.
Name_____
Address_____
City_____ State ____ Zip____
Credit Card: ☐ Visa ☐ MasterCard
Signature _____
Mail to:
Brady c/o Prentice Hall
P.O. Box 512, W. Nyack, NY 10994

////Brady

Special volume discounts and site licenses are available for Brady books and Brady Utilities. Brady products are ideal for corporate use, training programs, and seminars, and can be customized as premiums for your business.

For information, please contact: Director of Special Sales, Brady, Simon & Schuster, Inc., New York, NY 10023 (212) 373-8232.

Important! Read Before Opening Sealed Diskette
END USER LICENSE AGREEMENT

The software in this package is provided to You on the condition that You agree with SIMON & SCHUSTER, INC. ("S&S") to the terms and conditions set forth below. **Read this End User License Agreement carefully. You will be bound by the terms of this agreement if you open the sealed diskette.** If You do not agree to the terms contained in this End User License Agreement, return the entire product, along with your receipt, to *Brady, Simon & Schuster, Inc., One Gulf + Western Plaza, New York, NY 10023, Attn: Refunds*, and your purchase price will be refunded.

S&S grants, and You hereby accept, a personal, nonexclusive license to use the software program and associated documentation in this package, or any part of it ("Licensed product"), subject to the following terms and conditions:

1. *License*

    The license granted to You hereunder authorizes You to use the Licensed Product on any single computer system. A separate license, pursuant to a separate End User License Agreement, is required for any other computer system on which You intend to use the Licensed Product.

2. *Term*

    This End User License Agreement is effective from the date of purchase by You of the Licensed Product and shall remain in force until terminated. You may terminate this End User License Agreement at any time by destroying the Licensed Product together with all copies in any form made by You or received by You. Your right to use or copy the Licensed Product will terminate if You fail to comply with any of the terms or conditions of this End User License Agreement. Upon such termination You shall destroy the copies of the Licensed Product in your possession.

3. *Restriction Against Transfer*

    This End User License Agreement, and the Licensed Product, may not be assigned, sublicensed or otherwise transferred by You to another party unless the other party agrees to accept the terms and conditions of this End User License Agreement. If You transfer the Licensed Product, You must at the same time either transfer all copies whether in printed or machine-readable form to the same party or destroy any copies not transferred.

4. *Restrictions Against Copying or Modifying the Licensed Product*

    The Licensed Product is copyrighted and may not be further copied without the prior written approval of S&S, except that You may make one copy for backup purposes provided You reproduce and include the complete copyright notice on the backup copy. Any unauthorized copying is in violation of this Agreement and may also constitute a violation of the United States Copyright Law for which You could be liable in a civil or criminal suit. **You may not use, transfer, copy or otherwise reproduce the Licensed Product, or any part of it, except as expressly permitted in this End User License Agreement.**

5. *Protection and Security*

    You shall take all reasonable steps to safeguard the Licensed Product and to ensure that no unauthorized person shall have access to it and that no unauthorized copy of any part of it in any form shall be made.

6. **Limited Warranty**

    If You are the original consumer purchaser of a diskette and it is found to be defective in materials or workmanship (which shall not include problems relating to the nature or operation of the Licensed Product) under normal use, S&S will replace it free of charge (or at S&S's option, refund your purchase price) within 30 days following the date of purchase. Following the 30-day period, and up to one year after purchase, S&S will replace any such defective diskette upon payment of a $5 charge (or, at S&S's option, refund your purchase price), provided that the Limited Warranty Registration Card has been filed within 30 days following the date of purchase. Any request for replacement of a defective diskette must be accompanied by the original defective diskette and proof of date of purchase and purchase price. S&S shall have no obligation to replace a diskette (or refund your purchase price) based on claims of defects in the nature or operation of the Licensed Product.
    The software program is provided "as is" without warranty of any kind, either expressed or implied, including but not limited to the implied warranties of merchantability and fitness for a particular purpose. The entire risk as the quality and performance of the program is with You. Should the program prove defective, You (and not S&S) assume the entire cost of all necessary servicing, repair or correction.
    Some states do not allow the exclusion of implied warranties, so the above exclusion may not apply to You. This warrant gives You specific legal rights, and You may also have other rights which vary from state to state.
    S&S does not warrant that the functions contained in the program will meet your requirements or that the operation of the program will be uninterrupted or error free. **Neither S&S nor anyone else who has been involved in the creation or production of this product shall be liable for any direct, indirect, incidental, special or consequential damages, whether arising out of the use or inability to use the product, or any breach of a warranty, and S&S shall have no responsibility except to replace the diskette pursuant to this limited warranty (or, at its option, provide a refund of the purchase price).**
    No sales personnel or other representative of any party involved in the distribution of the Licensed Product is authorized by S&S to make any warranties with respect to the diskette or the Licensed Product beyond those contained in this Agreement. **Oral statements do no constitute warranties,** shall not be relied upon by You, and are not part of this Agreement. The entire agreement between S&S and You is embodied in this Agreement.

7. *General*

    If any provision of this End User License Agreement is determined to be invalid under any applicable statute or rule of law, it shall be deemed omitted and the remaining provisions shall continue in full force and effect. The End User License Agreement is to be governed by and construed in accordance with the laws of the State of New York.